ELMHURST COLLEGE LIBRARY

The Unruly School

The Unruly School

Disorders, Disruptions, and Crimes

Robert J. Rubel

Lexington Books
D.C. Heath and Company
Lexington, Massachusetts
Toronto

Library of Congress Cataloging in Publication Data

Rubel, Robert J.
   The Unruly School.

   Includes bibliographical references and index.
   1. School violence–United States. I. Title.
LB3013.3.R8   373.1'5'0973   77-3837
ISBN 0-669-01668-3

Copyright © 1977 by D.C. Heath and Company.

All rights reserved. No part of this publication may be reproduced or transmitted in any form or by any means, electronic or mechanical, including photocopy, recording, or any information storage or retrieval system, without permission in writing from the publisher.

This book was developed under Visiting Fellowship Grant number 76-NI-990077 from the National Institute for Juvenile Justice and Delinquency Prevention, Law Enforcement Assistance Administration, U.S. Department of Justice. The points of view or opinions stated in this document are those of the author and do not necessarily represent the official position or policies of the U.S. Department of Justice.

Second printing, October 1978.

Published simultaneously in Canada.

Printed in the United States of America.

International Standard Book Number: 0-669-01668-3

Library of Congress Catalog Card Number: 77-3837

Contents

	List of Charts	vii
	Foreword, *Peter D. Blauvelt*	ix
	Acknowledgments	xi
Chapter 1	**Introduction**	1
	Statement of the Problem	1
	Definitions of Terms	1
	Significance of the Study	4
	Purpose of the Study	5
	Questions To Be Answered	6
	Scope and Limits of This Study	9
	Method of Analysis	11
	Organization of the Remainder of the Study	12
Chapter 2	**Scope of the Most Significant Literature and Research**	17
	In-depth Local Studies	17
	Special-interest Group Studies	29
	Statistical Studies	35
	Summary	39
Chapter 3	**Disorders**	47
	Introduction	47
	Differing Views of School Disorders	49
	Major Trends in Student Disorders	58
	Summary and Conclusions	70
Chapter 4	**Disruptions**	83
	Introduction	83
	Differing Views of School Disruptions	84
	Major Trends in Student Disruptions	92
	Summary and Conclusions	100
Chapter 5	**Crimes**	109
	Introduction	109

	Differing Views of School Crimes	111
	Major Trends in Student Crimes	119
	Summary and Conclusions	151
Chapter 6	**Conclusions and Recommendations**	161
	Summary	161
	Conclusions	163
	Extrapolations	168
	Recommendations for Further Study	170
Appendix A	**Major Social and Educational Activity Relating to Juveniles between 1950 and 1975**	173
Appendix B	**Uniform Report Format**	177
Appendix C	**Incident Reports**	181
	Author Index	187
	Subject Index	189
	About the Author	195

List of Charts

1-1	Differentiation of School Offenses	2
1-2	The Action/Reaction Cycle	8
2-1	Actual Percent Increases in Arrest Rates of Fifteen to Seventeen Year Olds	37
4-1	U.S. House of Representatives Survey	86
4-2	*New York Times* Articles on School Disruptions	93
4-3	*U.S. News and World Report* Articles on Student Disruptions	94
4-4	Major Statistical Studies on Student Disruptions	96
4-5	National Education Association's Teacher Opinion Polls on Pupil Behavior	98
5-1	*U.S. News and World Report* Articles on Student Crimes	121
5-2	Basic Data Concerning Pupils, Teachers, and Schools	124
5-3	Total Part I Arrests of Fifteen to Seventeen Year Olds	127
5-4	Total Part II Arrests of Fifteen to Seventeen Year Olds	128
5-5	Gross Changes in Arrest Rates of Fifteen to Seventeen Year Olds	129
5-6	Growth of Membership in the National Association of School Security Directors	130
5-7	Assault Arrest Rates	132
5-8	Teacher Assaults from 1956 to 1975	133

5-9	Teacher Assaults from 1956 to 1975	134
5-10	Arson Arrest Rates	136
5-11	School Fires: Costs and Numbers	137
5-12	Value of All School Property from 1950 to 1974	138
5-13	School Values Compared to School Fires	139
5-14	Percent School Fires of Incendiary Origin	140
5-15	*School Product News'* Annual Survey	144
5-16	Vandalism Arrest Rates	146
5-17	Larceny/Theft Arrest Rates	147
5-18	Burglary Arrest Rates	148

Foreword

I had been involved with this book long before the format was developed. As long ago as 1971, when Bob Rubel was working at the Law Enforcement Assistance Administration, he became an active participant in the National Association of School Security Directors—especially in the Mid-Atlantic Chapter. He was instrumental in the development of a Uniform Incident Reporting Format by the National Association of School Security Directors. Throughout his period of research, Bob has continually sought and received help and guidance from all levels of our Association; I commend the final product.

The issue of crime and violence in public schools is receiving a great deal of attention from politicians, educators, and parents. Almost daily, newspapers and television present grisly details of various violent and disruptive acts committed in schools throughout the country. The public has become increasingly convinced that the vivid scenes portrayed in the *Blackboard Jungle* of two decades ago are common occurrences in schools today. We accept the notion that society has somehow become the hapless victim of marauding bands of adolescent vandals, arsonists, and extortionists. Though this may be an accurate picture, there is compelling reason to believe that the real story has greater depth and complexity.

Persons involved in the operation of a school security program—or of a public school—find themselves pressured by fears and frustrations caused by the belief that horrible events occur in most schools on a daily, if not hourly, basis. One result of such pressure is that school systems across the country find themselves attempting to respond in rational ways to irrational stimuli. These stimuli come in the form of individual events: a teacher is assaulted in a junior high school; an elementary schoolchild is sexually molested on the way to school; or arsonists cause a million-dollar school fire. Such problems force school administrators to respond to random events, whose importance has been defined by others. These extramural definitions are often based on misinformation and invalid conclusions derived in a haphazard fashion, lacking the benefit of insightful research. An additional complication is that school administrators and security directors are engaged in a massive effort to combat increased levels of violence in schools without the help of an historical perspective in which to place overall problems, either on a local or a national basis.

The issue of changes in student crime and violence in schools over a period of time has never before been addressed on a national scale. This is equally true of a host of spin-off questions: are actual numbers of crimes in schools increasing? If so, in what areas? If not, what accounts for the appearance of increased crimes? What impact has the formation of Offices of School Security had on student crime and violence? Based on current data and past trends, what reasonable future can be projected for schools and students?

This book focuses on these and other questions. Such an approach is important on several counts: it is historically interesting; the issues raised—especially relating to problems that use data about crimes in schools—are of very real assistance for educators and security directors when confronting problems presented by seriously misbehaving youths. This book is also useful for evaluating the effectiveness of programs specifically designed to assess issues of crime and violence in schools. This work is not only an academic study of a social phenomenon, but it also represents a practical treatment of a complex and ongoing problem.

Peter D. Blauvelt

Acknowledgments

This book is the result of four years of intensive research, one year of writing, and of the unstinting encouragement and counseling of a few close friends. The early support and guidance provided by Dr. Warren O. Hagstrom of the University of Wisconsin has been invaluable. I am particularly indebted to my mentor, Dr. Ruby B. Yaryan, not only for her wholehearted support, but also for her assistance in making sense out of diverse and largely noncomparable information. Her recommendations enabled me to avoid many pitfalls in research and writing.

In the field of school security, I found the members of the National Association of School Security Directors to be open, generous, and friendly. For continued support and technical help, I warmly thank Joe Grealy, Director of Internal Affairs for Broward County, Florida, schools, and Peter Blauvelt, Director of Security, Prince George's County, Maryland, schools. Joe Grealy is the founder and current President of the National Association of School Security Directors; and Peter Blauvelt, the Vice President.

Within the Law Enforcement Assistance Administration, Office of Juvenile Justice, I am indebted to John Greacen—former Director of the National Institute for Juvenile Justice and Delinquency Prevention and now Director of Research for the Police Foundation—who originally supported my request for a Visiting Fellowship in LEAA; Buddy Howell, the current Director of the Institute, who continued that support; Phyllis Modley, who has graciously and helpfully given me the freedom to develop my projects for this fellowship year; and Tom Albrecht, who for many years has been a close friend and adviser.

I also want to thank my father, John Rubel, for assisting in the writing style of this book, and my wife Margo for maintaining an even keel under the pressures I placed on our home.

For exhaustive editorial assistance, I am grateful to Marion Levy of the University of Maryland.

I dedicate this work to The Dock, who didn't live to see this book completed.

1 Introduction

Statement of the Problem

The climate for all kinds of unwanted behavior by students in the public schools of America has changed radically during the last generation. Not only has violence increased, but also much of what is now taken for granted would have been shocking twenty years ago; that is, the character of the violence has undergone drastic changes. The actions and viewpoints of school administrators in dealing with violence have also changed; there is some indication that these altered actions and viewpoints may in turn have influenced student violence or may influence it in the future.

Many people observed or read about increasing violence in the schools. But to prove such increases, to collect data that give a quantitative assessment of these changes, is extremely difficult—because the methods for recording disruptive incidents are nonuniform; some offenses are not reported, whereas others are overreported; and reporting procedures involve overlapping categories that preclude drawing hard, precise conclusions from the available data. Finally, it is difficult to verify an increase in violence because the available data represent at best only an incomplete biopsy, since the kinds of data recorded in one school may not be recorded in another. Despite these difficulties, an examination of the data below offers logical findings that validate the intuitions developed by those who have observed what is occurring in schools in the United States.

Definitions of Terms

This study attempts to present material as clearly and precisely as possible. The few words that are used in specific and rather technical ways will be clarified now. Since writings of authors from different disciplines are combined in this study, forcing of terms sometimes becomes unavoidable. To prevent any misunderstanding, therefore, terms consistently used (misbehavior, violence, disorder, disruption, and crime) are defined in the following paragraphs. (Chart 1-1 further assists understanding these words and their usages.)

Misbehavior

Misbehavior refers to any act judged unacceptable by the school administration. Such acts may range from talking out of turn in the classroom to riots and

Chart 1-1
Differentiation of School Offenses

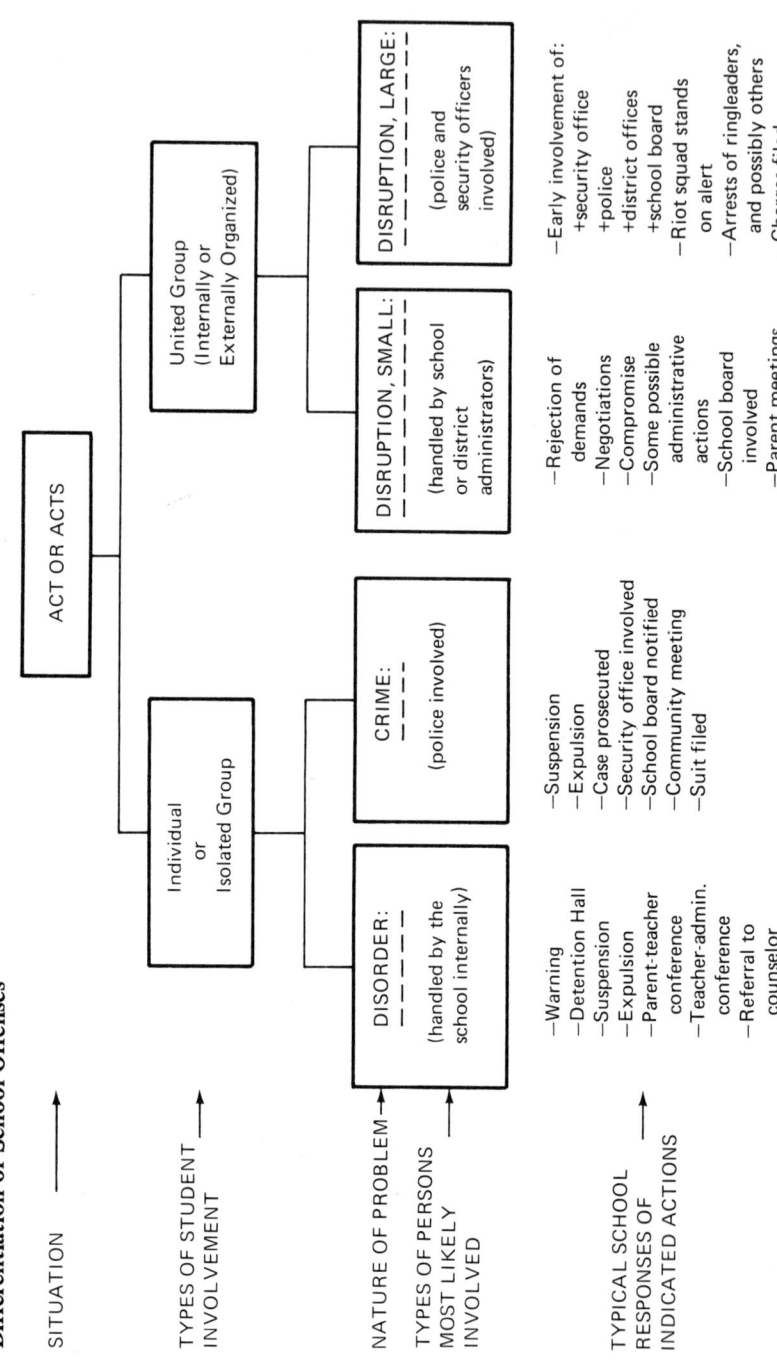

murder. Within the general term, there are three specific groups: disorders, disruptions, and crimes.[1] Misbehavior may or may not involve violence. Truancy is an example of nonviolent misbehavior; assault, of violent misbehavior. Finally, misbehavior is an act which might result in administrative action, such as a vice principal's referring a youth to a counselor or requesting a conference with a teacher. (Misbehaviors handled internally within the classroom are not of concern to this study. The difference is discussed in detail below.)

Violence

Violence, either physical or mental, is implicit in the three categories of misbehavior; that is, disorder, disruption, and crime. Violence in the disorder category may range from the relatively mild trauma of a student talking back to the teacher (and being sent to the office for the offense) to the more serious trauma felt by an entire science class when a youngster poisons all the laboratory animals (and is suspended).

Violence, or the threat of violence, is increasingly associated with disruption and crime in schools. Violence directed against students, teachers, or administrators amplifies the fear that it might recur. The threat of violence, both explicit and implicit in the climate created wherever violent acts have occurred, increasingly infects many schools, and is a major concern of this study.

To summarize, three general groups of high school student misbehavior are under investigation here. All three (disorders, disruptions, and crimes) involve either physical or mental violence, and if reported to school authorities will usually cause those authorities to make some kind of disciplinary response. The remaining discussions of definitions pay close attention to each of the three types of student misbehaviors.

Disorders

Disorders are noncriminal acts committed by individuals in violation of school rules. Often such offenses result in the classroom teacher or school administrator taking some form of action (reprimand, detention hall, or suspension), short of calling the police.[2] The action taken is usually carried out entirely under the authority of the school itself. A typical example is as follows:

A student is continually tardy to class. The teacher has repeatedly warned that continued tardiness will result in a referral to the assistant principal's office. The tardiness continues. One day, the teacher refuses to admit the student to class and sends him to the office with an explanatory note.

At the office, the assistant principal reads the referral note and decides on the administrative action of calling a teacher conference, also involving the guidance counselor and the registrar. The student is told to report back to class and an explanatory note is given to the teacher.[3]

Disruption

Disruption, unlike disorder or crime, is defined exclusively as a group event. With or without outside influence, a disruption is specifically characterized as an activity designed to accomplish a planned goal or establish a point of contention (Erickson, 1969:10).[4] To be considered a disruption, these goals or contentions must be judged "significantly [to] interrupt the education of [other] students" (Bailey, 1971:2). Boycott is a classic example of disruption.

Crime

Crime is seemingly the easiest term to define. A crime is an act that is forbidden by public law and that, if committed, can cause an adult to be arrested.[5] Specifically excluded from this definition are "status offenses," crimes which can cause only a juvenile to be arrested (by virtue of age status).[6]

This study demonstrates the ebb and flow of student disorders, disruptions, and crimes from 1950 to 1975. All three types of misbehavior have occurred, to a greater or lesser extent, throughout this time period.

Significance of the Study

As people who deal with students and the problems of school administration know very well, the climate within schools in nearly every community in America has changed swiftly and dramatically in the last few decades. The attitudes of students toward authority have certainly changed in that period—indeed, they seem to be changing all the time. The attitudes of teachers and administrators have changed, too, as school personnel have been replaced by new and often younger people and in response to the changing acts and attitudes of students.

However certain one may be that changes have occurred, it is not easy to study the changes in a definitive and quantitative way. There is no doubt that violence and the threat of violence by students in public schools have increased substantially in twenty-five years; but it is not always easy to pin down the ways in which the violence has grown. Are Americans facing new kinds of violence? Are incidents of violence occurring more often? Is there more or less unreported violence? Are the schools themselves unwittingly influencing trends in student violence either by encouraging or diminishing violence through administrative actions? The answers to such questions are often mired in conflicting or overlapping definitions, and are severely limited due to the different methods by which relevant data have been recorded and presented. The same kinds of difficulties arise when one tries to analyze not only violence, but also crimes committed by students, especially in schools, and disruptive behavior that may almost destroy the school staff's ability to teach.

Though a great deal has been written about students, schools, and crimes, there has not been a study showing how student misbehaviors, ranging from simple classroom disorders to crimes, have changed over time. Nor has there been a study attempting to show how school administrators have reacted to changing types of student misbehaviors. Finally, there appears to be no study that attempts to show how the student misbehavior is affected by administrative responses, though such a study might be useful for indicating how school administrations can do a better job of selecting the strategies and tactics best suited to dealing not only with current disciplinary problems, but also with what appear to be near-term trends.

This book has been written in an effort to fill these gaps. Solely by examining published historical and statistical data (without conducting field research), this study presents the findings and conclusions relating to changes, over time, in student misbehaviors in secondary schools. It also presents conclusions relating to the school's responses to student misbehaviors, and the students' counteractions to the school's responses. The particular significance of this approach is that a researcher or school administrator armed primarily with the historical perspectives (provided here) and warned about weaknesses in statistics that are continually produced (as warned here) can develop conclusions about specific schools or specific school districts by noting how his own school's specific trends have changed (and continue to change) over time.

Purpose of the Study

The purpose of the study is to examine the trends of secondary school students vis-à-vis the kinds, frequency, and intensity of their misbehaviors and the schools' responses to those misbehaviors from 1950 to 1975. Specific attention is paid to the types of crimes and disruptions that most strongly affect school administrations and generally require administrative responses either for school management or public relations reasons. In recent years, anyone in close contact with schools as a teacher, administrator, or law-enforcement officer is well aware that the key trends highlighted below have been taking place. This study demonstrates some of the more intuitive judgments of such individuals. Specifically, it shows that:

1. Since the 1950s, the kinds of misbehavior most frequently reported among high school students have changed from classroom disorders, such as

truancy and insubordination, to acts of violence against persons and property in the 1970s.
2. The frequency rate of certain acts of student misbehavior has increased out of proportion to the growth in high school population from 1950 to 1975.
3. The intensity of some acts of misbehavior among high school students has changed between 1950 and 1975. School fights, which have existed ever since kids started going to school, have taken on an entirely new aspect; whereas the fights were previously limited almost entirely to words and fists, now there are aggravated assaults with dangerous weapons and murder. Throwing stones at windows is an age-old problem, but for Mesa, Arizona, schools to have to cover their windows with sheet aluminum indicates an entirely different level of intensity (Neill, 1975:2).
4. The ways schools deal with misbehavior—ranging from disorders requiring suspensions to crimes requiring prosecution—have changed during the past few decades. No longer are students simply suspended; procedural due process is increasingly becoming an issue. From *Gault v. Arizona* (99 Ariz. 181, 407 P. 2nd 720, 1965), which established the requirement that police follow due process in cases affecting juveniles, to *Goss v. Lopez* (419 U.S. 565, 95 S. Ct. 729, 1975), which established that schools must follow due process in discipline cases involving suspensions lasting up to ten days, the protection of youths' legal rights in cases involving almost any disciplinary action has become an important concern among school administrators.

Less frequently do teachers have to break up fights; school security guards—armed, in many large urban districts[7]—are on the alert, specially trained (often by police academies) to deal with these problems. In most schools, custodians no longer have sole responsibility for making sure all is well when they lock up at night. At a minimum, urban school districts in the nation are equipped with entry alarms; many districts are also equipped with more sophisticated gadgetry, such as ultrasonic detectors or perimeter fence alarms.
5. During the past decade, the handling of many aspects of student violence in urban secondary schools became institutionalized (possibly in response to the schools' increasing toleration of violent student behavior).[8] The entire nature of the problem of student violence was intensified when schools first brought armed police on campuses in the late 1960s, ostensibly to quell disruptions. It is during this period that Offices of School Security first began to appear; that the threshold of tolerated behavior expanded to include increasingly violent forms of student misconduct; and that the first statistics on violent misbehaviors in schools became available.

Questions To Be Answered

Four questions fundamental to this study are discussed here. Answers to these broad questions will present a comprehensive view of the trends in student misbehaviors and possible roles the schools may play in curtailing such misbehaviors.[9] The following questions are addressed:

1. How can available statistics be used to hinder or help the problems faced by schools in reducing crime and violence?

First, statistical data can hinder schools in finding solutions to problems if that data are improperly collected or reported. If an improper analysis of data results in an overrepresentation of the seriousness of the problems, then an overreaction by the public (and presumably also by the schools) may well result. If an improper analysis of data results in the seriousness of the problems being underreported, then neither the public nor the schools have the opportunity to take timely action to curtail the problems.[10]

A second way statistics can hinder schools in finding solutions to misbehaviors among students centers on improper presentations of statistical data. Two examples of this problem are: first, citing a percentage increase in the occurrence of a certain kind of crime over a specific time period without accounting for changes in the "population at risk";[11] and, second, presenting a group of crimes that show percentage increases over a specified time span without presenting the raw numbers from which percentages were derived.[12] Reporting the percentage increases of crimes that have different base numbers causes infrequent crimes—for example, murder—to be exaggerated, and more frequent crimes—for example, assault or vandalism—to be de-emphasized.[13] This issue is discussed in much greater depth later.

Statistics depicting the results of experimental programs aimed at reducing or preventing school misbehaviors can help administrators who face similar problems elsewhere. Also, in an age where data are often necessary to help justify funding, good backup data may enable a school district to obtain research or pilot-program funding from federal, state, or local sources.

2. How do administrative or technological school responses to student actions lead to additional changes in the kinds, frequency, or intensity of student actions?

The proposed concept (examined extensively in chapters 3, 4, and 5) is that as "the system" develops an administrative or technological response to a behavior problem, the misbehaving youths alter their behavioral actions in ways designed to circumvent the schools' response to the original problem. The schools, perceiving a new student problem, begin the cycle over again, perhaps perpetually. Chart 1-2 graphically displays this phenomenon and provides some examples.

It is interesting to note that in the instance in which school administrators anticipated and prepared for disruptions (the period from the beginning of college disruptions in 1964 to that of high school disruptions in 1968) and used well-planned, if excessive, countermeasures (police in large numbers), disruptions for all but racial issues ceased to occur after about 1971.[14]

Chart 1-2
The Action/Reaction Cycle for Assisting Trend Analysis of Student Misbehaviors

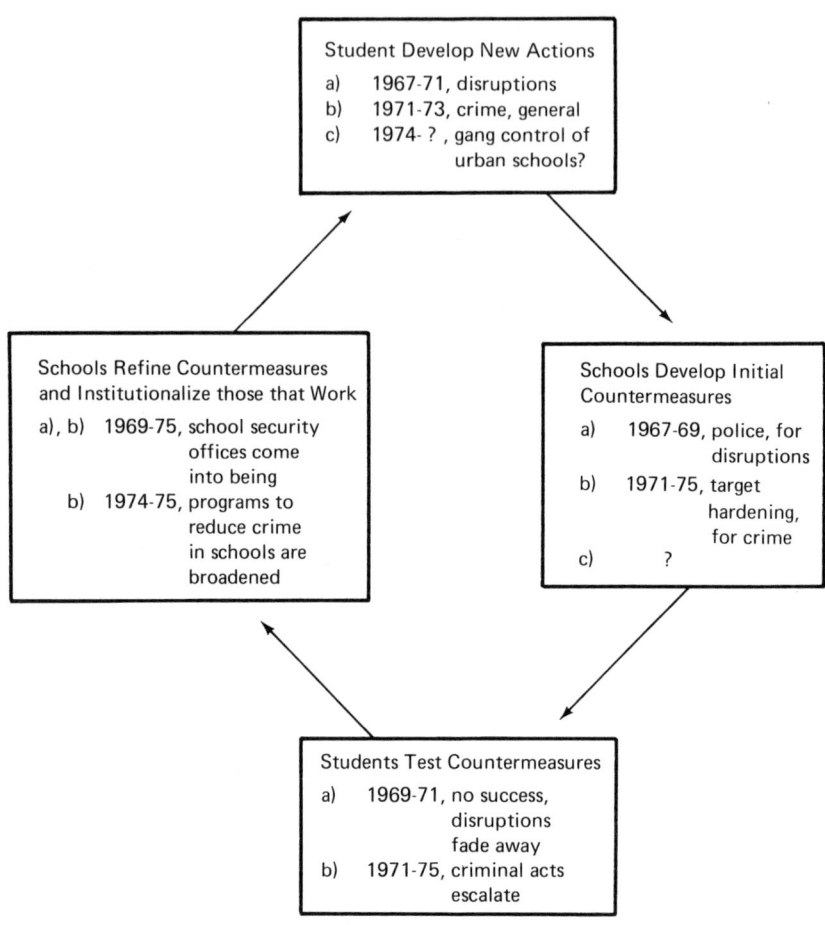

3. What actions or programs can the schools develop to help curtail problems of violent misbehavior, such as vandalism and assault?

What generalizations can be made about programs that succeed in reducing school violence? As is often noted, the issue of whether or not students develop a vested interest in the success of a certain project often becomes the single most important factor in the success of that project. Additionally, Berger (1974:11) suggests that students' vested interest is best shown through conscientious student government; Marvin (1976:56) suggests that one of the most important issues in a program's success in schools may be the cooperation of counselors;

and Larson (1972:84) stresses the intellectual fairness and internal consistency of the program's principles as key points in its success.

Of course, there are also "target-hardening"[15] solutions: bigger and better locks, more closed-circuit monitoring, plastic (polycarbon) instead of glass windows, and so forth. All these have arguable merits that are considered later in this chapter. It is important to keep in mind, however, that a school which resorts to target-hardening to the exclusion of basic programs addressing the needs of the pupils will end up with a facility that is little different from a jail without bars. When pupils have to pass through metal detectors to get into the building and show a plastic-laminated identification card at the same time, can only be in the halls with permits, and have prescribed hours of entry and exit, real questions arise as to what kind of education they are receiving.

4. How can an understanding of the historical trends of school disorders, disruptions, and crimes be helpful in planning intervention programs and techniques to curtail misbehaviors in the future?

If responsible people can establish a relationship between student actions on the one hand and school responses and student counterresponses on the other hand (see question 2), they would create a powerful tool for prediction and management. They could then take a systematic look at any school district and determine probable future student action in response to the institutional reactions operating at that time. Though it is unlikely that anyone can foretell the future, there are opportunities for using research results better to define the variety, scope, and probable utility of alternative administrative policies.

Scope and Limits of This Study

Before beginning the body of this work, it is necessary to discuss some of the general limitations placed on the research. The following section is divided into two parts: scope and technical limits.

Scope

1. The study is primarily concerned with validating commonsensible notions, demonstrating unusual conclusions, and suggesting new directions in dealing with student misbehavior in public secondary schools.
2. The period of study is from 1950 to 1975.
3. The discussion of student misbehavior includes those acts which usually cause the school to take some form of administrative action.
4. The study includes examination of the ways by which schools have often attempted to curtail student misbehavior.

5. Though the primary emphasis for student acts and school countermeasures assumes an urban school system, the national data are only available aggregated to include all schools. The general trends, then, are national in scope, while the problems addressed in chapters 3, 4, and 5 are those most frequently experienced by urban school systems.
6. The study is not concerned with the analysis of specific programs to combat youthful misbehaviors, though it does mention some programs as examples of reasonable solutions.[16]
7. Due to the complexity of the problems of model development, this study is not concerned with the development of educational models for the reduction of student misbehaviors. The literature confirms that approaches to crime reduction appropriate in parts of New York City may be wrong for Denver. In a similar fashion, rural programs seldom can succeed in urban areas. Though this study will provide both urban and rural administrators with historical trends in the areas of school disorders and crimes, and will provide administrators with suggestions as to paths students are likely to take in reaction to administrative responses to behavioral problems, it leaves the formulation of specific programs to individual school districts.
8. The study does not develop theories proposing to explain why individual students misbehave; however, some conclusions are reached about why overall student behavior changes at certain times. It develops theories about changes in student tactics and about how to anticipate such changes in response to administrative countermeasures.

Technical Limits

1. The absolute levels of juvenile criminality have probably gone up during 1950-1975. The primary source for information on juvenile crime is the FBI's *Uniform Crime Reports* (*UCR*). When using the *UCR* statistics, certain points must be kept in mind. First, there is no way to determine the number of actual crimes committed; many are not reported. Second, many acts are reported to official sources other than the police.[17] Third, the types of crimes that are of interest to police change with time (often because of local pressures exerted by such groups as churches, parents, civic leaders, or the city council). Fourth, particularly in cases involving juveniles, arrests are often made rather reluctantly and only after the police have gone through a number of counsel-and-release cycles. Though the available arrest figures indicate dramatic increases, one cannot possibly be sure whether those increases are due to changes in reporting methods, increases in the reporting of certain juvenile offenses, or actual increases in juvenile crimes.
2. The reporting of kinds and frequencies of school offenses was fundamentally altered after the mid-1960s by the creation of school security offices

(currently found in every large urban school district throughout the country). Before school security offices came into being, the individual school administrator often had a vested interest in understating the degree and seriousness of crimes and violence going on in his or her school. The typical seasoned administrator had learned that if the public (or the district offices) realized that disorder or crime was excessive or not under control by the principal, then his or her personal chances for advancement were lessened. Proof of good administration often lay in an administrator's running a good school: obviously, a good school cannot have problems with disorders or crime that cannot be handled within the school.

With the advent of school security offices operating out of schools' district offices, a new situation arose. Now the director of school security had a vested interest in getting facts concerning the extent and costs of crime and vandalism throughout the district to justify budget increases for programs intended to prevent such misconduct. Because principals have had to conform to these more rigid districtwide reporting requirements, statistics became increasingly comprehensive between 1972 and 1975.

3. Nonuniform terminology between school districts, even to describing what would seem to be common criminal categories, has made national comparisons of offenses in schools very difficult. In 1973, at the national conference of the National Association of School Security Directors (NASSD), the issue of uniform terminology arose when it was found that assaults, arson, vandalism, and so forth were being defined quite differently between the many school districts represented at the conference. The association adopted the position that uniform definitions of common terms would be of crucial importance for presenting a united position to a federal funding source or congressional investigating committee. In the years following that conference, the association undertook a program designed to identify the nature, extent, and cost of school crime and vandalism by using the uniform terminology developed by the FBI's *Uniform Crime Reports.*
4. Crime is becoming increasingly tolerated in America. People are becoming accustomed to, and perhaps even resigned to, violent misbehavior at all levels of our society. Because of this, the kinds and frequencies of acts tolerated by schools and communities significantly affect the kinds and frequencies of violent acts that are reported. This situation has only recently begun to receive public attention. Betchkal (1971), Berger (1974), and Nemy (1975) all discuss this phenomenon as it affects the reporting of criminal acts in public schools.

Method of Analysis

During the research period, data were gathered relating directly to the issues of student misbehavior in public secondary schools from as many sources as possible. Analysis of this information, with particular emphasis on certain types of student misbehavior between 1950 and 1975, permits a number of preliminary observations:

1. Schools and the public perceived and treated classroom rowdiness differently from crime, though both were generally acts of individuals.
2. Disruptions (demonstrations and riots) were group events that seemed to be treated by schools and public alike as quite different from acts of criminality.
3. Many of the statistics revealed in the data were contradictory.
4. Special-interest groups were collecting and publishing specialized, self-serving data prolifically.

These observations lead to a set of procedures that assist in sensible and consistent data analysis:

1. Data collected from all sources are indexed according to various characteristics such as:
   a. Individual act, disorder
   b. Group act, disruption
   c. Individual act, criminal offense
2. Statistics are analyzed for:
   a. Hidden assumptions
   b. Advantage to the research group in presenting a biased report
   c. Use or nonuse of rate-of-change data
   d. Consideration of changes that affect the absolute numbers as well as percentage changes
3. Reports of special-interest groups are analyzed to account for:
   a. Vested interests in showing increases or decreases in the statistics.
   b. Ramifications of increases or decreases in the statistics
   c. Vested interests in having the problem continue

Each chapter stands on its own in relation to the presentation and analysis of the data.

Organization of the Remainder of the Study

Chapter 2 scans the scope of the major literature pertinent to this investigation (including strengths and weaknesses of the most significant material) and presents an analysis and critique of many of the available statistics. Chapters 3, 4, and 5 consist of the presentation, analysis, and interpretation of the issues set forth in the statement of the problem: chapter 3 deals with disorders, chapter 4 discusses disruptions, and chapter 5 looks at crime. Chapter 6 includes a summary of the study, along with conclusions, extrapolations, and recommendations for further research.

Notes

1. The terms were chosen for convenience, but they may suggest meaning not intended. Naturally, every disorder will be disrupting; all disruptions cause disorder; and most crimes are sources of both. The text clarifies the use of these terms.

2. There is one act, truancy, which may or may not involve the police. This study considers truancy a disorder. The principal justification for this placement of a juvenile crime act within a category supposed to be limited to noncriminal acts is that it does not fit logically in the "crime" section. The crime section, as stipulated, considers adult-type offenses that are committed in schools by juveniles.

3. Some real disruption of the teacher's classroom may well have resulted from the student's behavior and the teacher's response; however, the reader is asked (with the author's apology for its imperfections) to accept the use of the word disorder as set forth here to explain this incident.

4. To the extent possible, the terms disorder, disruption, and crime as they are used here conform with their use in the literature. Unfortunately, all authors do not employ the same terms or define the ones they use in ways that allow direct comparison.

5. Though the study stipulates that the offense must be of the type that could cause the perpetrator to be arrested, it has not insisted that the perpetrator be booked or convicted of the criminal act in which he was engaged, before such student misbehavior is counted as a crime.

6. Examples of status offenses include complaints related to truancy from school; runaway; child neglect; curfew violation; and stubborn child. Though most of these categories have no bearing on this paper, truancy does. As mentioned in note 2, the study is considering truancy in the disorder class of misbehaviors.

7. Sworn officers who carry weapons are currently known to be employed in these school districts: Washington, D.C.; Chicago, Ill.; Los Angeles, Calif.; Austin, Tex.; Minneapolis, Minn.; Indianapolis, Ind.; Atlanta, Ga.; Compton, Calif.; Lexington, Ky.; and Philadelphia, Pa.

8. By tolerated behavior, this study means those behaviors which the school considers acceptable. Many of the tolerated behaviors in the late 1960s and early 1970s would formerly have resulted in student suspensions or expulsions.

9. The study recognizes that schools tend to reflect the values and customs of surrounding communities and, in many ways, of our society as a whole. Where local crime is high, schools will suffer from it; where it is lower, school administrators and staff have an easier time.

10. The assumption that any bureaucracy, such as public schools, will take timely action merely based on correct research information is probably invalid. The only suggestion here is that the opportunity to make timely decisions is a function of well-analyzed and accurate information relating to whatever problem is under consideration.

11. The Bayh use of the National Education Association studies showing a 14.7 to 37 percent increase between 1964 and 1973 in the number of teachers reporting that they knew of some teacher in their school who had been physically assaulted in the previous school year actually represents a 1.9 percent decrease in the rate of assault, when the increased number of enrolled high school students is taken into account.

12. For an example of the use of percentage-change data in the analysis of school crimes, see the Preliminary Report of the Senate Subcommittee to Investigate Juvenile Delinquency (Bayh, 1975).

13. The absolute numbers are often very important in ways that are easily overlooked. For example, fifty disruptive students on a large campus have a very different impact than 150 do, as many major universities discovered in the 1960s and early 1970s. In fact, weeding out the ringleaders and keeping the dissidents down to a small enough number made a huge difference in the manageability of the entire university in those days. Clearly, the teacher in a classroom where the number of misbehaving students increases 100 percent in one year (from one to two misbehaving pupils) is faced with a much less serious problem than the teacher confronted with "only" a 10 percent increase in misbehaving students—from 10 to 11 in one year.

Considering now the implications of the study comparing small-incident crimes with large-incident crimes, the study notes the following hypothetical example: in small-incident crimes (such as homicide or rape), an increase from 400 to 600 incidents represents a 50 percent increase and involves an increase of 200 incidents. On the other hand, in large-incident crimes (such as vandalism or assault), an increase from 10,000 to 15,000 incidents is still an increase of only 50 percent. The difference, of course, is that instead of involving only 200 incidents, there has been an increase of 5,000 incidents.

14. It is difficult to generalize conclusions about the timing of the lessening of secondary school disruptions. The period of the early 1970s saw public concern focusing on issues more serious than student riots over dress codes and freedom to publish their newspapers. This is the period of the ending of the Vietnam war, the onset of economic recession, the preoccupation of the Nixon Administration with Watergate, and so forth.

15. Target-hardening refers to any physical or electronic means used to make building entry more difficult or more risky for the intruder.

16. Marvin (1976) and Brodsky and Knudten (1973) have done extensive work toward collecting and categorizing school programs aimed at reducing and preventing school crime and disorder.

17. That is, acts that would be treated as criminal by police and courts are reported to other authorities (such as welfare workers, parole officers, clergy, and so forth) and thus escape official statistical counts of the FBI.

References

Bailey, Stephen K.
    1971   *Disruption in Urban Public Secondary Schools.* Washington, D.C.: National Association of Secondary School Principals.

Bayh, Birch
    1975   "Our Nation's Schools—A Report Card: 'A' in School Violence and Vandalism." Washington, D.C.: Preliminary Report of the Subcommittee to Investigate Juvenile Delinquency, Judiciary Committee, U.S. Senate (April).

Betchkal, James (ed.)
    1971   "Violence in Schools: Now for the Solutions." *American School Board Journal* (January):27-37.

Berger, Michael
    1974   "Violence in the Schools: Causes and Remedies." Bloomington, Ind.: Phi Delta Kappa Educational Foundation.

Brodsky, Stanley L., and Knudten, Richard D.
    1973   *Strategies for Delinquency Prevention in the Schools.* Tuscaloosa, Ala.: University of Alabama Press.

Cobb, Marion M.
    1953   "Some Suggestions for Preventing Discipline Problems." *High Points* 35(October):12-13.

Erickson, Kenneth; Benson, George; and Huff, Robert
    1969   "Activism in the Secondary Schools: Analysis and Recommendations." Eugene, Ore.: Bureau of Educational Research.

Larson, Knute
    1972   *School Discipline in an Age of Rebellion.* New York: Parker Publishing Company, Inc.

Marvin, Michael et al.
    1976   *Planning Assistance Programs to Reduce School Violence and Disruption.* Philadelphia, Pa.: Research for Better Schools.

Miller, Walter B.
    1975   *Violence by Youth Gangs and Youth Groups in Major American Cities.* Interim Report of Grant 74NI-990047. Washington, D.C.: Law Enforcement Assistance Administration.

Neill, Shirley B.
   1975   *Violence and Vandalism: Current Trends in School Policies and Programs.* Arlington, Va.: National School Public Relations Association.

Nemy, Enid
   1975   'Violence in Schools Now Seen as Norm across the Nation." *New York Times* (June 14).

U.S. News and World Report
   1968   "Violence Hits Schools, Colleges, as Rebellion Spreads to High Schools." (May 20):36-40.

2 Scope of the Most Significant Literature and Research

There are many research studies concerned with aspects of juvenile delinquency and about what schools should do to teach students more effectively. But research efforts of national scope focusing on misbehaving youths in secondary schools—longitudinal studies that encompass a broad range of problems—are not extensive, either because of the complexity of the variables involved or because of limited public interest in a macroscopic view of school misbehaviors. Therefore, to piece together pictures of changes in relationships between students and schools, the study examines a number of related issues from varying vantage points. This chapter reviews the scope of the literature that deals with these issues. It is useful and convenient to study the available literature under the subheadings: in-depth local studies, special-interest group studies, and statistical studies.

Though there is some overlap among these three categories, to a large extent they are separable. The in-depth local studies are often topical, but not national; the special-interest group studies are often large and national, but informal and somewhat biased in the presentation of data; the statistical studies are often national, but noncomparable. An additional point of interest in this literature review is the change in the types of misbehaviors researched over time. By reviewing the literature in these three subgroups, instead of in the three misbehavior categories (disorders, disruptions, and crimes), the year of authorship stands out much more clearly in relationship to the subject of the research. This comparison of the year of authorship to the subject of the research gives a general indication of the trends in academic and governmental research in the field of student misbehaviors in schools.[1]

In-depth Local Studies

There have been few notable reports or studies dealing primarily with issues of disorders, disruptions, or crimes in public schools. Of those that are available, however, the most important are: disorders—National Education Association, 1956, pupil behavior; Hagstrom and Gardner, 1969, disorders (classroom rebellion); Children's Defense Fund, 1975, suspensions; Robert F. Kennedy Memorial, 1973, pushouts; and Polk and Schafer, 1972, delinquency in general.

Reports on disruptions include—Erickson, 1969, riots; Havighurst, 1970, confrontations; Bailey, 1971, disruptions; Vestermark, 1971, collective violence; and Meyer, 1971, disruptions/apathy.

Studies on crime include—Greenberg, 1969, vandalism; Panel on School Safety, 1972, crime in schools; Brodsky and Knudten, 1973, anticrime programs in schools; Marvin, 1976, crime in schools; and Miller, 1975, gangs.

Disorders

Disorders are the least-studied of the three focal areas, probably because they represent a residual category which includes a wide variety of offenses that are difficult to catalog. Where this kind of nonuniformity exists, research tends to be slow. The following reports deal with disorders.

National Education Association: The only study of national scope that really focused on disorders was the "Teacher Opinion on Pupil Behavior, 1955-56" conducted by the Research Division of the National Education Association. This analysis was undertaken because the misbehavior of children and youth appeared to be one of the most critical social problems of the day. "Newspaper accounts of juvenile gangsterism, stealing, armed assault, and even murder are being viewed with growing concern" (National Education Association, 1956:52). The study, which used a stratified random sample based on the geographic distribution of teachers in the United States, received 4,270 responses to its 10,000 mailed questionnaires. The data, which were carefully and responsibly presented, covered pupil behaviors in relation to teachers, the school, the family, the community, and various miscellaneous factors.

The findings were extensive and valuable; among the more interesting conclusions were:

1. Most public school teachers said the situation in their school neighborhoods and communities was not nearly as bad as the impression presented by mass mediums of communication.
2. Almost all teachers (95 percent) described their pupils as either exceptionally well-behaved or reasonably well-behaved.
3. As classroom teachers became older and gained more experience, they tended to have less trouble with pupils; however, after having taught twenty-five to thirty years, the troubles of the typical classroom teacher began to increase once again.

Hagstrom and Gardner: Though not national in scope, this research study specifically focused on disorders. Concentrating not on the pervasiveness of disorders, but rather on the identification of the characteristics of eleventh grade youths most likely to "openly challenge the authority of the school," the findings were that boys, more than girls, may exhibit this rebellious behavior. Further, Hagstrom and Gardner's findings indicated that the boys showing this behavior were especially likely to be those who did not expect to attend college. Going one step further, this research found that boys and girls from high-socio-economic-status families who did not expect to attend college were more likely to be rebellious than other students (Hagstrom and Gardner, 1969:18).

For the purposes of this study, the utility of the Hagstrom and Gardner findings is lessened somewhat due to the suburban Wisconsin student population they used. Differences between the goals and objectives of urban and suburban youth populations make it difficult to generalize the findings to students in the predominantly urban settings of this study. For suburban schools with pupil behavior problems, however, the findings of the Hagstrom-Gardner work become quite useful. Such districts can use the information about the characteristics of disorderly pupils to assist in planning overall crime-reduction programs. Studies discussed later, for example, have correlated disorderly schools with high rates of vandalism. It is assumed that disorderly schools have their roots in disorderly pupils.

In addition to these two studies on disorders, two subjects falling within the general parameters of the term "disorder" are discussed. The two subtopics are: the school's role in relation to suspending, expelling, and pushing out public school students; and the school's relation to delinquency.

Children's Defense Fund: The most comprehensive study on suspensions and expulsions was by the Children's Defense Fund (1975). This research analyzed *why* children were suspended, *who* got suspended, the *racial implications* of suspensions, and the *harm* suspensions could inflict on children.[2] The results of this study on suspensions and expulsions will be used in the discussion of the school's responses to misbehaving students. Among the most important Children's Defense Fund findings were:

1. Of the 24 million students covered by the survey of the U.S. Department of Health, Education and Welfare's Office of Civil Rights, over 1 million students (4.2 percent) were suspended at least once during the 1972-1973 school year (Children's Defense Fund, 1975:56).
2. School administrators were most likely to suspend children who were in secondary school and were black, male, and poor (Ibid.:60).

Whereas the Hagstrom and Gardner study report on a predominantly suburban population in Wisconsin, this effort by the Children's Defense Fund utilized a national population sample (which, as a result of American demography, resulted in a sample population that was largely urban). The Defense Fund's findings, based on their national sample, closely paralleled those of other studies. As noted, they found that pupils most frequently suspended were in secondary school and were "black, male, and poor." This was consistent with a commonsensible feel for the location within the educational system where suspensions would be most frequent. The next major study to be discussed picks up on this issue about the racial overtones that often accompanied suspensions and expulsions.

Robert F. Kennedy Memorial: In the early 1970s, the Robert F. Kennedy Memorial and the Southern Regional Council conducted a large study of pushouts.[3] The work focused on the southeast. Its findings showed that as desegregation became court mandated in the 1960s and integrated schools became more of a reality, de facto discrimination and classroom segregation persisted through the use of such techniques as ability tracking, and disproportionate suspension and expulsion of black students (Robert F. Kennedy Memorial, 1973:14). (Whereas blacks often made up only 15-30 percent of the district student population, the research findings indicated that 50-80 percent of all the youths suspended or expelled in the course of a year were black [Ibid.:4, 51]). Other findings include the following:

1. A pushout problem clearly existed. From about 1968 to 1973, disproportionate numbers of minority students had been suspended, expelled, and induced in other ways to drop out of many recently desegregated school systems.
2. The pushout problems seemed to be related to large-scale desegregation, especially in school districts where desegregation was poorly handled and the community resisted it.
3. The pushout problem was not necessarily a consequence of desegregation. Many school districts were found where de facto segregation through pushing out pupils was not an issue.
4. Suspensions were often imposed for reasons that did not warrant such extreme action (Ibid.:10, 11).

Limitations in the Kennedy study, with respect to this study, stem from a combination of regionalization and focus. Choosing the southeast because of its extensive "pluralistic education" (Ibid.:x) and targeting only "victims of racial discrimination or arbitrary actions of school authorities" (Ibid.:viii), the Kennedy study looked at the school's response to a racial group, rather than to student misbehavior itself.

Polk and Schafer: The topic of schools and delinquency became increasingly popular during the early 1960s and the early 1970s. Disorders and delinquency simply were not big issues in the 1950s; however, the nature of acts of juvenile delinquents became so serious by the 1970s that publications and studies were referring not to juvenile delinquency but to juvenile crime.

The most complete study of the school's role in contributing to or reducing juvenile delinquency in the broad sense was Polk and Schafer's *Schools and Delinquency* (1972). Expanding on two articles appearing in *The President's*

Commission on Law Enforcement and the Administration of Justice: The Task Force Report on Juvenile Delinquency and Youth Crime (1967), Polk and Schafer did a remarkable job in analyzing *where* and *how* schools affected the lives of youths. Critical for understanding the pressures students feel, in school as well as in the community, this work not only presented an orderly review of the leading theories of delinquency causation, but was also one of the earliest works to suggest that schools themselves played a role in the creation and nurture of misbehaving youths. In addition to the finding that schools contributed to youthful delinquency, this work's primary observations were as follows. First, the ways schools were organized conceptually and functionally exacerbated the problems of youthful misbehavior; second, programs to reduce, prevent, or control delinquency could not refer only to technological issues of control, but had to address the underlying conditions that helped produce educational failure, perceived irrelevancy, lack of commitment, and exclusion— and, therefore, delinquency (Polk and Schafer, 1972:240).

The work was particularly valuable for establishing the groundwork on which later changes in the interrelationships between students and schools would be regarded. The findings in Polk's work remained valid throughout the period of this study. Particularly useful were Polk and Schafer's generalizations about the roles of schools vis-à-vis educating youths. Though Polk did not discuss issues of student violence and school crime as problems in themselves, he presented a thorough treatment of the school's role in parenting frustrated, highly stressed, delinquency-prone youths.

Disruptions

Studies focusing on disruptions are reasonably plentiful. From the earliest papers that sounded almost as if they were thinking out loud about the possibility that disruptions might become political at the high school level (Hagstrom, 1969:20), through the definitive work on collective violence in schools (Vestermark, 1971), the most significant aspects of high school disruptions have been studied.

Erickson: In 1969 Erickson introduced the concept that *disruptive unrest* represented student actions entirely different from past violations of school disciplinary codes.[4] Disruptions shared three characteristics that held them apart from simple violations of discipline (disorders): disruptions involved *groups*; the student activity undertaken was *calculated* to disrupt the functioning of the school; and the groups utilized *techniques of collective protest* (Erickson, 1969:10).

Havighurst: One of the earliest studies actually designed to analyze the nature and scope of student activism and conflict was Havighurst's *A Profile of the Large-City High School* (1970). Some findings of that work's eighth chapter have been replicated in later studies, and bear mention here. First, Havighurst found that student activism resulting in conflict had the greatest likelihood of developing in schools where students generally were *high in socioeconomic status* and where *most of the students were black* (Havighurst, 1970:8-3. Emphasis in the original.). Second, student-student confrontation was highest in racially mixed schools and drop off as the school enrollments were increasingly either black or white (Ibid.:8-7). Third, high-status schools, either black or white, resorted to calling for police assistance less frequently than other schools (Ibid.:8-13).

The Havighurst study was notable because its mention of the relationship between a school's racial mixture and the amount of student conflict was historically early. Also, its sample size was large enough (700 high schools in 45 cities with population exceeding 300,000) to give a fair profile of the problems facing urban schools. The study did not research the conflict issue very extensively, however. The Bailey study can be viewed as an expansion and refinement of chapter 8 in Havighurst.[5]

Bailey: The study devoted by Stephen K. Bailey at Syracuse University in 1971 is titled *Disruption in Urban Public Secondary Schools*. This work gathered information on disruptions from nineteen cities across the country, and, in the course of the investigation, its author visited twenty-seven schools. At the same time that school personnel were interviewed, community persons (police, parents, and school district personnel) were also interviewed. The broad-based findings from Bailey's study were:

1. School size was more important than city size; larger schools had more problems.
2. Disruption was positively related to integration. Schools that were almost all black or almost all white were less likely to be disrupted.
3. Integrated schools with high percentages of black staff were less likely to be disrupted than schools with low percentages of black staff.
4. Average daily attendance and disruption were inversely related.
5. Principals with least experience in office:
   a. Reported greater black enrollments
   b. Endorsed more active responses to disruption in contrast to "riding it out"
   c. Reported greater concern for positive prevention training programs
   d. Were more hesitant to project the blame for disruption onto external, nonschool factors (Bailey, 1971:10-12).

Bailey's seemingly valuable findings were muted somewhat by their juxtaposition (by Bailey in the actual publication) to some earlier, somewhat uncritical studies. The weaknesses of the three sources cited in his section on "previous research" in the area of disruption are explained below.

The first source Bailey mentioned was a National Association of Secondary School Principals (NASSP) survey in the 1968-1969 school year that reported only 10 percent race-related protests. But even Bailey pointed out that "in defining protest, the NASSP included almost any activity that was 'out of the orindary' " (Ibid.:7). That finding was not very spectacular. The second source Bailey cited was the Westin study. This work originally appeared as an eighteen-page chapter in a book titled, *The School and the Democratic Environment.* In Westin's chapter, only about one full page discussed the author's study. Though Bailey and others have cited this work by Westin as having developed an indication of the extent of the school disruption problem by conducting a "systematic survey of American newspapers" (Ibid.:7),[6] there are two problems with these data.

The first problem was though Westin developed his data by subscribing to a newspaper clipping service for November and December 1968, and January and February 1969, the months that he used may actually have hindered his ability to employ the survey for verifying the reasonable accuracy of other studies (Westin, 1970:65). Those winter months are historically periods of the least student activity and of the greatest number of student holidays. Though the study was systematic to the extent that presumably all newspaper articles on disruptions were sent to Westin, it remained a time sample that may well be nonrepresentative of the entire school year on which other studies were and still are based.

The second problem was, as Bailey intimated (but failed to state), that Westin did not scale his data. A three-person disruption had the same weight in the latter's work as a 1,000 person riot. As a consequence of this scaling issue alone, Westin's finding of "239 serious disruptions in 348 high schools in 38 states" (Westin, 1970:65) told nothing of either the frequency or the intensity per school. (Westin added further confusion by failing to mention whether or not he controlled for multiple articles on one disruption.) A tangential issue involved in the scaling problem is that since the questions were not scaled, there was no real definition of serious disruption. Lacking that definition, it is impossible to determine what types of student activities were being counted (or even what types of student activities were sent to Westin by the clipping service, for that matter).

Quite separate from any problems that were internal to the Westin study is one issue that revolves solely around Bailey's use of Westin's material. The problem seems to be an error of interpretation on Bailey's part, and strongly influences the conclusions Bailey drew from Westin. For example, Westin (p. 65): "During November, December, January and February, there were 239 serious disruptions involving 348 high schools in 38 states and the District of Columbia." Bailey (p. 7): "[Westin] reported that 348 high schools in 38 states had undergone some form of disruption between November, 1968, and February, 1969, and that *an additional* 239 schools had suffered 'serious' episodes" (emphasis added).[7]

Though the effort by the House Subcommittee on General Education is cited in the "statistical studies" section below, it is noted here as the third source on which Bailey relied; this study considers it to have significant weaknesses. The House Study was evidently not considered a strong research project, and its validity was questioned by other House Committee members quite early. Though sponsored by the House of Representatives, the work was not "reported out of Committee." Instead of being reported out of Committee (which means that a majority of the Committee approved the study), it was entered in the *Congressional Record* in the form of a "Chairman's Report." What weaknesses precipitated the vote of no confidence remains a mystery; however, the released findings concluded that there were not many riots in schools nor many disruptions.[8]

The actual study Bailey conducted was divided into two sections: field interviews of twenty-seven schools in nineteen cities; and a supplementary survey consisting of 2,000 questionnaires sent to public schools with enrollments exceeding 750 pupils (having addresses in areas with populations exceeding 50,000). The findings discussed previously were determined largely from the field interviews. The supplementary findings resulting from the questionnaires, however, have not yet been discussed; they should be examined with a critical eye.

Of the 2,000 questionnaires mailed, only 35 percent (683) were returned. Of the 638 respondents, 85 percent (581) indicated "some type of disruption *in the past three years*" (Ibid.:8; emphasis added). This generalization raises a plethora of sticky questions, including: What kind of disruption? How intense a riot? What issues? How many disruptions: one, two? Why did Bailey use such a wide time band? And what is a *normal* rate of school disruption over time? Are the data that 581 respondents out of 2,000 mailings experience some kind of unspecified disruption over a three-year period an unusual finding? Bailey failed to address any of these issues. However, the findings from the interviews did validate commonsensible notions of where disruptions take place. Had disruptions been in existence longer, there would doubtless have been studies more empirically grounded.

Vestermark: Shortly after Havighurst and Bailey had produced works analyzing *who* did the disrupting, and *what correlates* to disruptions could be developed, S.D. Vestermark produced a remarkable document that focused on *collective violence* in all its aspects. In this well-written document (supported under a grant from the Law Enforcement Assistance Administration's National Institute of Law Enforcement and Criminal Justice) Vestermark devoted some 100 pages exclusively to disruptions in high schools. He discussed not only the philosophical relations between law enforcement agencies and schools, but also why high schools were particularly vulnerable to violence. He also devoted an extensive chapter to the police's tactical role in violent high school disruptions.

For the purposes of developing these tactical responses, Vestermark divided disruptions into two groups: *situational violence* and *guided violence*. Vestermark pointed out that the functional differences between these types of collective violence involved whether or not someone intended (guided) the violent incident to turn out the way it did (Vestermark, 1971:26-28).

One of the many intriguing findings in the Vestermark study was that "student rioters had developed more systematic theories of police tactics than the police had [developed] of rioter tactics"—or, at least, the rioters had written and disseminated more than have police (Ibid.:54). The Vestermark materials were so extensive that a presentation of them must wait until chapter 4. Suffice it to say now that Vestermark's work was solidly analytical of policy and practice and presented virtually every imaginable situation and the tactics available as countermeasures.

Meyer: No sooner had the Vestermark study been received by the Law Enforcement Assistance Administration (LEAA) than the final report of another LEAA study was turned in. Also commissioned by the National Institute of Law Enforcement and Criminal Justice, the second project was titled "The Expansion of the Autonomy of Youth: Responses of the Secondary School to Problems of Order in the 1960s." Conducting this study in 1970-1971, authors Meyer, Chase-Dunn, and Inverarity stumbled onto a most unusual situation. Having proposed a study of crime and disruption in secondary schools to determine "whether increased community support and involvement might play some part in reducing such problems" (Meyer et al., 1971: Preface), the authors had to revise their stated objectives after having already begun the research. The difficulty, it seemed, was that school administrators did not experience their primary problem as one of discipline and order (Ibid.:6). The researchers pointed out that the actual problem was school nonparticipation—student apathy.

The finding by the Meyer team that school administrators were not concerned with disruptions but rather with apathy, presented a turning point for this study. Though discovered by accident, the phenomenon demonstrated by Meyer et al. became clear in later years through retrospective analysis of dozens of other, more informal sources. These informal sources, as well as the findings of the Meyer study, form the transition between chapters 4 and 5.

The Meyer study, which was conducted under the auspices of the Stanford Research Institute, inspires confidence. Two relevant earlier studies of national scope were discussed there and, unlike Bailey's study, Meyer's work carefully examined the strengths and weaknesses of each previous study. The studies (Coleman's "Equality of Educational Opportunity" and the Bailey work) each contained seven to nine questions, the answers to which were reanalyzed by the Meyer group and provided justification for their early direction. That the research was carefully planned yet nonetheless had to be redirected, is valuable knowledge for this book and will be discussed later.

Crime

As the Meyer study found, by 1971 disruptions were becoming less of a critical concern to school administrators. In the brief lull that followed the disruptions of the 1968-1971 period, the public slowly focused on a new problem—juvenile crime. Reports on crime are discussed below.

Greenberg: Also in the Stanford Research Institute, Greenberg was an early researcher who noticed increasing vandalism in schools across the nation. Though Greenberg's use of the word "vandalism" combined many terms that were listed separately by later researchers as discrete categories (for example, burglary, theft, and arson), it did not seriously affect the findings. The work proposed to discuss the many interrelated problems of school vandalism, and to identify solutions that had been applied in selected school systems (Greenberg, 1969:3). Having done this, Greenberg came up with four findings that were, in retrospect, quite interesting. At the time Greenberg conducted his study, no national data existed on any type of school crime. School security offices were still in their infancy, and the Senate was just producing its study on riots. This must be kept in mind regarding the Greenberg findings, which were:

1. Most schools had a vandalism problem.
2. In the average district, losses were not large enough to justify the costs of electronic alarm systems.
3. The failure of staff security precautions was a significant reason for vandal loss.
4. A system of vandal prevention based on apprehension of the vandal was generally ineffective.

The report ended by urging diagnostic as opposed to symptomatic approaches to the "determination of the causes and manifestations of school vandalism" (Ibid.:36).

The Panel on School Safety: New York, the first city to experience many of the problems that later beset large urban areas throughout the country, was the first community to prepare a districtwide analysis of the safety within their public schools. Commissioned by the New York Board of Education, this excellent 1972 study titled *A Safer Environment for Learning* developed the following findings:

1. Flexible and relevant curriculum was crucial, since oversized and overcrowded schools which offer irrelevant[9] courses to disinterested students inevitably discourage the students.
2. More personalized school environments were desirable, and these were to be achieved through smaller school units and greater student involvement with

all phases of decision making relating to issues affecting the quality of school life of the youths themselves.
3. The involvement of the entire school, as well as the outside community, in the development and maintenance of a school safety program was essential.
4. To concentrate on the prevention of crises rather than on always responding to crises represented a correct step toward solving problems rather than just covering them up. (*A Safer Environment for Learning*, 1972:2-4)

The Panel on School Safety derived its findings from sampling a respectable cross section of opinion. Because of its interviews with New York school administrators, commissioning special papers by individuals actively involved with school security-related fields, and reading a good selection of the available literature, the final report presented hard recommendations rather than just more statistics. The investigators, furthermore, took an objective view of all they were reporting. Anomalies in the data were brought to the reader's attention, and where different viewpoints were expressed by members of the research group, the differences were discussed.

It is interesting to note that by the time this study was being prepared in 1972, the authors were already noting discrepancies between the media representation of school problems, the political discussions about the extent of school problems, and the actual extent of these problems that their panel of experts could discover (Ibid.:18).

Brodsky and Knudten: In 1973 the U.S. Department of Justice's research branch began what has become a continuing interest in issues relating to the nature and extent of crime and violence in schools. The first tentative study on school crime was commissioned by the National Institute of Law Enforcement and Criminal Justice, Law Enforcement Assistance Administration (LEAA). Prepared by Stanley Brodsky and Richard Knudten, the study (*Strategies for Delinquency Prevention in the Schools* was written primarily for LEAA, and presented many recommendations to the agency based on surveys of all fifty superintendents of state boards of education and a sample of 390 superintendents of local school boards of education. Of the 440 questionnaires sent out, 219 (49.7 percent) were returned. Questions focused on only two topics: first, what school systems were doing in the areas of delinquency prevention and control; second, what suggestions could be made about new programs in these areas (Brodsky and Knudten, 1973:43).

The data from the Brodsky and Knudten study were very helpful, because the focus of the work was tightly limited and the integrity of the final report was unblemished. As opposed to being a broad-based project (for example, a study of school delinquency), this research very thoroughly and competently answered only the two questions mentioned above, and the answers were unadorned by rhetoric. Brodsky and Knudten's study responded well to a specific request for technical assistance by a federal agency. They not only provided needed information, but the information was not biased. The report was objectively written and the data were concisely presented. The Brodsky-Knudten study was particularly useful to this book, because they developed the first national assessment aimed at determining what actual steps school districts took to reduce delinquent behavior. Understanding the timing of that effort has assisted this study to set time periods of federal interest in issues of school-based crime.

Marvin: A federal study titled *Planning Assistance Programs to Reduce School Violence and Disruption* was completed in January 1976. Though released one month after the time period studied for this book, it has received sufficient national publicity that it must be acknowledged. Directed by Mike Marvin and produced by Research for Better Schools (RBS), this work was also commissioned by the Law Enforcement Assistance Administration. The Marvin study differs from this book in that the Marvin study did not analyze existing statistics or attempt to develop new conclusions from an understanding of the available sources. The Marvin study was a planning project which assumed that the problems of violence and disruption in the schools were widespread and that there was sufficient interest and concern about the problem to justify a national effort. As a consequence of this difference of purpose, Marvin's "Nature and Extent" chapter reports findings as given by their respective authors, whereas this book provides analysis and interpretation of various studies. Given the above assumptions, mere reportage is probably acceptable for the planning document, but must be considered a basic weakness from a research perspective. Therefore, the Marvin work is not often considered in this book.

The objectives of Marvin's study were threefold: first, to establish a working relationship with LEAA and with the educational community; second, to provide an information base for LEAA for planning purposes which included study of (1) the nature and extent of the problem, (2) current efforts underway, (3) overview of help desired by local schools, and (4) experience of other federal agencies in this area; third, to develop a recommended national program.

The Marvin study is recommended reading because it provides additional information as to the kinds of programs used to combat juvenile crime and violence. Marvin accomplished this research by conducting telephone interviews in 147 school districts to determine, in depth, the types of prevention and control programs focused on misbehaving youths. His overall approach was similar to that of the Brodsky-Knudten study in that some of Marvin's questions also concentrated on school programs to prevent and control school crime, and also sought recommendations for new programs. Unlike the Brodsky-Knudten study, Marvin's targets were local school administrators and school security directors rather than state or local school superintendents.

Miller: The Miller study dealt with juvenile gangs and their changing relationships to secondary schools. Walter B. Miller, in his extensive 1975 study on *Violence by Youth Gangs and Youth Groups as a Crime Problem in Major American Cities* (funded by a grant from LEAA's National Institute of Law Enforcement and Criminal Justice and conducted through Harvard's Center for Criminal Justice), discussed schools at some length. Miller pointed out that the traditional view of schools as *neutral turf* had dissolved into a new picture of schools as being "owned" by rival gangs in Los Angeles and other large cities. And one ramification of ownership was that the gangs charged admission either to the school facility itself or to certain parts of the building, such as the cafeteria (Miller, 1975:123).

Miller's study, which was an exploratory pilot effort, was not intended to be a definitive work in the area of gang activity in public schools. It does, however, provide an excellent feeling for the nature, scope, and intensity of a problem that is only now becoming an issue throughout the nation. Miller conducted interviews at many levels within communities, and placed his findings in the context of historical gang activity in schools. Miller's work will be particularly useful in the final part of this book, for gang activity in schools is a phenomenon that represents a new form of student actions to which schools will have to develop countermeasures.

Special-interest Group Studies

In the category of school misbehavior, especially in the more serious and hence more topical problem areas, specialized groups have evolved which conduct research and prepare papers on well-focused concerns. These groups—often professional associations—generally have restricted audiences, for whom the reports are designed. The categories of concerns addressed by these groups and of interest to this study are:

1. legal rights of children;
2. suspensions, expulsions, and pushouts;
3. disruptions;
4. discipline (mild to severe) and vandalism; and
5. data gathering in all areas.

Legal Rights of Children

In 1971 the National Organization on Legal Problems of Education (NOLPE) published three monographs on aspects of the law and youths. Two of these monographs were particularly important. One was concerned with "the legal basis for student suspensions and expulsions and ... the procedure that school officials must follow when they suspend or expel a student" (Phay, 1971:1) and the other monograph was concerned with "rights and freedoms of public school students" (Gaddy, 1971:1). These works reviewed the more significant court decisions that shaped the limits placed on school administrators, especially in the following areas: freedom of expression, freedom of association, freedom of dress and appearance, freedom of religion, freedom from discrimination, freedom from unauthorized searches, freedom from vague regulations, and access to due process.[10] The monographs by Phay and Gaddy were very important, for unlike works that were meant primarily for lawyers (for example, Tractenberg, 1970; Midonick, 1972), they provided background history and court philosophy that allowed the layperson to digest the meanings of the various rulings. They were also quite readable.

Suspensions, Expulsions, and Pushouts

Quite naturally, from the attention paid to the "correct" way to suspend or expel a student came public interest in knowing how many students were indeed suspended, how many were expelled, and how many were pushouts. The Children's Defense Fund of the Washington Research Project, Inc., began its book *Children Out of School in America* (1974) with the observation that an analysis of the Census Bureau data on nonenrolled youths produced the fantastic figure that 1 million youths between the ages seven to fifteen were not in school. Of that group, three-quarters were in the seven to thirteen age bracket. Discussing such topics as barriers to school attendance, exclusion of children with special needs, and school discipline and its exclusionary impact on students, this work was aimed at building public awareness of the concept of social stratification through the use or misuse of school discipline.[11]

Expanding on the theme of "damage to the student through suspensions," the Children's Defense Fund published a second report in 1975 titled *School Suspensions: Are They Helping Children?* This is the most definitive work to date on this topic.[12] The strength of these works lay in their scholarly and thorough treatment of the literature: they provided close analysis of many of the studies listed in this chapter.

Disruptions

As later chapters point out in greater depth, disruptions did not seem to have presented much of a problem in high schools, though they had received spectacular press coverage. Secondary school administrators had from the

Berkeley uprisings in 1954 until about 1968 to prepare themselves for large-scale group demonstrations. When the disturbances finally arrived in about 1968, two groups published useful handbooks focusing on co-opting as well as legal procedures for dealing with disrupting groups of youths.[1][3]

Prepared for rapid referencing, *Dissent and Disruption in the Schools: A Handbook for School Administrators* (Benton, 1971), produced by the Institute for Development of Educational Activities, Inc. (I/D/E/A/), not only traced the legal trends being confronted in the federal courts, but also analyzed school tension situations beginning with their early indications, continuing through peaceful student actions, and ending in violent conflicts. A particularly valuable aspect of this *Handbook* was that at every step where tactical intervention was recommended, it clearly presented the moral and legal considerations that the school administrator must confront.

Unlike the I/D/E/A/ *Handbook*, the work of the National School Public Relations Association (Gudridge, 1969) addressed a number of broader issues in relation to secondary school disruptions. Among the issues were such questions as: how we got here; where we are; what to do about it; and where we are going. Titled *High School Student Unrest: How to Anticipate Protest, Channel Activism, and Project Student Rights*, the work relied heavily on educational practitioners to provide actual examples of the types of issues about which students were protesting in the late 1960s. It also paid a great deal of attention to the nature of the protests. Moreover, it provided discussions of ways by which to co-opt the anger of protest leaders, ways to head off troubles before they became demonstrations, and the desirable types of school rules and regulations that were firm, fair, and legal.

The Gudridge work was helpful for this book because of its forthright discussion on co-opting roles schools could and did play vis-à-vis disruptions. Though co-opting has negative connotations, this work treated the topic in an objective fashion, pointing out that if the school administration would consider the students' requests before they became "demands" and agreed to those that were least likely to arouse the school board and the community, the disruption could be successfully co-opted (Gudridge, 1969:5).

Another noteworthy article appeared in the June 1969 issue of *School Management*. Titled "Strategies for Coping with Student Disruption," it divided disruptions into three subcategories: sit-ins, boycotts, and violence. The article included case studies of each of these kinds of disruptions and discussed each incident from the perspectives of *initial reaction, result,* and *aftermath*. At the end of each section, there was an analysis of the information covered in the anecdotes. Though "Strategies for Coping with Student Disruptions" was a short article, it had a number of strong points. First, it presented and analyzed various real plans of action, covering strategies implemented under numerous conditions which can now be assessed for success or failure based on the anecdotes provided. Second, the article appeared in a journal serving school administrators and thereby received extensive coverage among the group of school persons who had line responsibility to prevent disruptions.[14]

Though the article had numerous strong points, it also contained certain weaknesses, such as the following: first, the samples were probably selected editorially to fit the story being told; second, there were no assurances of accuracy in the case studies and most of the incidents were sketchy, sounding as if they were developed out of summaries of news articles; third, the original causes of some of the incidents were not indicated, resulting in a feeling that the case studies were incomplete. Methodology aside, however, this work was insightful, logical, and well written, and will be considered further in chapter 4.

Discipline (Mild to Severe) and Vandalism

The National School Public Relation's Association (NSPRA) had a valuable function: from 1969 to 1975, it combined information from most other specialized educational associations and produced topical, timely reports covering the nature and scope of specific problems. Since 1969, four NSPRA reports bore heavily on student misbehaviors. These reports were Gudridge (1969) *High School Student Unrest*;[15] Wells (1971) *Vandalism and Violence: Innovative Strategies Reduce Cost to Schools*; Jones (1973) *Discipline Crisis in Schools: The Problem, Causes and Search for Solutions*; and Neill (1975) *Violence and Vandalism: Current Trends in School Policies and Programs*.

All four reports had two generic weaknesses. First, they were largely informal and anecdotal, drawing heavily on other publications. Rather than introducing new data, the NSPRA papers merely synthesized relevant newspaper, journal, and academic reports. Second, data were never questioned; statistics in these NSPRA reports were taken without comment from the research source. The combination of these two weaknesses conspired to produce reports that were informal and sometimes misleading. Whether or not the reports' weaknesses were outweighed by possible advantages of timeliness and editorial clarity is a matter of opinion. Nowhere else were such national state-of-the-art papers prepared on such specific topics;[16] however, nowhere else was statistical misrepresentation on the nature and extent of school misbehaviors so likely to be disseminated to school administrators.

Data Gathering, in All Areas

Though it is perhaps odd to think of it this way, the U.S. Congress serves as a primary stimulus insofar as national data collection is concerned. Before passing legislation directing the Executive Branch to perform any kind of new function, Congress conducts, or asks a federal department to conduct, a needs assessment.

Particularly in cases where entirely new legislation is being proposed, the research required by Congress may be extensive. Examples of congressionally inspired studies are highlighted below.

When riots in secondary schools became an issue, the House Subcommittee on General Education (Pucinski, 1970) conducted a survey regarding the nature, breadth, and scope of the problem.[17] This report also served as the nucleus of the U.S. Office of Education's publication on the same topic. The Senate in 1970 conducted a survey of 155 urban school districts on the topic of school violence and disruptions between 1964 and 1968. Representative Jonathan Bingham (1971) introduced the findings into the *Congressional Record* as part of the summarizing statements about his "Safe Schools Act." In 1975 the Senate's Subcommittee on Juvenile Delinquency conducted a similar survey (Bayh, 1975). The next Senate survey covered 757 school districts, the issue was crime, and the time period analyzed was 1970-1973.

It is crucial to understand that the purposes of these reports were not primarily research. The Senate was concerned with raising public awareness to the nature and extent of changes in pupils in public schools. To that end, there was less interest on the part of the Senate in mounting large-scale projects. Though it is unfair to subject these studies to close examination for research errors, readers do need a minimal understanding of the more obvious errors which exclude these works from consideration in this study.

1. 1970 Survey of 155 School Districts (Bingham, 1971): Usually informally called the "1970 Study of 110 School Districts," the fact is that the 110 figure represented *respondents only*, rather than the total population sampled. Apart from the problems that the data returned to the Senate for inclusion in their report were fantastically spotty and probably noncomparable between school districts, a number of research errors contaminated the findings. First, this report did not compute incident *rates* in relation to total student population. As a result, large school districts were compared with small school districts in terms of numbers of incidents. Second, the actual incident chart from which the summary data were drawn contained many more nonresponses than responses. Since the Senate's summary data noted a percent change of the 1968 number of incidents over the 1964 number of incidents, this meant a nonresponse was treated as if it were a nonproblem. When these data were reprinted in reports used to demonstrate the existence and growth of such problems, the danger of communicating possibly incorrect impressions existed. Third, no caveat was provided explaining that much of the violent crime in schools was perpetrated by outsiders illegally on the school grounds, and that the survey could not distinguish between crimes committed by students or nonstudents. Fourth, no attention was paid to changes in overall school enrollment or to changes in age-grouped populations for these years. Using high school enrollment exclusively, the figures (provided by the Bureau of the Census) were: 1964, 11.4 million; 1968, 12.8 million; and 1973—relating to the 1975 Senate study,

below—14.2 million. The Bingham report never mentioned the obvious conclusions that *some increases* in the national counts of crime incidents in schools were likely to be *normal* due to these population increases.

2. The 1975 survey of 748 of the largest school districts in the United States (Bayh, 1975): Usually called "Our Nation's Schools—A Report Card: 'A' in School Violence and Vandalism," this study was similar in format to Bingham's 1970 survey and included some of the same data-gathering and analysis problems discussed above. Primarily meant to raise public awareness of the growing problems of crime and violence in public schools, this report—and the hearings associated with it—have been instrumental in raising public awareness in this critical area.

Since these studies were not primarily research efforts but state-of-the-problem papers, great care must be taken when trying to draw conclusions from them. They represent a valiant attempt to quantify an undefined problem; however, this book does not use data from either survey.[18]

The above studies were only those directly conducted by Congress, and legislation was occasionally passed that required the Executive Branch of government to conduct various types of studies relating to school misbehaviors. Examples of such congressionally mandated studies are: first, the Juvenile Delinquency Prevention and Control Act of 1971, which called for a determination of federal emphasis on all aspects of juvenile delinquency;[19] and, second, the Education Amendments of 1974 to the Elementary and Secondary Schools Act charging the Department of Health, Education and Welfare (HEW) with determining the types and frequencies of school crime and property loss as well as with determining effective security systems and crime offense rates.[20] By 1975, the National Center for Education Statistics was compiling the first part of that request, and the National Institute of Education was working on the second part. In addition to these congressionally mandated studies, Public Law 93-380 directed HEW "to request each state education agency to take steps necessary to establish and maintain appropriate records to facilitate the compilation of information," listed above (PL 93-380 Sec. 825). Due in part to long time lags required to develop a staff to plan and implement such studies and in part to the long time lag required to analyze the survey returns, neither of these HEW efforts will produce reports until late 1977. The mere existence of these HEW projects is of interest to this book, however, since they provide an indication of the current research focus of both Congress and HEW.

The influence of Congress of course reaches far beyond actual legal mandates. In 1973 at the national conference of the National Association of School Security Directors, the decision was made to establish a uniform crime and property-loss reporting system. The determination came about because the association's membership felt such information could help Congress in relation to national legislation which might be passed in this area.

Statistical Studies

Statistics that are relevant to this study are scarce. In very few cases are the data both national in scope and broad enough over time. Statistics of interest to this study cover the following areas:

1. Public opinion   1969-1975
2. Public concern   1950-1975
3. Census data   1950-1975
4. Juvenile arrests   1953-1974
5. Vandalism costs   1970-1974
6. Riots   1968-1969
7. Fires   1950-1975

Public Opinion (1969-1975)

The Lou Harris "Poll" in *Life* magazine, May 1969, was the first public opinion survey focusing on misbehavior problems in schools. Growing out of public concern over racial tensions and issues of student protest and dissent in the late 1960s, the "Poll" found that students not only wanted a greater voice in what went on in schools, but that they were also aware of their powers and abilities to achieve greater voice. The Harris "Poll" also uncovered a surprise: in issues of discipline, a loose alliance existed between student and teachers—"it [was] the parent, with his differing standards and priorities, who [was] the odd man out" (Harris, 1969:29).

In the Lou Harris "Poll," discipline referred to minor classroom misbehaviors. In the early Gallup "Polls," discipline still referred to minor classroom misbehaviors but shifted toward crime and violence by 1975. The "Gallup Polls on Attitudes toward Education" ran from 1969 to 1975. In every year except 1971, discipline was the issue of greatest concern to the respondents. In 1969, 1970, and 1971 pollsters asked questions about discipline from the standpoint of its strictness. Since the 1971 "Poll" had not listed discipline as the first public concern, the 1972 "Poll" asked no in-depth questions on that topic. But in 1972 discipline again headed the roster of problems of greatest concern to respondents. Given the persistence of this topic and the broad interpretations of the term "discipline," Gallup introduced questions in the 1973 "Poll" about what discipline meant to the public.

In 1974 several questions designed to differentiate between various types of discipline violations first appeared. One question dealt with student gangs disrupting schools and another, with stealing in schools. Much more detailed questions appeared on the noninterested student and the recalcitrant student.[21]

The Gallup "Poll" for 1975 again tried to get a grip on the school discipline problem. Questions on drugs and alcohol, alternative schools featuring strict discipline and making students work harder all nibbled at the edges of the larger issue of discipline. The problems with the Gallup "Polls" were twofold. First, the content of their questions changed from year to year; second, in only two of the seven years were data collected on the sex, race, education, and occupation of respondents. Had this data been collected every year, there might have been shifts in the population sample of persons expressing their concerns in the "Polls."

Public Concern, 1950-1975

For this book, charts have been developed based on actual counts of the numbers of articles written by the *New York Times* and the *Chicago Tribune* on public secondary school occurrences of: (1) crimes, assaults, violence, and vandalism; and (2) riots or disruptions.

These charts purport to show changes in the media concern (and presumably the public concern) over the seriousness of the school crime/disruption issues.[22] The problem with developing these counts is endemic. First, when are assaults, particularly gang fights, included as small riots? Second, how are multiple articles counted on the same riot or crime? Third, how are Parent Teacher Association-type meetings (held to discuss disruptions or crimes) kept separate from the articles on the actual incidents?

The approach taken in this book to minimize these problems was to have instructed the researchers compiling counts to be consistent in their tabulations, at all costs. That the *Tribune* group (actual *Tribune* employees) and the *Times* group did not count the same universe of events is not critical; slopes of the graph may not look the same, but they should occur at about the same points in time.

Census Data, 1950-1975

The U.S. Department of Commerce, Bureau of the Census, provided two charts: (1) population of fifteen to seventeen year olds, for each year, 1950-1975; and (2) high school enrollment figures for each year, 1950-1974.

Juvenile Arrests, 1953-1974

The only statistics that served as an indicator of rate increases in juvenile crimes were the increases in the rates of juvenile arrests (fifteen to seventeen year olds) that can be computed from the FBI's *Uniform Crime Reports* (*UCR*).[23] The U.S. Department of Justice's Federal Bureau of Investigation, Uniform Crime Reports Section (Statistics Division), went over its juvenile arrest data and extracted arrests exclusively for fifteen to seventeen year olds. This was done for the following categories:

1. Total Part I offenses. (This category includes criminal homicide, forcible rape, robbery, aggravated assault, burglary, larceny/theft, and auto theft.)
2. Total Part II offenses. (This category includes other assaults, arson, forgery, fraud, embezzlement, stolen property offenses, vandalism weapons, sex offenses, and so forth.)
3. Aggravated assault.
4. Burglary.
5. Larceny/theft.
6. Arson (1964-1974).
7. Vandalism (1964-1974).

By accounting for variables of change in the U.S. population of fifteen to seventeen year olds (figures available from the Bureau of the Census) and changes in the numbers of law enforcement agencies reporting data to the FBI (figures available in each *Uniform Crime Report*), the actual rate of change in arrests of fifteen to seventeen year olds can be calculated. The calculations show, for example, that the arrest rate of fifteen to seventeen year olds in 1964 for Part I crimes is 230 percent above the 1953 rate, whereas the 1974 arrest rate for assaults is 440 percent above the 1953 rate (see chart 2-1). Discussion of these data appear throughout chapter 5.

Chart 2-1
Actual Percent Increases in Arrest Rates of Fifteen to Seventeen Year Olds (1953-1974)[a]

Offense	Population,[b] 1953	Arrest Rate,[c] 1953	Population,[b] 1974	Arrest Rate,[c] 1974	Percent Increase of Arrest Rate: 1974 over 1953[a]
Assault	6,490	2.5365	12,651	13.6909	440
Burglary	6,490	32.7037	12,651	80.3479	150
Larceny/Theft	6,490	43.1557	12,651	142.8089	230
Total Part I	6,490	87.2347	12,651	291.2210	230
Total Part II	6,490	160.3079	12,651	511.6645	220

[a]The actual percent increase controls for: (1) changes in the *UCR* arrest population over time by using rates per 100,000 population and (2) changes in the number of juvenile arrests as a function of changes in the youth population of the same age group.
[b]Population expressed in thousands.
[c]Rate expressed in terms of 100,000 population.

Vandalism Costs, 1970-1974

The most comprehensive analysis of vandalism costs was the annual study conducted by *School Product News* (Slaybaugh, 1975). Not only did this report discuss "how the vandalism dollar is consumed," but it also analyzed vandalism costs as a function of school district size. Though the 1974 survey return rate was only 15 percent (561 of 3,810 questionnaires), Slaybaugh pointed out that this information was very reluctantly given to anyone but the federal government. Interestingly, the *School Product News* analysis showed that urban fire damage was lower (cost per pupil) than suburban;[24] property destruction, glass breakage, and equipment theft were much greater in large than in small districts; and arson was about the same in large, medium, and small districts.[25]

The weaknesses of the *School Product News* studies were as follows. First, in notations of changes in the dollar costs of vandalism over the years, inflation's effect on the value of the dollar had not been considered. Second, rates of vandalism costs could not be computed because the data were not provided. Third, the return rate of the questionnaires was slanted toward suburban schools. (The result will undoubtedly underrepresent the extent of vandalism costs.) Fourth, there was no discussion about nonreporting or underreporting districts. Fifth, there was no discussion about differences in reporting procedures between responding districts.

Riots, 1968-1969

Though not a longitudinal study, the effort by the House Subcommittee on General Education to assess the depth and scope of the riot issue deserves mention here. In 1970 Congress (Pucinski, 1970) sent out a survey to every (50,000) high school district in the nation. The response rate was 52 percent (15,086) and of these, 18 percent of the schools reported some form of protest activity. Only 1 percent (149) reported one or more riots as protest activity. Of those reporting riots, 64 percent indicated that there were only one or two riots that year, and 70 percent indicated that less than 10 percent of their students were involved. If one were profiling riots in the nation's schools from this survey, the following could be said:

In the 1968-1969 school year, most schools (99 percent) experienced no riots. Those that did were small schools (with enrollments less than 1,000) located in urban areas (70 percent urban). The mean income of the parents of students attending riot-torn schools ranged from $5,000 to $10,000. Enrollment was evenly mixed with respect to race. About half the time, there had been increased ethnic enrollment in the last five years. The riots usually involved injuries (66 percent) but to few members of the student body (70 percent of the reporting schools noted that less than 10 percent of their students were involved). Though property damage was slight (77 percent reported less than $500), police were often called in (83 percent called police). Racial issues were the catalyst for the riots most of the time (83 percent).

The Children's Defense Fund publication (1975:241) discussed the technical weaknesses of this study. The Defense Fund pointed out that the Pucinski study did not distinguish between legal and illegal protests, and did not ask whether violence in any form accompanied the protest activity. Again, the House study did not compute incident rates, so this book could not draw conclusions about city size of school district size and disruptive activity from it. As pointed out previously, this study was not reported out of committee, but was only published in the *Congressional Record* as a "Chairman's Report." This fact perhaps testifies either to the unsensational findings or to the committee's concern about releasing a study with such weaknesses.

Fires, 1950-1975

The National Fire Protection Association (NFPA) had three related studies: one in 1957, covering 300 school fires from 1946 to 1956; one in 1965, covering 650 school fires from 1957 to 1964; and one in 1973 covering 155 school fires from 1967 to 1970. The tables drawn by the association were of identical format for all periods. Among the findings were: first, there were shifts in the types of fires from *faulty wiring* in the 1945-1955 period to *incendiary* in the 1967-1970 period; second, there were extraordinary increases in the numbers and costs of school fires (3,000 in 1950 and 20,500 in 1971; cost, $16.1 million in 1950 and $87 million in 1971); and third, there was little or no attention paid to the secondary costs of fires (loss of materials and facilities, trauma loss in cases of deaths, split sessions or other inconvenience resulting from holding classes in another school, and so forth). In addition to the tables that aggregated these data, the NFPA has been able to provide the *actual numbers, estimated costs*, and *percent incendiary* for all school fires reported to their association. The figures on an annual basis only became available beginning with the 1968 data. Previously, available figures existed in multi-year blocks only.

The caveat accompanying these data was that the actual numbers reported to the NFPA annually came from every fire department in the country. Though the NFPA requested that certain categories of fires be accounted for, and school fires were one such category, errors in the NFPA numbers would by definition reflect possible reporting errors at the local level.

Summary

The reviewed literature fell into three categories: research that produced in-depth, but often local, studies; research and reports of special-interest groups, such as professional associations; and statistical data, often collected by government agencies. Of the major in-depth local studies, there were a sufficient quantity available to show general directions of consultant and academic research interest over time. Often studies were commissioned by federal agencies to answer specific questions about student misbehaviors. In these cases, this study concluded there were shifts in government research interests in student misbehaviors over time from disorders (from about 1950 to 1968) through disruptions (from about 1968 to 1971) to crimes (from about 1970 to 1975).

With respect to the studies conducted by special-interest groups, this book could determine the kinds of concerns such groups had over time by regarding the topics on which their reports focused year after year. Of the research that developed statistics over all or most of the study's time period, there were two general groups: statistics reflecting public opinion or public concern about student misbehaviors; and statistics attempting to chronicle absolute increases in crimes or misbehaviors. In later chapters, the book compares changes in the public's opinion about such misbehaviors with many of the official crime and population data.

Though many of these studies and statistics reappear in the following chapters, there is an especially important reason for grouping them here in this particular way. The groupings allow for a longitudinal look at the kinds of research being conducted, whereas the chapters that follow select pieces of these studies as they are needed to develop the required in-depth analysis of the specific kinds of misbehaviors being discussed.

Notes

1. The significance of this approach is as follows: by listing the major special-interest group studies in one subsection (for example), the study can observe that the topics of concern to these groups change from disorders in the 1950s to disruptions in the late 1960s to crime in the early 1970s. This represents, in other words, a horizontal cut of the literature (because it covers the entire time period), whereas the individual chapters that follow represent a vertical cut of the literature (because they address only specific subjects).

2. Suspensions are generally short-term actions taken by the school principal and usually last less than ten days. Expulsions mean exclusion from attending any schools in that school district and usually require more formal school district action than simple suspension.

3. The term "pushout" refers to any student who is either officially or unofficially restricted from coming to school. Within the last decade, this term is particularly used to connote an individual who has established a tacit understanding with the school administrator that if he does not come to school, the school will not press truancy charges.

4. The Bailey study tried to use Erickson's term "disruptive unrest" when conducting their interviews and noted that the term confused school administrators (Bailey, 1971:2). It seems that the terms, separately, had different connotations, so Bailey used only disruption. This study used only the term disruption, based on that precedent.

5. Both the Havighurst and Bailey studies were supported, to a greater or lesser extent, by the National Association of Secondary School Principals (NASSP). The Havighurst study was conceived and funded by the NASSP; the Bailey study was funded by HEW's Office of Education but was published by the NASSP.

6. The Westin study was also cited in the opening paragraph of the Preliminary Report of the Senate Subcommittee to Investigate Juvenile Delinquency (Bayh, 1975). The same kind of authority was ascribed to Westin in that report. Westin was also cited (and reviewed nonanalytically) in the Vestermark work.

7. The issue highlighted by the comparison of these two quotes is whether the 239 serious disruptions were a subset of a total of 348 high schools or whether the 239 serious disruptions were in addition to the regular disruptions reported in the 348 high schools. In one case, the total number of schools is 348; in the other case, 587. The correct interpretation probably is 348, of which 239 reported serious incidents. (This interpretation is also supported by Fish, 1970, in his book's introduction. Fish also used the Westin counts of student disruptions to establish the extent of the problem nationally.)

8. It seems that a riot is a violent disruption, and a disruption is a peaceful riot; however, since none of these studies define either term, and a number of the studies use both terms (as well as unrest), cross-interpretation of the data is difficult.

9. The problem of whether it was the student or the school that determined the curriculum's relevancy remained unaddressed. The disinterested student who proclaims grammar, composition, history, and algebra irrelevant may be interested in the entertaining performance of a charismatic teacher, instructing in subjects that are of little or no value in developing mental skills or intellectual discipline.

10. Not until 1975, in the *Goss v. Lopez* and *Wood v. Strickland* cases (Conway, 1975) were new legal issues added that modify these NOLPE publications.

11. School discipline is used here to mean suspensions, expulsions, or informal agreements that the pupil will no longer come to school.

12. The Robert F. Kennedy Memorial in Washington, D.C., published *The Student Pushout: Victim of Continued Resistance to Desegregation.* Discussed in the previous section of this chapter, it had a much narrower focus than the Children's Defense Fund's books, since it fundamentally looked at indefinite

suspensions and the like as semiofficial ways of removing minority race members from public schools. Legal avenues of recourse were listed, and the federal laws prohibiting these kinds of de facto expulsions were provided.

13. Concern over issues covered in these works first surfaced publicly in a 1969 House Education Subcommittee report. The issues were generally those repeatedly mentioned in the media at that time: racial tensions, dress codes, inequalities of society, and so forth.

14. The same statement about coverage cannot be said about the I/D/E/A/ or the NSPRA (Gudridge) documents, which lacked the subscribing membership necessary for large-scale dissemination of their ideas.

15. *High School Student Unrest* was discussed in the "disruptions" section.

16. Though congressional testimony contained presentations by the presidents of the same organizations used in the NSPRA reports, congressional documents lacked the editorial sense made by NSPRA. Reports made from congressional testimony were also less frequent and usually more broadly focused on general topics.

17. This report on school riots is analyzed in the "statistics" section.

18. An example of the difficulty in analyzing the *first* survey where raw data were available is the following: in 1968 New York reported that it expelled 5,942 pupils, whereas the city reporting the next highest number of pupils expelled noted only 261. Of the 110 reporting districts, over half (67) indicated zero expulsions. That New York expulsions were so far out of line with even the next highest city answering the survey and that so many cities reported no expulsions casts doubt about the analyzability of these data.

19. The actual laws requiring a reporting of the federal juvenile delinquency efforts are Section 409 of Public Law 92-31 and Public Law 92-381.

20. The actual law covering this study is Public Law 93-380, Section 825.

21. Meyer (1971) first picked up on the apathy theme (see under "general studies") quite by accident. Gallup first introduced the question in the 1971 "Poll," but dropped it in 1972 and 1973.

22. The logical assumption, quite clearly, is that frequency of news articles in the *Times* and the *Tribune* reflects anything other than the frequency of news articles in the *Times* or the *Tribune*. For the sake of this study, if only from a phenomenological viewpoint, this information should not be rejected out of hand. These charts do show peaks—especially in the area of disruption—that correspond closely with findings of the preponderance of formal studies.

23. Weaknesses in the *UCR* data were discussed in the "technical limits" section of chapter 1.

24. The lower urban fire damage rate may be due simply to faster response times of fire departments.

25. That the large districts experienced about the same dollar loss for arson as medium and small districts may suggest that though there are a few arsonists in every crowd, there are not a lot of arsonists in a large crowd.

References

Bailey, Stephen K.
    1971   *Disruption in Urban Public Secondary Schools.* Washington, D.C.: National Association of Secondary School Principals.

Bayh, Birch
    1975   "Our Nation's Schools—A Report Card: 'A' In School Violence and Vandalism." Washington, D.C.: Preliminary Report of the Subcommittee to Investigate Juvenile Delinquency, Judiciary Committee, U.S. Senate (April).

Benton, A. Edgar
    1971   *Dissent and Disruption in the Schools: A Handbook for School Administrators.* Dayton, Ohio: Institute for Development of Educational Activities, Inc.

Bingham, John
    1971   "Safe Schools Act: H.R. 3101, and H.R. 10641." Washington, D.C.: 92nd U.S. Congress (February and September).

Brodsky, Stanley L., and Knudten, Richard D.
    1973   *Strategies for Delinquency Prevention in the Schools.* Tuscaloosa, Ala.: University of Alabama Press.

Chicago Tribune
    1976   "Chicago Tribune Count of Articles on High School Disruptions and Crime, 1950-1975" (by special contract).

Children's Defense Fund (Cambridge: Mass.)
    1974   *Children Out of School in America.*
    1975   *School Suspensions: Are They Helping Children?*

Conway, Lenny
    1975   *Suspensions and Due Process.* Washington, D.C.: Robert F. Kennedy Memorial (February 28).

Elam, Stanley (ed.)
    1973   *The Gallup Polls of Attitudes toward Education 1969-1973.* Bloomington, Ind.: Phi Delta Kappa, Inc.

Erickson, Kenneth; Benson, George; and Huff, Robert
    1969   "Activism in the Secondary Schools: Analysis and Recommendations." Eugene, Ore.: Bureau of Educational Research.

Fish, Kenneth L.
    1970   *Conflict and Dissent in the High School.* New York: Bruce Publishing Company.

Gaddy, Dale
    1971   *Rights and Freedoms of Public School Students: Directions from the 1960s.* Topeka, Kans.: NOLPE Monograph Series, no. 2.

Gallup, George
    1974   "Sixth Annual Gallup Poll of Public Attitudes toward Education." *Phi Delta Kappan* (September):20-32.
    1975   "Seventh Annual Gallup Poll of Public Attitudes toward Education." *Phi Delta Kappan* (December):227-240.

Greenberg, Bernard
    1969   *School Vandalism: A National Dilemma.* Menlo Park, Calif.: Stanford Research Institute (October).

Gudridge, Beatrice
    1969   *High School Student Unrest: How to Anticipate Protest, Channel Activism, and Protect Student Rights.* Arlington, Va.: National School Public Relations Association.

Hagstrom, Warren O., and Gardner, Leslie L.
    1969   "Characteristics of Disruptive High School Students." Technical Report Number 96. Madison, Wis.: Wisconsin Research and Development Center for Cognitive Learning, University of Wisconsin (September).

Harris, Lou
    1969   "Crisis in the High School." *Life* (May 16):23-39.

Havighurst, Robert J.
    1970   *A Profile of the Large-City High School.* Washington, D.C.: National Association of Secondary School Principals (November).

Jones, J. William
    1973   *Discipline Crisis in Schools: The Problem, Causes and Search for Solution.* Washington, D.C.: National School Public Relations Association.

Marvin, Michael et al.
    1976   *Planning Assistance Programs to Reduce School Violence and Disruption.* Philadelphia, Pa.: Research for Better Schools.

Meyer, John; Chase-Dunn, Chris; and Invarity, James
    1971   "The Expansion of the Autonomy of Youth: Responses of the Secondary School to Problems of Order in the 1960s." Menlo Park, Calif.: The Laboratory for Social Research, Stanford University.

Midonick, Millard L.
    1972   *Children, Parents and the Courts.* New York: Practicing Law Institute.

Miller, Walter B.
    1975   *Violence by Youth Gangs and Youth Groups in Major American Cities.* Interim Report of Grant 74NI-990047. Washington, D.C.: Law Enforcement Assistance Administration.

National Education Association
    1956   "Teacher Opinion on Pupil Behavior, 1955-1956." Washington, D.C.: *Research Bulletin of the National Education Association* vol. 34, no. 2 (April).

Neill, Shirley B.
    1975   *Violence and Vandalism: Current Trends in School Policies and Programs*. Arlington, Va.: National School Public Relations Association.

Panel on School Safety
    1972   *A Safer Environment for Learning*. New York: Panel on School Safety, appointed by the Academy for Educational Development (October 31).

Phay, Robert E.
    1971   *Suspensions and Expulsions of Public School Students*. Topeka, Kan.: NOLPE Monograph Series, no. 3.

Polk, Kenneth and Schafer, Walter
    1972   *Schools and Delinquency*. Englewood Cliffs, N.J.: Prentice-Hall.

Pucinski, Roman C.
    1970   "Results of a Survey on Students' Unrest in the Nation's High Schools." *Congressional Record* (February):E1178-E1180.

Robert F. Kennedy Memorial (Washington, D.C.)
    1973   *The Student Pushout: Victim of Continued Resistance to Desegregation*.

Slaybaugh, David J.
    1975   "School Security Survey." *School Product News* (June):10-15.

Tractenberg, Paul
    1970   *Current School Problems*. New York: Practicing Law Institute.

U.S. Department of Commerce
    1976   "U.S. Population of 15-17 Year Olds from 1950 to 1975." Compiled by special request by the Statistics Division, Bureau of Census.
    1976   "High School Enrollment Figures, 1950-1974." Compiled by special request by the Office of Congressional Liaison, Bureau of Census.

U.S. Department of Justice
    1976   "Arrests of Youths Ages 15-17 from 1953 to 1974." Prepared by special request by the Statistics Branch, Uniform Crime Reports Division.

Vestermark, S.D.
    1971   *Responses to Collective Violence in Threat or Act*. Vol. 1: *Collective Violence in Educational Institutions*. Springfield, Va.: National Technical Information Service.

Wells, Elmer
    1971   *Vandalism and Violence: Innovative Strategies Reduce Cost to Schools*. Arlington, Va.: National School Public Relations Association.

Westin, Alan F.
    1970   "Facing the Issues: Responding to Rebels with a Cause." In *The School and the Democratic Environment*, Danforth Foundation and Ford Foundation (eds.), pp. 65-82. New York: Columbia University Press.

Public Laws Cited

Amendments of 1971 to the Juvenile Delinquency Prevention and Control Act of 1968 (Public Law 92-31).

Amendments of 1972 to the Juvenile Delinquency Prevention and Control Act of 1968 (Public Law 92-381).

Education Amendments of 1974 to the Elementary and Secondary Schools Act of 1965 (Public Law 93-380).

3 Disorders

Juvenile delinquency is not of the schools' manufacture, nor is it of the schools' cure, but there is a role to be played.

Right now, all the future delinquents are sitting in a classroom, some classroom, in the Nation's schools. The last crops of delinquents are recently from the Nation's schools. Some will come back to the Nation's schools. ...

[The youngster with whom we are concerned] often gets a bankruptcy statement for a report card. When he brings it home, it indicates that he is perhaps good for nothing. He is a youngster who shows a marked dislike for schools, and often exhibits a confusion-bred hatred that pushes into rebellion. ...

A youngster who often has very limited aptitude, he is often caught in the vise of an academic curriculum, and is given a squeeze, with the hopes that some learning will drip out. What drips out often is a delinquent.

(Kvaraceus, 1959:37)

Introduction

The schools' handling of disorders (noncriminal acts)—the least severe student misbehavior for this study—often represents a pivotal point in the educational life of youths. The act that the pupil commits may be treated in any number of ways—these are often subjective and vary according to individual orientations and circumstances. In the handling of disorders, the critical subjective issues seem to include the following: first, who observes the act; second, who reports the act; and third, to whom the act is reported (Polk, 1972:155). The way the child perceives the fairness of its treatment for an act of disorder may well affect its reaction to school for years to come.

As Kvaraceus' quote implies, schools may play a part in the creation of youths who ultimately get into additional trouble either within their communities or with the police. This chapter looks at that part. Disorders are critical in this respect because, unlike punishments for disruptions or crimes, punishments for disorders often seem to take into account such subjective variables as race, sex, age, and previous school and social history of the child. Also unlike crimes, offenses that are punishable as disorders are often established by the local school administration; there may be large variations between schools (even within the same school district) as to the kinds of rule infractions or the frequency of rule breaking that will cause the school administrator to take a formal action.

This chapter looks at disorders from two fundamental viewpoints, and then at the trends in the major types of responses to disorders. However, two initial digressions are required: first, a reminder of the definition of disorder as discussed in chapter 1, and second, a stipulation concerning the questions addressed by this chapter.

Definition of Disorder

Disorders represent a residual category including acts that are neither criminal nor group disruptions. The primary utility of this category is that it is helpful for understanding a large body of student misbehaviors. Disorders are differentiated from disruptions in that the student or students involved are acting out in their own behalf, not for the sake of some greater issue; the entire functioning of the school is not purposefully interrupted by the commission of the disorderly act or acts. Disorders are differentiated from crimes in that the offense committed could not result in the youth's being arrested by law enforcement officials.

Major Questions about Disorders

To understand problems faced both by pupils and schools in relation to student disorders, consider the following major questions:

1. To what extent does an understanding of the differing views of student disorders contribute to an understanding of the interactive relationships between students and schools?

In illustrating the nature of the roles schools and students played, vis-à-vis perpetration of (and punishment for) noncriminal violations of school rules, the study looks at the roles played by the principal actors from two vantage points; first, how pupils saw disorders and their possible reasons for engaging in them; second, how school personnel feel about student disorders.

2. How did different levels of authority figures (teachers, school administrators, school security officers, or aides) respond to school disorders?

Groups with different concerns for pupils probably had different responses to disorderly students. Although teachers and administrators both work in schools for the betterment of youths, those groups often approach discipline differently. As an example, a "nice guy-tough guy" distinction sometimes seemed to be in evidence between the teacher and the school administration when it actually came to disciplining a misbehaving student. Such potential teacher-administrator dichotomies in relation to student problems probably changed over time. In periods when noncriminal rule infractions were so frequent as to impinge on the orderly functioning of schools, one might have expected to have seen greater alignment between teachers and administrators toward controlling aggressive pupil behavior.

3. What changes have taken place in the period from 1950 to 1975 in the kinds, frequency, or intensity of disorders in schools?

The primary problem involved in answering this question is that the keeping of incident statistics became largely a phenomenon of the early 1970s, when school crime became an issue. Since there were few national statistics on noncriminal school rule infractions, almost all the supporting data addressing this question had to be drawn from often subjective reports that appeared in news articles and educational journals. Even though many of these articles did not supply statistical data, shifts in the descriptive language they used to discuss student misbehaviors in secondary schools were very helpful in acquiring an historical perspective.

4. Over the twenty-five year period from 1950 to 1975, what general national activity was going on that might have affected issues relating to the handling and treatment of disorderly pupils in schools?

Because the answer to this question could be developed into book length, this chapter includes only the most important aspects of national life. Appendix A details in a time outline such issues as resolutions of professional educational associations, general education legislation, and major federal activity.

Differing Views of Student Disorders

In studying any action to which some kind of trend is ascribed, the objects of that trend should be examined for internal consistency before the trend concept is accepted. In this study, it is important to compare the perceptions of pupils on the one hand, and school personnel on the other (in relation to what indeed constitutes a disorder), before drawing conclusions about student actions and school reactions. Such a step is essential, for until the issue of similar or dissimilar perceptions of what disorders were all about can be resolved, the study's establishment of changes in the kinds, frequency, or intensity of disorders (or in reactions to them) is suspect. The purpose of this section is to determine whether the relevant participants in disorder situations were all speaking about the same types of concerns.

Pupils' Views of Disorders

To achieve a perspective of pupils' views of disorders, it was necessary to look at writings of and about students in secondary schools. In the categorization of pupils' views respecting disorders, some fairly clear-cut observations emerged: first, though misbehaving is fun—it is a natural part of being young and almost all youths get into a little trouble at some time or other—the issue was not so much the act of misbehaving, but rather who the students were and who observed them; second, some kinds of misbehaviors in classes were a prelude to the loss of pupils' respect for the teacher and could lead to general class lawlessness; third, misbehavior was sometimes a student's reaction to chronic failure.

Category One: Here, one of the most important observations was that outcomes of the process of handling disorders were as much a function of the pupils' social and academic reputation as they were a function of the kinds of acts committed, combined with the school status and personal mood of the individual who observed and reported the act (Polk, 1972:155). Guilt of the pupils was often assumed in cases where pupils had records of past offenses, whereas innocence was often assumed where pupils were academically talented and had little or no record of past offenses (Larson, 1972:103).

This problem involving the subjective nature of how pupil disorders were handled became further complicated when racial issues were involved. Though this book would like to be able to state conclusively that there was some kind of correlation between the outcomes of disciplinary actions taken for disorders and the racial combinations of persons engaging in the acts and reporting them, the literature did not provide any guidance. Indeed, all sorts of combinations of actions and reactions were evident, as the following examples show.

The Children's Defense Fund (1975:67) noted a case involving a fight which a white youth initiated against a black youth. The black student was the one to be handcuffed and removed from the school by police, despite protestations that he was the victim, not the perpetrator of the fight.[1] In contrast, an article in *U.S. News and World Report* (April 1975:39) discussed white students being yelled at and reprimanded, while minority-group students were not censured.

The reason given by white teachers for this differential treatment was their fear of being called racists for yelling at minority-group students.

Category Two: A large part of one book was devoted to the second category (too much misbehaving in classes could be a prelude to loss of student respect for the teacher[2] and to consequent general lawlessness). Gerald Levy, in his imaginative work, *Ghetto School* (1970),[3] discussed—hyperbolically—tendencies relating to continual testing and retesting of teachers by students. Levy dramatized the polarization of teachers, referring to them as chronic and acute. The major discriminating factor between these two types of teachers was the disciplining of students as a function of their attitudes about the students. Chronic teachers tended to be more experienced—usually having taught for a few years—and committed to helping the youths receive a meaningful school experience at almost any cost. They "accepted the notion that control must precede education" (Levy, 1970:26). Acute teachers tended to be recent college graduates with liberal outlooks who began the school year by trying to make friends with their students. Levy called this an "indirect plea to the children for exemption from the battle over control" (Ibid.:41).

The pupil response to these teacher types was fairly clear cut. Levy found the chronic teacher had philosophized that control preceded learning (while sincerely interested in seeing that pupils did learn), so "a chronic teacher could hit a child and think it beneficial to the child" (Ibid.:26). Sensing this, pupils in the Levy model avoided giving chronic teachers the need for disciplining. The acute teacher had a reputation for caring mostly about education from books and for not being concerned with a straight line; therefore the children adopted the pose: if teachers failed to clamp down on talking, eating, and moving around, they would talk, eat, move around, and leave the classroom as much as possible (Ibid.:41).[4] Levy observed that in a relatively short period of time, acute teachers were destroyed. They either had to evolve into seasoned chronic teachers or leave teaching altogether.

An interesting case where teacher-testing became more generally school-authority testing was seen in the following example. A *Los Angeles Times* article (July 4, 1975) quoted a student as saying that as directives from the principal were announced over the public address system, groups of students caucused in the halls to devise strategies for testing the order (McCurdy, 1975: Part I, page 3).

That much of this behavior was a fairly harmless and natural outlet for adolescent emotions did not lessen the problems that disorders presented to the smooth running of a bureaucratic educational institution. As the numbers of students engaging in disorders increased in a school, the ability of that school to carry on the traditional functions of education was hindered. At some point, as the disorders increased, a "critical mass" was reached and change took place in either the administrative policy of the school or in the school administration itself. This critical-mass theory, as it applies to cases of classroom disorders, has been investigated only with respect to gang activity in schools. Miller (1975:121) reported gang members "gradually increasing their numbers in particular classrooms until they had achieved a 'critical mass'—a presence which defeated the capability of the teacher to exercise discipline."

Category Three: In this category of disorder, failing—especially unwarranted or continual failing—often resulted in behavior that was disorderly. In the case of this kind of disorder, most frequent discussion of the problem occurred in the 1969-1972 period, probably resulting from the numerous books about ways schools failed pupils. Yet the problem had been discussed as early as 1956. In "Delinquents in the Classroom," Beck (1956) noted that youths who experienced being culturally "shut off" from the majority society tended to react by rejecting certain of that society's symbols. Among the things often rejected, Beck listed: conforming dress (aggressive pupils will wear a uniform of rebellion); polite speech; honest behavior; and social cooperation. Indeed, these youths ranked schools "with the enemy" and saw themselves as "putting in time until they could legally quit school."[5] While attending school in this state of antagonism, these pupils would have been disinclined to cooperate with a teacher who was "to their eyes, a representative of the big community who shuts them out" (Beck, 1956:486).[6]

An additional observation relating to disorders as a by-product of continual failure was Liddle (1964). Writing about "normal" middle-class youths in public high schools, Liddle discussed the greater problem of creeping competition and its relation to failing students. He considered the ego hurt and emotional (and intellectual) withdrawal resulting from high school students who were not the prettiest, smartest, most clever, or best spellers. He discussed the lessons students learned when teachers taunted classes, "You did pretty well on yesterday's test; you should have, you've had it three times now" (Liddle, 1964:147). And when teachers kept the papers as "ammunition when your parents come in to find out why their little darling got a C on the report card" (Ibid.:147), the message came through clearly. Some of the messages pupils received from such behaviors on the part of teachers were: first, when students finally did learn something, after a lot of teacher effort, it was too little and too late; second, the teacher was not working with the parents—indeed, saw parents as the enemy; and third, since the teacher was sarcastic and clearly antagonistic to students, they were well within their rights to retaliate by being sarcastic to and antagonistic toward the teacher. Hence, disorders arose. Or was it first disorders; hence, teacher sarcasm?

This complex relationship, however, between pupils perceiving teachers as antagonistic and not helpful (see also Graubard, 1969:120) and acting out in response to seeing their lives as failures (see also Glasser, 1970:44) as well as acting out to get back at the teacher (as noted throughout Levy, 1970) was really central to the thesis (so aptly worded by Polk, 1972:146) "that underachievement, misbehavior and early school-leaving are properly and most usefully to be seen as adverse school-pupil interactions, and not simply as individual acts, carried out by students as natural responses to damaged psyches or defective homes." As this study will later demonstrate, these adverse school-pupil interactions changed with time, and are meaningful for its purposes.

School Personnel Views of Disorders

School personnel manifest some very general attitudes toward disorders that tend to be timeless. These views tend to modify almost any school response to disorders. This subsection briefly outlines these general, grouped attitudes, as expressed in various educational journals and publications from 1950 to 1975.

Teachers: The ways teachers viewed student disorders were often polarized. Basically, teachers seemed unwilling to admit that there was a problem or that they wanted to "get tough" about what they saw as a tremendous problem. The teacher view about disorders that "it's not much of a problem" was represented by such authors as Cobb (1953), who felt that simply paying attention to pupils and giving them love and attention would prevent what few discipline problems did come up, and Satlow (1959), who made suggestions about room orderliness and teacher dress as ways of keeping good discipline.[7] Even though it was written much later, Levy's picture of the chronic teacher (1970) portrayed someone who did not see a "disciplinary problem" in itself, but only one part of the "whole youth" that may have required some fine adjusting. The chronic teacher maintained that pupil disorders were simply a part of growing up, and since he was a professional teacher, the youth's pranks simply did not bother him. According to Levy, the teachers were not affected because they were in control of the situation.[8]

One probable cause relating to teachers not publicly acknowledging pupil disorders as particularly extensive in their own classes may well have been the administrative responses they often received when complaining about the nature and extent of discipline control problems. Examples of pressure against reporting the nature or scope of classroom problems can be seen in the writings of authors such as Edgar (1955) and Wells (1971).

Alvin Edgar, in a ten-point admonition to teachers about the dos and don'ts of handling the discipline problems, wrote that teachers should: "Never call upon the principal or superintendent for help. [Every] case referred to the principal or superintendent weakens your professional standing with them because of your inability to handle your own problems" (Edgar, 1955:60). Elmer Wells stated: "Teachers, too, often fail to report all incidents. As one observer noted: 'Unless a teacher is really hurt or scared by a threat, the incident often is not reported. The teacher is fearful of adverse criticism. He or she might be blamed as the cause of the attack, either by superiors or parents, called a troublemaker, or accused of not being able to maintain discipline. Also, teachers often think they can handle the situation without outside help' " (Wells, 1971:9).

Senate testimony focusing on teacher nonreporting of all incidents relating to school misbehavior developed an estimate that between 30 and 60 percent of the reportable disorders (and crimes) went unreported (Bayh, 1975:6). Major reasons given for this phenomenon in the testimony and elsewhere were primarily that teachers were unable or unwilling to admit that they could not control students in their classes, or that teachers feared reprisals from students if they reported what had happened to them. This last issue—fear of reprisal from the students—became particularly acute in cases involving crimes and criminality (see discussion in chapter 5); however, even at the low level of intensity that comprised disorders, fear of the students was not infrequently mentioned as a real concern and problem.

Opposing the attitude that "disorders were not a problem" was the attitude that disorders were very much a problem, and that only by taking a tough stand against offenders was it possible to control the class as a whole or to educate the class.

Root assumptions of the position that teachers must control their classes to be "good teachers" were made particularly well in Arthur J. Prescott's "Classroom Control or Classroom Chaos" (1963). An academic study finding teachers expressing a need to control their students' behavior (as a prerequisite to teaching the subject matter of the course) was presented in Vinter and Sarri's "Malperformance in the Public School: A Group-Work Approach" (1965). The many variations on this theme were discussed carefully in Joan Roberts' *Scene of the Battle: Group Behavior in the Urban Classrooms*. One of Roberts' observations of special relevance for this study, was the distinction between the "conferred authority of headship and the earned authority of leadership" (Roberts, 1971:21). She also noted that in classes where teachers viewed the course content as a means of establishing control and in classes where concern for control superceded that for education, students often obeyed primarily because they were coerced. On the other hand, in classes where the teacher had the genuine respect of the students (born of such virtues as knowledge, caring, and patience), the control was earned, not illusory. This view fitted very well with that of Levy as well as other authors mentioned above.

One of the more classic ways by which pupils "tested" teachers' authority (according to Roberts) was to challenge their leadership competence and observe their reactions: if teachers acted responsibly and reasonably, they earned the students' respect; if poorly, they lost the respect of the class. Another point Roberts made was that if a teacher handled a discipline situation by using methods the pupils felt were unreasonable, the students lost faith in the teacher's general academic capabilities in the classroom (see also Levy, 1970:43; and Piety, 1972:3, note 2).

School Administrators: School administrators had three reasonably major concerns that affected the ways they handled student actions. These concerns, in relation to disorders, were: first, disorders did not prevent the school from being a safe place for students and staff; second, disorders did not prevent teachers from teaching; and third, principals defined their own role concerning disorders in such a way as to provide clear direction for the remainder of the staff.

The school safety concern is not relevant in this chapter, but becomes critical in the chapters on disruptions and crime. The overall safety of the school was not severely threatened by excessive truancy or a few student fights. To the extent that overall school disorders became serious (perhaps in terms of frequency[10]), administrators had to take a stand. Clearly, if only one or two out of 100 teachers complained about school disorders, the school administration probably would not take a very hard look at its own administrative position vis-à-vis disorders. However, if over half the teachers were unable to conduct the business of teaching due to schoolwide disorders such as pulling of fire alarms or raucousness resulting from excessive class cutting, the school administration would have to undergo some change in philosophy and approach to disorders simply to avert educational disaster.

The second reasonable concern of most secondary school administrators was to curtail and contain classroom disorders so that teachers could teach. Prescott (1963) and Herrick (1961:219) expressed the common sense of the early 1960s in relation to teachers taking responsibility for controlling their own classes. That disorders affected the classes of newer teachers (Levy, 1970:chapter 3) because these less experienced teachers were assigned to fill urban school vacancies (Subcommittee to Investigate Juvenile Delinquency, 1959:18) was also of concern to the administration.[11] Recognizing the teachers' responsibility for most problems of classroom disorder, principals responding to a Michigan study (Hicks, 1963)[12] indicated they were willing to take responsibility for counseling teachers on problems in classroom control, and even to handle the chronic student offenders, but resolution of everyday classroom problems rested solely on the teachers (Hicks, 1963:32).

The third area of administrative concern focused on unresolved questions of the principal's own role at the school in relation to disorders. Hicks (1963:32) observed that lack of clear-cut universal directions relating to their own public image (vis-à-vis handling disorderly youths) often resulted in principals becoming overly circumspect about how soon and how deeply they became involved with cases. Most commonly, when assigning the various roles played in handling disciplinary issues in schools, it is felt that the principal of the school was the key figure in determining the climate of that school.[13] A compounding problem throughout this period was that as chief administrative officers of schools, principals were subject to harangues by their own staffs, school district offices, and communities if they failed clearly to think through and communicate their positions about misbehaviors in general or in specific instances. It was perhaps this compulsion not to "look bad" that caused De Cecco and Richards (1974) to suggest that bureaucratic overreaction to the need to be responsible for students had led to compulsive counting and recounting of them, almost as if schools were retail businesses in which it was necessary to keep an ongoing "inventory [of the goods] every forty or fifty minutes [to account for] possible transient loss" (De Cecco and Richards, 1974:11).

Security Officers: Between 1969 and 1975, city and county school district offices throughout the country increasingly developed divisions of school security. Though the next two chapters of this study specifically deal with the timing and ramifications of these offices' development, the interactions between security officers and students in relation to disorders deserves some mention at this point.[14]

There were two major concerns for security personnel in the area of student disorders: first, that disorders would not expand to crimes; second, that principals would keep adequate records of the types of offenses occurring in their schools. Though security officers had many different kinds of tasks and responsibilities,[15] one common concern—especially in relation to deterrence of crime—was with the prevention of those disorders which the normal in-school channels could not handle.

A hypothetical example of such a situation is: in a classroom setting, an insolent pupil is sent to the main office, escorted by another student; the offending pupil breaks away from the escort, runs back to the classroom, and yells at the teacher. When other teachers come to help the verbally assaulted teacher, a fight breaks out among the class members. It is at this point—and perhaps even at the escort phase—that school security officers should have played a role and had an interest in the outcome of the fray. Since the ramifications of this kind of altercation (suspension, or possibly pressing criminal charges) would have inevitably involved the security office in more work, that office, if only out of self-interest, would have developed a vested interest in helping to prevent such situations from mushrooming in the first place. As potentially serious disorders increasingly concerned urban school systems in the 1970s, security officers were increasingly involved in individual schools. This issue and its ramifications are discussed throughout the book.

The second area of concern for the Office of School Security was the adequate keeping of records. Though security offices were primarily interested in records for court use in criminal cases or for insurance claims in damage cases, records of youthful misbehavior were also useful in the aggregate for determining the general level of misbehavior within schools of the district.[16] All this record keeping forced school administrators to categorize activities in a new way: criminal or noncriminal. For this study, the change in reporting is of vital interest since the public (1973-1975) had been deluged with statistics proving remarkable increases in school crime and violence. It may well be that these remarkable increases can be attributed to changes in the reporting categories used by schools in compliance with instructions issued by the district superintendent through the district director of security, and not entirely to changes in absolute levels of violent or criminal behavior.[17]

Summary and Conclusions about Differing Views of Disorders

From the pupils' perspectives, persons who observed them engaging in disorders and persons to whom they were reported affected the types of reactions the school administration displayed. Though a certain amount of disorderly classroom behavior had traditionally been accepted by pupils as "fun" and by staff as "normal," excessive misbehavior (often in the form of teacher-testing) at times led to students losing respect for the teacher. This could in turn have led to even greater classroom and school lawlessness. In addition to expressing frustrations toward schools and teachers by engaging in misbehaviors such as teacher-testing, pupils often reacted physically and emotionally to continual personal failure. Since the school curriculum in the early 1960s was being revised, this was perhaps a period of somewhat greater confusion, failure, and misbehavior for many pupils.

From the standpoint of the teachers, there seemed to be a continuum of viewpoints, ranging from "there is no discipline problem in my class" to "there are continual discipline problems in my class." The polarity of these responses took an interesting twist when certain teacher variables were considered. A correlation was found in conservative or liberal views of the concept of education by teachers and their control of the classroom. More conservative (the Levy term was chronic) teachers did not seem to have as many problems with disorders, and those that did occur were viewed as part of the youths' normal maturation behavior. This approach seemed to lessen the impact of specific disorderly offenses.

Administrators had primary responsibility for the overall school climate. To that end, their views of disorders focused mainly on those disorders which: potentially had the capability of threatening the safety of students or staff; were capable of preventing a teacher from conducting the class; or would indicate to "outsiders" that the administrator did not have a clearly defined or clearly communicated understanding of his or her role in relation to student disorders.

School security personnel, though relatively new arrivals on the secondary school scene, played a catalytic role. Since their primary duties centered on the prevention and investigation of crimes, they were often concerned with preventing and controlling disorders before noncriminal acts became crimes. Part of the process of sorting between noncriminal and criminal acts forced the schools to keep records consistent with the definitions of misbehaviors held by the director of school security, who operated at the school district level. These definitions varied widely between districts.

The most comprehensive conclusions this study can draw from the preceding discussion are little more than empirical confirmations of common observations. First, the basic views of disorders by pupils and teachers were fundamentally the same. Different perspectives provided by pupils, teachers, and administrators, all had implications in relation to the action-reaction-action cycle this study is demonstrating. Second, the slight difference between the focal concerns of the local school administration and the district-based Office of School Security presented a possible area of conflict. Unless the local school administration and the district offices agreed on what constituted disorder versus disruption or crime, the actions and reactions of the local school administration to the local school disorder would be out of step with district policy.

From these conclusions, this book sets the following directions: first, pupil, teacher, or school administration responses to disorders mean those relatively minor actions and reactions which originated in classrooms; and second, responses made by local school administrators (and to a lesser extent by district directors of school security) mean that other than strictly educational considerations sometimes came into play, affecting counteractions taken in relation to disorderly pupils. With the development of some general directions based on analyses of major viewpoints of students and school staff members (in relation to noncriminal student misbehaviors), and with the conclusion that disorders were a separate subject throughout the literature, this book now outlines some major trends in American schools during the past twenty-five years.

Major Trends in Student Disorders

Though this study is confident there were changes in some kinds of student misbehaviors and in the schools' and the public's reactions to some of the misbehaviors, empirically establishing these changes is difficult. In this section, the study endeavors to demonstrate the following general patterns:

1. Pupil disorders, which existed throughout 1950-1975, seemed to have three distinct phases: pranks, from 1950 to 1964; teacher-testing, from 1964 to 1971; and withdrawal/apathy, from 1971 to 1975.
2. From about 1950 to about 1964, teachers "passed" their more seriously misbehaving youths to the school administrator, and the school administrator often passed these youths out to the community through suspensions and expulsions.
3. As the sheer numbers of suspensions and expulsions grew in 1965-1975, court suits were filed that questioned some of the rights of school administrators. These suits ultimately established the need for schools to set up due process procedures in disciplinary cases: no longer could principals arbitrarily suspend or expel youths.

Caveats

Before going into further explication of trends in student disorders, it might be useful to examine two caveats. The first caveat deals with the various resources available to schools and school districts; the second caveat discusses the merits and demerits of using aggregate responses as an indication of activity.

Funds: It was often the case that variations in the school's handling of minor (and even some major) rule infractions varied as a function of many things—not the least of which were local-level variations in resources (Smith, 1952:88).

Though this study is not concerned with the multitude of helping services available outside the school (team centers), the resource issue would affect the availability of some in-school services. If the community was rich in referral resources, then school counselors were likely to involve the community in the treatment of the student's in-school problems. If the community was poor in resources, then schools had to develop much more comprehensive programs on their own (if they were intent on helping the youths) or push out the pupil from public education altogether.

Other in-school issues also hinged on the economic condition of the school district. Since staff were costly, any staff in nonteaching capacities became, in a sense, extra cost or fringe expenses on the part of the school. Whether or not the school had an "opportunity room," for example, was an economic consideration on a basic level.[18]

On a less obvious level, economic considerations surrounding specific schools were often ultimately connected with both the personality and the philosophy of the school administrator and the pupils. Suburban pupils may have been more interested in getting good grades (perhaps because they wanted to continue their education), and this may have led them to maintain some semblance of education in the schools. In many urban core schools, pupils did not seem to have an interest in education, and their schools closely resembled battlefields.

Aggregate Response Patterns: People with different backgrounds (especially those from different disciplines) viewed the causes of disorders from different perspectives. These different perspectives often led to different responses to similar problems.[19]

To establish control over the major trends in the handling of youths by schools, a common denominator was needed, something that would indicate that an action of some kind was significant. In the consideration of historical changes, larger variations in behavior often showed up as common movement—traveling together. It was these aggregate changes that the book wanted to report. The data sacrificed to this kind of macroscopic analysis were the microscopic actions and reactions taking place in individual classrooms, schools, and school districts. The chief asset of this approach, however, is in the overall historical perspective it can yield.

The common denominator developed to help analyze this "traveling together" of actions relating to student disorders is a sort of maxim. Called the "rule of problem progression," the maxim states that "if you cannot handle the problem, pass it on." This rule may be usefully applied in the case at hand, because a school's administrative hierarchy was so set up that problems were continually referred to higher authority. If a teacher could not handle a problem, a range of choices was available: main office, counselor's office, parental conference, and so on. If the main office or counselor's office could not handle the problem, it might be referred to school district offices or to school security offices (after about 1970). If the school organization could not handle the problem, school officials might always call on outside resources.

Data about the nature and extent of the "passing" of problems (either by teachers to administrators or by administrators to the surrounding community) were used as *indicators* of the extent of pupil disorders. For indicators regarding pupil reaction to being passed out of the school system, this book used court decisions.[20]

Kinds, Frequency, and Intensity of Student Disorders

In both what was said and what was left unsaid in the literature of this period (1950-1975), there seemed to be an emphasis on three generally separable types of disorders:

1. From 1950 to about 1964, disorders seemed to be patternless and occurred at levels of frequency and intensity usually within an acceptably tolerable range for educators and the public.
2. From about 1964 to about 1971, the most prevalent disorders represented some kind of teacher-testing. This form of disorder seemed a problem particularly affecting young teachers in urban schools.
3. From about 1971 to 1975, disorders were again difficult to separate (largely due to the public concern over school crime), but were probably such self-directed offenses as absenteeism and alcohol abuse.

1950 to about 1964: This period was perhaps the most difficult to study. Due to long-standing and unchallenged practices of expelling seriously misbehaving pupils and suspending students who did not cooperate with the school administration (Goldstein, 1969:380), the pupils who remained tended to conform to school and community expectations respecting pupil behavior.

Perhaps the most important indications of the frequency and intensity of student disorders were found in the National Education Association's 1956 study of "Teacher Opinions of Pupil Behavior," which presented the findings of the only national survey concerning disorders conducted in this time period.[21] It found that "nearly two-thirds (64.2 percent) of the public-school teachers of the United States reported that real troublemakers accounted for fewer than 1 in every 100 pupils; almost 95 percent described the boys and girls they taught as either exceptionally well behaved, or reasonably well behaved" (National Education Association, 1956:105).

The overall tone of the 1956 NEA report was best captured in its last paragraph. In the section of their summary devoted to the causes of misbehavior, the authors wrote that: "The factors most frequently associated with misbehavior in school, in the opinions of classroom teachers, are related to the home and family of the children and youth. . . . This feeling on the part of classroom teachers was evident not only in the statistics collected but also in the thousands of comments sent in with the questionnaires. If classroom teachers were given one choice of the many ways to improve behavior in school, the majority of them would say: 'First, give the boys and girls competent mothers and fathers . . . who care what happens to their children.' " (Ibid.:106)

An additional indication of the low levels of concern over student misbehaviors during this period could be seen in the Senate reports resulting from hearings on the topic of juvenile delinquency. As late as 1957, the "Education Report" of the Senate Subcommittee to Investigate Juvenile Delinquency (Committee on the Judiciary) failed to mention juvenile delinquency in schools. Though when used technically, the term "juvenile delinquent" means a juvenile formally found to be delinquent by a judge, the Senate hearings were investigating all aspects of misbehavior that could conceivably lead to the ultimate declaration of delinquency by a court. Considering the extensive scope of the Subcommittee's interest in the 1950s,[22] this omission was a particularly important indication that school disorders (or crimes, for that matter) had not yet reached the attention of one of the first groups of investigators in this country to receive and report on practically everything out of the ordinary. (In 1957[23] if student discipline could not have been handled in schools, that certainly would have been out of the ordinary.)

The issue with the Senate report, as with that of the National Education Association, is that its omitting to mention high levels of student disorders can be taken as an indication that the problem was not a major problem at the time. Pranks and the like—the occasional breaking of school windows—were evidently occurring at acceptable levels in this period. Only in later years (see chapter 5) did the frequencies and intensities of these pranks begin to take on an aspect of maliciousness that required criminal prosecution and incarceration.

By the late 1950s, judging from reports of school responses to disorders (see, especially, the Juvenile Delinquency Subcommittee hearings of this period), small hints appeared that discipline problems in public secondary schools were becoming a major issue. As in many other areas of the economy and the urban experience, New York City was one of the first cities to have to acknowledge that pupil attitudes and actions were getting out of hand. A Senate juvenile delinquency investigating team, focusing on schools in 1958, observed that even in the schools specifically designed to deal with troublesome youths:

> ... we were told that there was a continual war of nerves between the teachers and the students. The students continually test or try the teachers to see just how far they can go and what the limits are to their behavior.... We were told of incidents of the smuggling into school of guns or knives and other forbidden articles. However, in the majority of cases, it was felt that this was merely a test on the part of the youngsters to see if they could get away with entering the school with contraband material and leaving at the end of the day without being detected (Senate Subcommittee to Investigate Juvenile Delinquency, 1959:21).[24]

Also, by the late 1950s psychologists and psychiatrists had begun to influence educational policy, and school district administrations had begun to develop a "psychiatric model" for treating disorderly pupils. As explained by Hypps (1959:318), the root of this approach was that if early patterns of maladjusted behavior could be identified by teachers, and follow-up counseling and care provided for the youths, future delinquency proneness would be lessened because of the close attention and supervision offered.[25]

One of the unexpected consequences of this step, however, was that a critical mass was reached time after time in classes, in terms of the sheer numbers of maladjusted youths sitting in one room. Disorder became contagious, and teachers found they had to develop a tough stand, surrender the classroom, or turn over the more troublesome[26] pupils to the school administration.

1964 to about 1971: This period was chaotic. Revised science and math curricula were being implemented nationally; compensatory education was in full flower; popular books were being written about why schools fail children; the country was involved in the Vietnam war; and the college riots eventually trickled down to the secondary schools. Urban high schools were hiring masses of new teachers to help cope with a 22 percent student population increase (from 11,517,000 in 1965 to 14,057,000 in 1971–U.S. Department of Commerce: Bureau of the Census). Many of the new teachers were men seeking assignments in the urban core schools to receive army deferments. These and other developments seemed to have produced what, in retrospect, was a fairly intense and short-lived period of teacher-testing, the principal disorder for this time period. An example of the mixing of many of these issues in such a way as to demonstrate the almost natural development of teacher-testing among students is suggested below.

As long as youths had to go to schools, some surely felt that schools were worthless places in which to spend the day. Increasingly, however, youths—

particularly in urban schools—came to realize (perhaps because of the mass media) the breadth of the gap between what the schools offered by way of "success" and the realities of a lifetime of failure that would very likely be theirs without schooling. As the pointlessness of study and schooling loomed in their faces, and as teachers were unprepared to deal with such a crisis, "the youths [were] forced to reassess the whole school, the teachers, the routines, the bribes, the punishments and the control" (Levy, 1970:90). Wilkerson (1969:120) also noted "that very many children of the poor [perceived] their experience in the slum school as meaningless or oppressive." Wilkerson's view was seconded by William Kvaraceus (1971), who wrote that:

As they first enter school, most children—rich or poor, black or white—are immediately absorbed into a massive educational system; they enter school only on the school's terms and on the basis of unconditional surrender. These terms often demand renunciation of self and a constant submission to processes of conformity and standardization. Most schools achieve their goals at the price to the individual of some loss of privacy, personal identity and individuality. They require at least outer conformity to external authority and subservience to the strong pressures of the peer group. They invoke the severe competitive processes of selection and survival of the academically fit. All too frequently they provide an artificial separation between the classroom and the life stream of everyday problems and issues. Those who are unable or unwilling to submit to the social system frequently join the ranks of the failures, the troubled and troublesome, the dropouts and the delinquents or, in defense, they may set up their own ego-supporting institutions in the form of the underground press, the delinquent gang, or the anti-establishment political party (Kvaraceus, 1971:2, 3).

One of the consequences of schools' forcing youths into unconditional surrender in terms of conformity and standardization of behavior was that some youths developed feelings of hostility, resentment, and disassociation.[27]

In an urban setting, teacher-testing to determine whether teachers were part of the problem or part of the solution (to use a phrase of the period) became a kind of safety valve whereby the pupils, though causing a lot of trouble in the classroom, were at least remaining in school and venting their anger verbally.[28] The question of the teacher's integrity was brought out in Levy's *Ghetto School* (1970), among other places. Levy pointed out that if teachers were firm and honest, students would tend not to begin the destructive campaign of teacher-testing. It also seemed that even if the teacher did not maintain attitudes agreeable to the pupils, but the pupils felt that the teacher was sincere, teacher-testing was seldom initiated. If teacher-testing went to far, the teacher— in the face of what may have been seen as nearly total disaster—"may [have felt] a desperate need for exercising rigid control within the classroom to inspire that at least the outward appearance of constructive effort [was] maintained" (Snow, in Kerber and Bommarito, eds., 1965:227, 228). For a teacher to begin using control as a countermeasure to teacher-testing was, as Levy pointed out, the final signal to students that they had won.

1971 to 1975: This was also a difficult time, but for reasons almost opposite from those of the 1950 to 1964 period. The influx of students that caused massive teacher hiring in 1964-1971 stopped: from 1971 to 1974, the student high school population increased only 1.9 percent (from 14,057,000 to 14,275,000—U.S. Department of Commerce: Bureau of the Census). Moreover, the lottery system for selecting draftees was implemented in January 1970; no longer did young male college graduates have to teach in the ghetto to win deferments.

The combination of these data with Levy's notes about the transformation of acute teachers[29] led to the not surprising observation that the high frequency of teacher-testing as it existed in 1964 to 1971 was a thing of the past. So, too, most of the riots (discussed in chapter 4) largely subsided by the end of 1973. Between 1971 and 1975, however, violence on school campuses became such a major issue that practically everything written about schools in this period used such words as violence, vandalism, crime, assault, and extortion. With the implementation of Offices of School Security (discussed in greater detail later), which had a mandate to keep crime records, many offenses previously disguised as disorders suddenly became crimes. Fights became assaults; trash-can fires became arson; broken windows became vandalism or breaking and entering, depending on whether or not there was entry; lost articles became thefts; and so on. Due in part to changes in the types of misbehaviors considered noncriminal, writing about the noncriminal acts during this time was difficult.

It is this study's best guess that after the teacher-testing period died down and after riots subsided, student behavior in secondary schools evolved in three general directions: first, violent crime increased in terms of absolute numbers; second, large portions of the student body simply took no outstanding action, positive or negative; and third—viewed as a counterbalance to violent crime—increased numbers of pupils exhibited withdrawal and self-destructive behavior.[30] Some symptoms, or proxy measures, of withdrawal and self-destructive behavior of interest here are absenteeism and the use of alcohol.[31]

The earliest real indication that a shift in trend was occurring grew out of a research project undertaken in 1970 by the Stanford Research Institute under a grant from the Law Enforcement Assistance Administration, U.S. Department of Justice. The original purpose of the grant was to establish the nature and extent of school disorders (meaning riots as well as disorders and crime) in the San Francisco Bay area.

As Meyer et al. (1971) completed the survey phase of this project, they found it necessary to redirect the entire study; they discovered that "most of the administrators with whom [they] talked, in fact, discussed student absenteeism and other forms of student nonparticipation in secondary schools, rather than the problem of disorder, as a major concern: (Meyer et al., 1971:9). Meyer also made the earliest observation that school administrations were "externalizing" their immense problems. School personnel looked at problems in schools and in society as a whole and declined to take responsibility for the students' behavior. The problems of the students, they told the Meyer interviewers, were no more than reflection of the problems of the country (Meyer et al., 1971:7). Morris (1972) agreed with the Meyer study, and his article in the National Education Association journal *Today's Education* said basically the same thing: "According to many experts, today's truant is simply a product of our frantic modern society. He is less inclined to accept parental order or explanation and more inclined to accept the tenets of his youth culture, including 'Never trust anybody over 30' " (Morris, 1972:1).

Questions concerning the extent to which absenteeism was a function of the modern society and of 2,000-pupil senior high schools was raised by the New York Panel on School Safety (1972:20). Absenteeism in New York in the early 1970s seemed to the panel specialists to be partially due to scheduling and curricular problems, endemic to schools that size. Though sympathy for the plight of students led some educators partially to excuse absenteeism,[32] proof that absenteeism was a school offense subject to disciplinary proceedings can be found in the statistics on suspensions for absenteeism previously discussed in this chapter (Children's Defense Fund, 1974:64).

Appearing toward the end of 1975, youthful *drinking* occurred more and more frequently as a new direction for student disorders. The "Gallup Poll of Public Attitudes toward Education" in 1975 noted that "this year, for the first time, 'drinking' (use of alcohol) is mentioned by enough respondents to establish a new category, although it is not one of the top 10" concerns about problems in the public schools (Gallup, 1975:228).

Two other reports supported this opinion. The first report was by the National Institute on Alcohol Abuse and Alcoholism (U.S. Department of Health, Education and Welfare, NIAAA, 1975). Titled "Drinking and Young People," it found that by 1975, "experimentation with alcohol has become almost universal among high school students; that the number of regular drinkers, the quantity of alcohol consumed, and the frequency of use in this population increase proportionately with age; and that these trends have been accelerating in recent years" (U.S. Department of Health, Education and Welfare, 1975:2). The second report was produced by the Center for the Study of Social Behavior, Research Triangle Institute. In their summary statement, the authors wrote: "While study procedures, definitions, and methodologies have varied greatly, the consistency of the findings indicates that adolescent alcohol consumption is a serious societal problem and is probably becoming increasingly so" (Center for the Study of Social Behavior, 1975:140).

Another interesting, if informal, study conducted in a Maryland high school by the staff of the school newspaper found that "90 percent of the seniors and 81 percent of the juniors and sophomores said they drink" (Baker, 1975:A-2).[33] Baker stated: "these polls support the finding in the NIAAA survey that alcoholism—not marijuana—is the so-called "drug of choice" of the mid-1970s"

(Ibid.:A-2). The primary findings of the NIAAA survey to which Baker alluded were that "93 percent of boys and 87 percent of girls in their senior year of school had experimented with alcohol..." (U.S. Department of Health, Education and Welfare, 1975:2). Though these sound like impressive quotes, readers are alerted that students were asked whether or not they had ever *tasted* alcohol. The logical leap made by both reports—for both failed to ask *how much* liquor was tasted—was that alcohol-tasting correlated with an alcohol problem.[34]

School Responses to Student Disorders

This section will discuss the ways both teachers and school administrators responded to student disorders from 1950 to 1975. The most interesting concept involved the school administration's often misused powers to "pass" its more annoying students out to the community. This "passing" concept is discussed in four stages. First, the study shows how teachers had been encouraged both to handle most of their own disciplinary problems and to pass on the more difficult ones. Second, the study notes the transition of the problem from teacher to school administrator. Third, it observes the administrator passing the problem out to the community. Fourth, it indicates some ways the community began resisting this "passing" pattern and through civil court action, challenged some of the school administrators' basic powers of authority. Though there was a great deal of overlap, temporal progression through these four stages from 1950 to 1975 can generally be seen by noting the dates of the sources cited.

Teacher Reactions to Pupil Disorders: For teachers as well as for school administrators, the range of responses to disorders ran the gamut from "hands-off" to "hands-on." One of the recommendations to teachers on the soft side of the spectrum in 1954, was to "deal individually with [misbehaving pupils] and look for underlying causes. If a child is difficult or unmanageable in class you will accomplish more by seeing him alone without an audience present" (Schubert, 1954:112). This statement from the *Journal of Education* implied a number of conditions, all of which are of intense interest to this study. First, for the situation to be handled in this way, such a low level of misbehaving activity must have existed that the teacher had time to look into the causes of only one pupil's misbehavior. Second, for the teacher to be able to take time out in this fashion without the entire class going to pieces presumed that the vast majority of the other pupils were extraordinarily well-behaved and cooperative. Third, the recommendation presumed that the serious offender so respected the teacher's judgment and opinions that the offender would respond to the individual attention that was given.

Additional recommendations occurring during this period, some of which tended more toward the "tough stands," were as follows. Prescott (1963:1) discussed the need for teacher control of the classroom and ways in which to achieve it. Neatness, spontaneity, and order on the teacher's part were key points. Vincent (1964:107 ff.) discussed the newly revived legal sanction authorizing the use of corporal punishment as an indication of community support for a tough disciplinary stand by teachers,[35] and Edgar (1955:59-61) explained how to maintain discipline. As an indication of the almost smug early 1950s approach to misbehaving pupils, Stullken went so far as to suggest that teachers should look forward to the opportunity of working with "a maladjusted or delinquent child."[36] The "business of every teacher," as Stullken would have it, was "not only to teach children what they otherwise would not know and to help them acquire skills which they otherwise would not acquire, but also to help them behave in a way that society expects them to behave" (Stullken, 1953:567).

Teachers Shift Some Disorders to the School Administrator: Some common types of frustrations that resulted in teachers passing their disorder problems onto the school administration were sadly noted in Cavan's synopsis of a 1960 *Chicago Daily News* article.

The teacher, Mrs. T., after eight years of successful teaching, found herself faced with serious disciplinary problems. Her case was heard by the Board of Education, which voted, although not unanimously, to dismiss her from the school system. In defense of her inability to maintain discipline, she and other school personnel listed some of the things a teacher might not do either because of definite rules or because of objections of the principal. They could not assign homework as a penalty; keep children after school as they were then exposed to street hazards after the crossing guards had left their posts; keep a child out of a class he especially enjoyed; ask parents to come to the school for an interview, as experience had shown nothing was gained; grasp a pupil by the wrist or arm to escort him to his seat since the child might later exaggerate the amount of force used; or isolate him from other pupils, as this tended to stigmatize the child. Although principals were expected to give teachers suggestions and to come to their aid in severe disciplinary cases, not all principals gave positive and firm help (Cavan, 1969:291,292).

After a few such cases, teachers viewed disorders as potential threats to their own economic survival. Teachers saw that they could get fired for not properly controlling the nature and extent of classroom disorders. Under the pressure of economic survival, the mechanics of handling potentially sensitive incidents became paramount. For teachers, the problem of student disorders was often handled by passing the disorderly pupils over to the school administration—in increasingly large numbers, as the years went by.

This shift of responsibility from teacher to school administration is highlighted in Roberts' *Scene of the Battle: Group Behavior in the Urban Classrooms* (1971). In the second chapter, Roberts discussed teacher reliance on the official role as "sanctioned leader" to maintain classroom order. When that failed, the teacher then called on the (presumably higher) authority of the school assistant principal. An early example of a recommended use of shifting the burden from teacher to school administrator appeared in the "Secondary School Administration" series titled *The High School Principal and Staff Deal with Discipline* (Parody, 1963). This publication touted one school's approach of bringing disorderly pupils to the main office after the efforts of individual teachers had failed to produce desired results. Once in the main office, "the group was given a 'discipline book' to carry, in which each teacher recorded the discipline facts for each day" (Ibid.:67).

Further support for the idea—or tradition—that the school administration should accept problems beyond the scope of the normal classroom teacher existed in Hicks' study of 112 schools within a fifty-mile radius of Ann Arbor, Michigan. His second finding stated that principals "... should be required to deal with chronic offenders and major disciplinary matters only. All others are to be dealt with in the classroom by teachers" (Hicks, 1963:32).

School Administration Reactions to Student Disorders: The inclinations of teachers to use the "law of problem progression" to pass on their burdens to the school administration also applied to school administrators. In his research findings, John Dailey discussed variations in the conceptual ways in which strict and tolerant junior and senior high school principals approached disorderly youths. In his Office of Education study into the prediction and prevention of delinquency in Washington, D.C., public schools, Dailey found a general polarity between tolerant principals who tried to involve even the worst of their pupils in the school community and strict principals who preferred keeping their schools unified as bastions of educational purity, and expelled pupils who prevented education from going forward (Dailey, 1966:13).[37]

In relation to school administrators passing their problems out to the community, perhaps the best proxy measures this study can offer are the data that appeared in the Children's Defense Fund publication, *School Suspensions: Are They Helping Children?* Its summary findings were: "Of all the suspensions recorded in our survey, 63.4 percent were for infractions of school rules, not for dangerous or violent acts. A large proportion were for victimless offenses: overall almost 25 percent were for truancy or tardiness, and in some of our survey districts, the numbers of children who were suspended for truancy and tardiness ranged from one-third to one-half of all suspensions recorded" (Children's Defense Fund, 1975:12).

Though in many cases suspensions were thoroughly warranted as a reasonable response to pupil misbehaviors, too often suspensions—particularly in the 1960s—were given to pupils for such ambiguous offenses as insubordination or improper dress. Often, especially in cases such as suspensions for noncriminal acts (see Kennedy Memorial, 1973), this administrative action had been the point at which principals passed their student misbehavior problems out of the school into the community.[38] That was the point at which principals relinquished authority and status in hopes that someone, somewhere—especially someone in another city agency—would handle a situation beyond their grasp or control.[39]

Community Nonacceptance of Administrators' Passing Action: Throughout 1950-1975 some interesting court cases had an impact specifically on this trend of suspending youths in large numbers[40] as justifications for prohibiting certain acts in schools. Though this chapter is not the place for a detailed consideration of the philosophies behind suspensions, it is appropriate for a discussion of historical changes in the use of suspensions in relation to disorders. From 1950 to the mid-1960s, suspensions were almost totally within the jurisdiction of school administrators.[41] For short three-to-ten-day suspensions, few limits or guidelines were provided for schools in one district, much less for school districts across the country.

When disruptions and demonstrations occurred in secondary schools in the mid-1960s, a number of court decisions clarifying the use of suspensions came up. *Burnside v. Byars* (1966) and *Tinker v. Des Moines School District* (1969) were typical and important examples, in that both set precedents for separating disorders from disruptions in relation to the ways schools could treat youths. In *Burnside* and *Tinker*, the rulings prohibited suspensions for wearing armbands and buttons with slogans unless their appearance interfered with the maintenance of order and discipline in the school (Ackerly, 1969:25).

The final logical legal positions summarizing the intent of such earlier cases as *Burnside* and *Tinker* were the Supreme Court guidelines set out by Justice Fortas, limiting the power of principals to suspend pupils. A summary of the most relevant point follows: "To justify prohibition of a particular expression of opinion in the schools, there must be something more than a mere desire to avoid the discomfort and unpleasantness that accompanies an unpopular viewpoint. Where there is no finding or showing that engaging in the forbidden conduct would materially and substantially interfere with the requirements of appropriate discipline in the operation of the school, the prohibition cannot be sustained" (Ackerly, 1969:27).

As issues which could invoke suspensions were being crystallized from about 1964 to 1971, another movement developed concurrently. The latter issue was that of juvenile rights under the Constitution. The *in loco parentis* power of the school administrator now came under attack not simply from a judgmental point of view, but also from a pragmatic point of view. Students had begun to challenge principals' rights to invoke disciplinary suspensions without following procedural due process rules laid down in *Gault v. Arizona* (1967). The trend-setting decisions came in the two 1975 cases of *Goss v. Lopez* and *Wood v. Strickland*. *Goss* says that "when a state provides education for its children, that education cannot be taken away for disciplinary reasons, even temporarily, without due process of law" (Children's Defense Fund, 1975:85). *Wood* says that if due process is not followed in a suspension situation, then the principal or other suspending party can be sued for monetary damages (Ibid.:87).[42]

To school administrators, these court rulings meant that the pendulum had swung back to them; whereas the law of problem progression had previously been used to move the teachers' problems to the principal, and the principals' problems to the community, the community (speaking through the Supreme Court) reversed the direction of the flow. The community now instructed the principal to handle internally the majority of school disciplinary cases. (If all suspensions were to follow procedural due process, as laid out by the Supreme Court decisions, the principal would need a staff just to handle the paperwork.)[43]

Summary and Conclusions

The major trends this study has been following are: first, from about 1950 to 1964, disorders were of no particularly consistent genre. Because of the well-established use of the judicial concept *in loco parentis*, pupils who failed to cooperate with public schools were subject to unguided disciplinary procedures by the school administrator. Suspensions or expulsions were considered reasonable school responses to unreasonable pupils. The progress of uncooperative pupils was documented by their being passed from teacher to administrator to community.

Second, from about 1964 to 1971, the problems of disorderly students were greatly amplified. At this time, large numbers of young idealistic teachers entered the teaching profession, and the nation entered a period of moral questioning concerned with students' rights, war, race, and so on. These young teachers were particularly susceptible to being emotionally baited by pupils; such emotional baiting was called teacher-testing. Teachers sent untold numbers of disorderly pupils to the school administration, which suspended vast numbers of them. In the courts, legal decisions began to favor the rights of juveniles and to limit the rights of school administrators to administer unchallenged discipline.

Third, from about 1971 to 1975, incidents of disorders were reduced substantially (even while evidence was beginning to mount that violence and crimes were increasing). The era of riots had passed; the high school student population had stabilized; and young male college graduates no longer sought sanctuary from the draft by teaching in urban schools. Teachers whose classrooms had been madhouses a few years before either learned to administer control or left the teaching field altogether. Court cases held that the *in loco parentis* concept was invalid in many respects and required school administrators to follow procedural due process when administering discipline to pupils. This added administrative burden forced principals to reevaluate the tradition of passing pupils through their offices back to the community. Suspensions of pupils came to require either clear demonstration that the pupil was causing immediate threat to persons or the functioning of the school, or access to a presuspension hearing for the pupil. Faced with these new administrative burdens—and the real possibility of being sued for noncompliance—school administrators adopted new attitudes as to who should be suspended and why. Increasingly, administrators began to avoid suspensions whenever possible, and looked to the teachers as those individuals primarily responsible for the maintenance of classroom discipline. Whether innocently coincidental or a by-product of new teachers' pressures placed on students in response to principals' pressures placed on teachers, one of the primary disorders of this period was absenteeism.

Notes

1. Supporting this observed differential treatment of minority-group members was Mackler (1967:289), who found that in New York, when two types of programs existed for troubled and troublesome youths, white students tended to be viewed as troubled, and minority-group students tended to be viewed as troublesome. See also the Robert F. Kennedy Memorial publication, *The Student Pushout*, for an extensive treatment of the thesis that black students were suspended, expelled, and pushed out of schools for reasons of de facto segregation, and that the charges precipitating the pushing out were among the most subjective: insubordination, dress codes, disobeying classroom rules, not cooperating and so forth (Robert F. Kennedy Memorial, 1973:ix, 14).

2. A minor notion tangential to the idea that classes as a whole could lose respect for the teacher was that when specific pupils reported specific problems and found the teacher could not correct the situation, a certain amount of withdrawal took place. In the eyes of the pupil who had failed, his teacher was "no longer as valuable to the child as an academic teacher . . . " (Piety, 1972:3).

3. Though *Ghetto School* was about an elementary school, the concepts discussed in it were fairly universal and had an application to high schools. Since I was an acute teacher in a ghetto high school, Levy's observations are particularly relevant to my own experiences.

4. See also Sherman (1972:10) for a discussion of the "homework game" pupils played on this type of acute teacher.

5. The logical inconsistency between youths rebelling against the majority society yet being concerned with staying in school until they can "legally quit" was Beck's. Since he was writing in the mid-1950s, he probably projected his

own lawfulness into an untested sentiment purportedly expressed by the subjects of his research paper.

6. This study felt that one particularly interesting, if tangential, observation could be developed by extrapolating from a comment that appeared in the introduction to *Tally's Corner: A Study of Negro Streetcorner Men* by Elliot Liebow. When discussing his research design, Liebow mentioned that in "looking at these men as fathers, husbands, lovers, breadwinners, and so forth, we look at them in much the same way they look at themselves" (Liebow, 1967:13). In much the same way, this study could extrapolate that troublesome youths in schools could be looked at as whole individuals living out the phenomenon of failure that they can see as their most likely future. If this is indeed the case, then constant "conning" and "gaming" becomes little more sinister than adjustment fronts for lives filled with constant frustration and anger.

7. Discipline seemed to be the word used throughout the 1950s and into the 1960s to refer to what this study calls disorders. Readers in the 1950 to 1968 period would no more have read "discipline" as "knife fights" than would 1970 to 1975 readers think "school crime and violence" meant talking excessively in the classroom. The entire "open classroom" movement of the late 1960s (and in many ways, the alternative schools development in the late 1960s and early 1970s) operated from the point of view that normal, healthy youths invariably raised a little hell, and that it was not necessarily healthy to channel this youthful exuberance (Holt, 1967:96).

8. For a good article presenting root assumptions of the use of teacher control in relation to being a "good teacher" see Arthur J. Prescott's "Classroom Control or Classroom Chaos" (1963). For an academic study finding teachers expressing a need to control their students' behavior as a prerequisite to teaching the subject matter of a course, see Vinter and Sarri's "Malperformance in the Public School: A Group-Work Approach" (1965).

9. The issue of "fear" in relation to disorders seems to affect teachers in Levy's "acute" category. It appears that teachers who put discipline control above book learning, are not the ones who feel "powerless to do anything." Those who feel powerless to do anything often see themselves as prisoners along with the students in the schools (Cavan, 1969:286).

10. The Law Enforcement Assistance Administration, Office of Juvenile Justice and Delinquency Prevention, when designing its "Serious School Crime Initiative" in 1976, defined "serious" in such terms as: so frequent as to impair the running of the school; so grave as to endanger the life or limb of people on the school grounds; so expensive as to involve a major capital loss. These distinctions are applicable at this point.

11. Mager and Pipe (1970) pointed out that often the issue was that people inexperienced in a situation simply did not know what things/acts to leave alone. Many disorderly cases revolved around that very point (see Polk, 1972:179).

12. The sample size for this study was as follows: 112 total schools, of which 43 were senior high, 25 junior high, and 44 elementary. Generally, the schools' communities were very small, encompassing a fifty-mile radius of Ann Arbor, Michigan. The return rate was 78.5 percent.

13. See note 41, below, concerning the concept of *in loco parentis*, as applied to the authority of school administrators.

14. The need for discussing the role of security vis-à-vis disorders is derived from the potentially intense relationship between security personnel and students. When someone can either arrest one or cause one to be arrested, one tends to be more cautious about behavior around that person. Suddenly, what *that person thinks* has been done is more important than what may actually have been done. In this respect, the mere presence of a security agent, or even a security aide, will cause a student reaction. It is the root assumption of school districts employing security agents that the students' reaction will be that of lawfulness.

15. Security officers had numerous different categories of responsibilities that were either allowed or restricted at the discretion of each particular school district. For example, one eastern school district had given its security director primary responsibility for investigating crimes against property, but the city police had to handle the school district's crimes against persons. In the adjoining school district, on the other hand, the security director had responsibility for investigating crimes against persons, but the custodial branch of that school district had the responsibility for the paperwork and investigations dealing with crimes against property. Moreover, in Prince Georges County, Maryland, the security director had responsibility for both physical and property crimes.

16. To a certain extent, these records would be used by the School Security Office to establish/justify their own budget requests. As such, the School Security Office had a vested interest in what data were collected, and how they were reported.

17. The concept that changes in the reporting of student misbehaviors rendered invalid many of the findings of national studies of student crime and violence in the 1970s is discussed in much greater detail at a later time. For now, an introduction to this concept is sufficient.

18. Though a number of such extra-cost items began appearing in the mid-1960s, many of them were curtailed during the economic recession of 1972-1973. The shrinking student population in the early 1970s also mitigated the implementation of many new ideas that were, at the outset, designed to reduce in-school disorders.

19. The situation wherein different academic disciplines looked differently for the causes of some actions was satirized marvelously by Gitchoff (1973:115-117). Gitchoff wrote one-paragraph summaries of the causes of juvenile deviancy from each of the following points of view: psychiatric,

psychological, medical, legal, sociological, social welfare, theological, educational, and criminological. The satire was amusing and left the reader with the uneasy feeling that Gitchoff thought problems of separating good youths from bad youths were made needlessly complex almost primarily because different disciplines liked to color their worlds with sophisticated theories that—in the final analysis—would still point their collective fingers at very similar youths and call them "rotten kids."

20. The interesting application of the "problem of progression" rule to pupils was that after repeatedly trying to resolve their daily problems (and ultimately getting passed back home, through suspensions), numerous court cases asked administrators, in effect, what rights they had to discipline pupils. Indeed, in the final years of this study's period, the community ultimately forced a change in the ways youths should be handled in schools.

21. This study is particularly trustworthy for the following reasons: first, use of stratified random sampling to develop the sample population; second, weighting of the sample to represent national distribution of teachers by city size and student population; and third, careful wording of sample questions to avoid bias.

22. To substantiate the study's position that "if there had been any, the Subcommittee would have found it," the reader may find the Subcommittee's own statement of objectives to be instructive:

Objectives of the Subcommittee

The subcommittee made investigations on the community level in every major geographical section to determine the total implications of the nationwide scope of the problem. At these community hearings, the subcommittee attempted to develop information within the community relative to the following:

(a) The extent and character of juvenile delinquency within the community.

(b) The existence, if any, of organized juvenile gangs; the extent to which these gangs operate, and the activities in which they are engaged.

(c) The extent of the use of narcotics and synthetic drugs among juveniles in the community.

(d) The existence in the community of living conditions which contribute to delinquency with particular attention to such conditions in relation to children of migratory workers and other socially disadvantaged groups of children.

(e) The use of alcoholic beverages by juveniles contrary to law, and the effect it may have upon their delinquency.

(f) The existence in the community of adult exploitation of juveniles by recruiting them into crime, by encouraging them to gamble, by directing their criminal activities, or by profiting from their criminal exploits, i.e., fencing stolen goods by juveniles, and white slavery.

(g) The extent to which communities have developed successful programs for the prevention of juvenile delinquency and for the rehabilitation of delinquent children and youths, including juvenile courts and probation procedures, detention facilities, etc. (Subcommittee to Investigate Juvenile Delinquency, 1957:2-3).

23. The year 1957 was hard for educators. In retrospect, it was a turning point. In 1957 *Sputnik 1* was launched, along with a barrage of indictments against the "gooey, precious romantic philosophy that stressed permissiveness and life-adjustment" that was at the base of Deweyian education (Postman and Weingartner, 1973:76). Schools were thrown into turmoil. Curricula were revised over and over for years to come, and new freedoms were given and taken from students. To a certain extent, school disruptions, discussed in the next chapter, were about uses and abuses of some of these freedoms. (For further readings, the Postman and Weingartner article is very good for providing a careful and quick overview of the background and results of the *Sputnik 1* launch in 1957 in relation to American education.)

24. The root of the youth's behavior appeared here to be a prank, not a crime. This is especially important to note since the schools being investigated in this particular hearing were New York's "700" schools. "700" schools were set up in 1958 specifically to absorb some of the 1,200 students who had been expelled from other New York schools in the previous academic year.

25. The next logical step suggested for efficiently putting this psychiatric model into effect was the convenience of grouping troublesome youths into homogeneous classes. One of the earliest references to the problems created by this kind of labeling of pupils, appeared in a book by Harlem Youth Opportunities Unlimited, titled *Youth in the Ghetto: A Study of the Consequences of Powerlessness and a Blueprint for Change*, New York, 1964. The authors comment about problems involved in isolating youths—particularly minority youths—into classes where "substandard performance is expected of them" (p. 37).

26. By "troublesome," this study means bothersome to the teacher in terms of frequency of acts or intensity of acts that the teacher was unwilling or unable to limit through personal, unaided interaction with the offending youth.

27. The concept of students disassociating themselves from the school has been discussed by Elliott (1968). The concept of students disassociating themselves from the teacher was mentioned in Haney and Zimbardo (1975).

28. The entire anatomy of teacher-testing was so well done by Levy (1970), that this study refers the reader to him. Eminently readable, Levy made the obvious somehow more obvious. See especially the section beginning on page 41: "The Acute Teacher Is Destroyed."

29. Levy concluded that acute teachers (who usually received the brunt of the teacher-testing) either quickly became chronic teachers (who no longer were as susceptible to the testing) or left teaching altogether after only a few traumatic years.

30. Granted that self-destructive behavior is only "self-destructive" in terms of the mores of the dominant society, nonetheless, that is how schools and school boards would look on this noted behavior.

31. Alcohol was largely decriminalized in the 1973-1975 period, so this study feels comfortable including it in this noncriminal section. Drug use also fits the pattern of withdrawal and self-directed anger; however, it is a criminal offense and therefore must be excluded from this subsection.

32. Forer, for example, saw absenteeism as a reasonable reaction by high school pupils who could not read (Forer, 1970:261). Fox felt that absenteeism was a normal student reaction against the socializing policies of schools (Fox, 1964:28). *U.S. News and World Report* saw absenteeism as an expression of apathy (February 21, 1972:48).

33. Quantity of drink was not specified, nor was the location of the drinking. The survey sample was 400 out of the total school population of about 2,400. Sample selection was not indicated.

34. In private schools, where nonacceptable behavior was grounds for expulsion, Baker noted that drinking on the campus of the private schools he surveyed was, indeed, grounds for dismissal from school. The headmasters with whom he spoke also indicated that drinking was (1975) a serious problem for them.

35. An indication that the authority to administer corporal punishment was "newly revived" in this period can be seen by the National Education Association's findings of the extent of authority to administer such punishment as of 1956. The survey conducted by the National Education Association of 10,000 teachers (4,270 returned) found "that only 5.0 percent of the teachers in school districts containing 1,000,000 or more people actually have the authority to administer corporal punishment..." (National Education Association, 1956:105).

36. Note the use of the "singular" here (delinquent child) as an indication of the degree of seriousness. It is also unclear whether Stullken was equating maladjusted with delinquent or he really meant them to be separate.

37. As might be expected, there are some easily drawn similarities between these two categories among principals and the two Levy categories among teachers.

38. Criticism over principals suspending pupils instead of using in-school and out-of-school resources to assist the child was also discussed in *School Suspensions: Are They Helping Children*, previously cited, p. 17.

39. Ahlstrom and Havighurst (1971:86) discussed the effects of suspending a truant, pointing out the brutalizing effect that this had on the youth. Rubenstein (1970:154) discussed these kinds of suspensions as administrative, middle-class swords hung over the heads of the Puerto Rican and black

communities in New York City. Principals passing the youths back to the communities read as a slap in the cultural face. *The Student Pushout* (Robert F. Kennedy Memorial, 1973) discussed suspensions for victimless crimes—and for noncriminal acts—as a form of de facto segregation and exclusion from education, especially in the South and as applied to minority children.

40. In *School Suspensions: Are They Helping Children?* (Children's Defense Fund, 1975:9) the figures derived from HEW survey sources showed that 1 million youths were suspended in the 1972-1973 school year. This count included school districts containing only about one-half the total national student population. This is what the study means by "large numbers" of suspensions.

41. In this country, the tradition that permitted school administrators to have almost exclusive rights to suspend a misbehaving pupil rested in the doctrine of *in loco parentis*. According to this doctrine, "the student is considered a child under the jurisdiction of the school, which stands in place of the parent; the school is thus given almost the same authority over the pupil while he is at school as the parent has over him at home. Courts were reluctant to question school actions with respect to the child except in extreme cases such as those involving serious bodily injury or malicious discipline . . . " (Phay, 1971:3).

For a thorough historical discussion of the *in loco parentis* doctrine, and how it has been distorted over time, see Goldstein's "The Scope and Sources of School Board Authority to Regulate Student Conduct and Status: A Nonconstitutional Analysis," 117 U.Pa. L. Rev. 373, 377-384 (1969).

42. See Conway (1975) for a thorough analysis of the scope and consequences of both these rulings.

43. It is fair to point out here that the "reasonable extrapolation" from this notion is that principals will now turn to their teachers and increasingly insist that they handle their own problems within the classroom situation, or work harder after the three o'clock bell to make contact with parents of troublesome youths, and that they not continue to pass problems to the main office. The further extrapolation is that teachers, not wanting to have the added burden of after-hours liaison, will become increasingly strict in classes. The whole tenor of American education is very likely to become much more rigid in the years following the cutoff point of this study's time period.

References

Ackerly, Robert L.
    1969   *The Reasonable Exercise of Authority*. Washington, D.C.: National Association of Secondary School Principals.

Ahlstrom, Winton, and Havighurst, Robert
   1971   *400 Losers: Delinquent Boys in High School.* San Francisco: Jossey-Bass.

Baker, Donald P.
   1975   "Lower Drinking Age Affects Schools." *Washington Post* (March 31):C-1.

Bayh, Birch
   1975   "Our Nation's Schools—A Report Card: 'A' in School Violence and Vandalism." Washington, D.C.: Preliminary Report of the Subcommittee to Investigate Juvenile Delinquency, Judiciary Committee (April).

Beck, Bertram M.
   1956   "Delinquents in the Classroom." *NEA Journal* (November):485-487.

Cavan, Ruth S.
   1969   *Juvenile Delinquency: Development, Treatment, Control.* New York: J.B. Lippincott Company.

Center for the Study of Social Behavior, Research Triangle Institute
   1975   "A National Study of Adolescent Drinking Behavior: Attitudes and Correlates." Rockville, Md.: National Clearing House for Alcohol Information.

Chicago Daily News
   1960   "Teacher Fired over Discipline Issue." (March 22, 24):16.

Children's Defense Fund (Cambridge: Mass.)
   1974   *Children Out of School in America.*
   1975   *School Suspensions: Are They Helping Children?*

Cobb, Marion M.
   1953   "Some Suggestions for Preventing Discipline Problems." *High Points* 35(October):12-13.

Conway, Lenny
   1975   *Suspensions and Due Process.* Robert F. Kennedy Memorial (February 28).

Dailey, John T.
   1966   "Evaluation of the Contribution of Special Programs in the Washington, D.C. Schools to the Prediction and Prevention of Delinquency." ERIC 010 431 ED (August).

De Cecco, John P., and Richards, Arlene K.
   1974   *Growing Pains: Uses of School Conflict.* New York: Aberdeen Press.

Edgar, Alvin
   1955   "Handling the Discipline Problems." *Music Educators Journal* 41(January):59-61.

Elliott, Delbert
   1968   "Delinquency, School Attendance, and Dropout," in J. Stratton *Prevention of Delinquency: Problems and Programs.* New York: Macmillan.

Forer, Lois G.
  1970 *No One Will Lissen,* New York: John Day, pp. 259-268.
Fox, Sterling Lee, and Shuck, Leslie Earl
  1964 "Relationship of Law Enforcement Agencies and School Districts in Selected Counties of California." A doctoral dissertation submitted to the University of Southern California. Ann Arbor, Mich.: University Microfilms, Inc.
Gallup, George
  1975 "Seventh Annual Gallup Poll of Public Attitudes toward Education." *Phi Delta Kappan* (December):227-240.
Gitchoff, G. Thomas
  1973 "The Dilemma of the Delinquent." *Criminology*, no. 1, 2(May):115-117.
Glasser, William
  1970 "Youth Rebellion—Why: An Interview with Dr. William Glasser." *U.S. News and World Report* (April 27):42-45.
Goldstein, Stephen R.
  1969 "The Scope and Sources of School Board Authority to Regulate Student Conduct and Status: A Nonconstitutional Analysis." Philadelphia, Pa.: *University of Pennsylvania Law Review*, no. 3, 117(January):373-430.
Graubard, Paul S. (ed.)
  1969 *Children against Schools.* Chicago: Follett Educational Corporation.
Haney, Craig, and Zimbardo, Phillip
  1975 "It's Tough to Tell a High School from a Prison." *Psychology Today* (June):268.
Harlem Youth Opportunities Unlimited
  1964 *Youth in the Ghetto: A Study of the Consequences of Powerlessness and a Blueprint for Change.* New York: HARYOU.
Herrick, Mary
  1961 "Discipline in the Schools." *Crime and Delinquency Abstracts*, no. 3, 7(July):213-218.
Hicks, Edward R.
  1963 "Principals and School Discipline." *Michigan Education Journal* 41(October):32-33.
Holt, John
  1967 *The Underachieving School.* New York: Delta.
Hypps, Irene
  1959 "The Role of the School in Juvenile Delinquency Prevention." *Journal of Negro Education*, no. 8, 28(Summer):318-328.
Kerber, August, and Bommarito, Barbara
  1965 *The Schools and The Urban Crisis: A Book of Readings.* New York: Holt, Rinehart and Winston.

Kvaraceus, William C.
- 1959 "Schools and Delinquency." *California Youth Authority Quarterly*, no. 3, 12(Fall):37-39.
- 1971 *Prevention and Control of Delinquency: The School Counselor's Role.* Boston: Houghton Mifflin Company.

Larson, Knute
- 1972 *School Discipline in an Age of Rebellion.* New York: Parker Publishing Company, Inc.

Levy, Gerald E.
- 1970 *Ghetto School.* New York: Pegasus.

Liddle, Gordon
- 1964 "Secondary School as an Instrument for Preventing Juvenile Delinquency." *High School Journal* 47(January):146-152.

Liebow, Elliot
- 1967 *Tally's Corner: A Study of Negro Streetcorner Men.* Boston: Little, Brown and Company.

Mackler, Bernard
- 1967 "A Report on the '600' Schools: Dilemmas, Problems and Solutions." In Robert Dentler, Bernard Mackler, and Mary Ellen Warshauer (eds.), *The Urban R's: Race Relations as the Problem in Urban Education*, pp. 288-303. Washington, D.C.: Frederick A. Praeger.

McCurdy, Jack
- 1975 "Teachers Urged to Report All School Violence." *Los Angeles Times* (July 4): Part I, page 3.

Mager, Robert, and Pipe, Peter
- 1970 *Analyzing Performance Problems.* Belmont, California: Fearon Publishers.

Meyer, John; Chase-Dunn, Chris; and Invarity, James
- 1971 "The Expansion of the Autonomy of Youth: Responses of the Secondary School to Problems of Order in the 1960s." Stanford, Calif.: The Laboratory for Social Research, Stanford University.

Miller, Walter B.
- 1975 *Violence by Youth Gangs and Youth Groups in Major American Cities.* Washington, D.C.: Interim Report of Grant 74NI-990047 to the Law Enforcement Assistance Administration.

Morris, Gordon T.
- 1972 "The Truant." *Today's Education* (January):41-42.

National Education Association
- 1956 "Teacher Opinion on Pupil Behavior, 1955-1956." Washington, D.C.: *Research Bulletin of the National Education Association* vol. 34, no. 2 (April).

Panel on School Safety
- 1972 *A Safer Environment for Learning.* New York: Panel on School

Safety, appointed by the Academy for Educational Development (October 31) (Preview copy: xerox).

Parody, Ovid F.
1963 *The High School Principal and Staff Deal with Discipline.* New York: Teachers College Press, Columbia University.

Phay, Robert E.
1971 *Suspensions and Expulsions of Public School Students.* Topeka, Kan.: NOLPE Monograph Series, no. 3.

Piety, Marilyn
1972 "School as a Delinquency Prevention Agency." *Delinquency Prevention Reporter* (May-June):3-4.

Polk, Kenneth, and Schafer, Walter
1972 *Schools and Delinquency.* Englewood Cliffs, N.J.: Prentice-Hall.

Postman, Neil, and Weingartner, Charles
1973 "A Careful Guide to the School Squabble." *Psychology Today* 7, no. 5 (October):76-86.

Prescott, Arthur J.
1963 "Classroom Control or Classroom Chaos." *Ohio Schools* 41(January):32-33.

Robert F. Kennedy Memorial (Washington, D.C.)
1973 *The Student Pushout: Victim of Continued Resistance to Desegregation.*

Roberts, Joan I.
1971 *Scene of the Battle: Group Behavior in the Urban Classrooms.* New York: Anchor Books.

Rubenstein, Annette (ed.)
1970 *Schools against Children.* New York: Monthly Review Press.

Satlow, I. David
1959 "Ounce of Prevention." *High Points* 41(May):56-61.

Schubert, Delwyn G.
1954 "Discipline without Disruption." *Journal of Education* 136(January):112-113.

Sherman, Stanley R.; Zuckerman, David; and Sostek, Alan B.
1972 *The Antiachiever: Rebel without a Future.* Boston: Boston University Center, Inc. (April).

Smith, Phillip M.
1952 "The Schools and Juvenile Delinquency." *Sociology and Social Research* 37:85-91.

Stullken, Edward H.
1953 "Schools and the Delinquency Problem." *Journal of Criminal Law, Criminology and Police Science* 43:563-577.

Subcommittee to Investigate Juvenile Delinquency
1957 "Report No. 130." Committee on the Judiciary, 84th Congress, 2nd Session.

1959 "Report No. 137." Committee on the Judiciary, 85th Congress, 2nd Session.

U.S. Department of Commerce
  1976 "High School Enrollment Figures, 1950-1974." Compiled by special request by the Office of Congressional Liaison, Bureau of the Census.

U.S. Department of Health, Education and Welfare
  1975 "Young People and Alcohol." Washington, D.C.: National Institute of Alcohol Abuse and Alcoholism.

U.S. News and World Report
  1972 "An Uneasy Truce in Troubled High Schools." (February 21):48-50.
  1975 "Violence in Schools: Now a Crackdown." (April 14):37-40.

Vincent, Harold
  1964 "Are Your Teachers Handcuffed on Discipline?" *School Management* 8(April):107-115.

Vinter, Robert D., and Sarri, Rosemary C.
  1965 "Malperformance in the Public Schools: A Group-Work Approach." *Social Work* 10:3-13.

Wells, Elmer
  1971 *Vandalism and Violence: Innovative Strategies Reduce Cost to Schools.* Washington, D.C.: National School Public Relations Association.

Wilkerson, Doxey A.
  1969 "The School, Delinquency and the Children of the Poor." In Paul S. Graubard (ed.), *Children against Schools.* Chicago: Follett Educational Corporation.

Legal Cases

Burnside v. Byars, 353 F. 2d. 744:5th Cir. (1966).
Gault v. Arizona, 99 Ariz. 181, 407 P. 2d. 760 (1965), rev'd, 387 U.S. 1:(1967).
Goss v. Lopez, 419 U.S. 565, 95 S. Ct. 729 (1975).
Tinker v. Des Moines Independent Community School District, 393 U.S. 503 (1969).
Wood v. Strickland, 420 U.S. 308, 95 S. Ct. 992 (1975).

4 Disruptions

S.I. Hayakawa, acting president of San Francisco State College, which has been racked by student violence, recently warned that "dirty, nasty revolutionary disruption" could be expected to spread to secondary schools. These predictions appeared to be borne out by events.

U.S. News and World Report

Introduction

Disruptions in secondary schools represent a transitional period of public concern between annoyance over student disorders in the 1950s and early 1960s and public alarm over student crimes in the 1970s. The use of techniques of disruption by secondary school students were short-lived but intense, covering the period from about 1968 to about 1971. There are two outstanding reasons for studying disruptions in the nation's schools: first, these group acts have a definable beginning and end that facilitates research; second, secondary school disruptions were so controversial that there was excellent media and research coverage.

This chapter looks at disruptions from two fundamental viewpoints and then at trends in the major types of responses to disruptions. First, however, the following two subsections remind the reader of the definition of the term "disruption" originally given in chapter 1, and stipulate the major questions this chapter addresses.

Definition of Disruption

A disruption is some kind of organized group misbehavior (criminal or noncriminal), specifically characterized as an activity designed to accomplish a planned goal or establish a point of contention (Erickson, 1969:10). Any such action undertaken must additionally have the effect of interfering with the education of other students (Bailey, 1971:2). Examples of actions that fit these definitions are: boycotts, sit-ins, walk-outs, and riots.

(Copyright: *U.S. News and World Report,* March 24, 1969:8. Reprinted with permission.)

Major Questions about Disruptions

To help understand the situation faced both by pupils and schools in relation to student disruptions, the study considers the following major questions:

1. To what extent does understanding the different views held by pupils and school personnel in relation to disruptions help to analyze disruptive actions taken by youths and countermeasures taken by schools?

   An understanding of the actions taken either by pupils against schools or by schools as countermeasures against pupils is predicated on an understanding of each group's respective point of view. To understand trends in disruptions in public secondary schools, the study looks both at the outcomes pupils expected of disruptions and kinds of disruptions school personnel expected.

2. To what extent can court cases from 1950 to 1975 relating to pupil rights in schools be used as an indication of the reasons for student disruptions that occurred in this period?

   Unlike college disruptions, which were often political protests, secondary school disruptions tended toward practical issues such as dress codes and smoking areas. In many cases, issues that sparked secondary school disruptions were ultimately settled in the nation's courts. Many issues often reported as the rallying points of student disruptions in secondary schools were also the focus of court cases of this same period. The study examines many of the more important rulings in such a way as to show changes in the ways school administrators were instructed to handle cases of student misbehaviors over time.

3. How did local school administrators tend to respond to student disruptions that may have threatened to close down the school?

   Principals, who had ultimate responsibility for the safety and climate of the school, had a great deal to say about the amount of force used to quell a disruptive situation. In some cases, a principal could use an influential teacher as a negotiator to settle a contested point before it became a crisis and the school was shut down. Other cases became so extreme as to require the city's school superintendent to do the negotiating while the school itself was occupied by riot police. On the assumption that there was some relationship between the amount of force used to counter student protests and the intensity of the protests, the study examines the range of choices available to school administrators as they were confronted with potentially disruptive incidents.

Differing Views of School Disruptions

In many cases, an understanding of an action taken in some situation rests on an understanding of the root assumptions motivating the action. Since disruptions were student actions taken to demonstrate specific issues, it is necessary to understand the root assumptions from the pupils' point of view. Correlatively, since schools are bureaucratic institutions which require reasoned explanations and budget justifications before any action or counteraction can be authorized, the root assumptions that school personnel developed relative to disruptions are relevant to this study. The following two subsections discuss the expectations and root assumptions of pupils and school personnel as they applied to secondary school disruptions from about 1967 to 1972.

Pupils' Views of Disruption: Studies

"Students do not want to take over schools—they want to be heard, and heeded" (Gudridge, 1969:5). This view, also expressed by Larson (1972:41), was an integral part of the character of secondary school disruptions, and set them apart from post-secondary school disruptions, as explained in this subsection. Larson astutely noted, though both high school and university disturbances often concerned issues of racism, unemployment, war, the military-industrial complex, ecology, and so on, secondary school disruptions placed an overriding emphasis on the operational aspects of their own schools and their own roles and freedoms within the schools. Among the operational issues that received a great deal of attention from the media and research studies were: "uninspired and downright bad teaching; oppressive regulations (especially in reference to clothing and hair style); censorship of student views; and no real voice for students in school affairs" (Larson, 1972:41). Substantiation of the kinds of issues concerning students in the 1968-1969 school year existed in a number of places. Two sources that serve as examples were: the 1969 House of Representatives "Survey of Student Unrest in the Nation's High Schools", and the Trump and Hunt 1969 survey of 1,982 secondary school principals.

House Survey of Student Unrest: In this House study, 15,086 schools (55 percent) responded to 29,000 mailed surveys. Chart 4-1 reflects the issues reported as responsible for troubles in the 2,710 schools (18 percent of the 15,086 respondents) that experienced some form of disruptive student behavior.[1] As the chart shows, issues of political concern were less frequent than issues of school rules and organization. This finding was further supported by the Trump and Hunt work.

Trump and Hunt Survey of Secondary School Principals: Also conducting a survey in the 1968-1969 school year, Trump and Hunt questioned 1,982 junior and senior high school principals to determine the nature and extent of student disruptions. According to the survey's findings, 68 percent of the nation's urban and suburban schools and 53 percent of its rural schools experienced disruption during this period. Trump and Hunt also reported that the issues raised by pupils

Chart 4-1
U.S. House of Representatives Survey Findings of the Causes of Student Disruptions in the 1968 School Year

Percent Schools Reporting This Concern	Numbers of Schools Reporting Incidents	Nature of the Issue Inflaming the Students
29	941	General disciplinary rules
28	913	Dress codes
15	489	Teachers or principals
15	487	Curriculum policy
13	410	Student political organization
100	3,240[a]	Total schools

Source: Roman C. Pucinski (1970:E1178).
[a]Some of the 2,710 schools reported multiple incidents.

centered on school regulations about one-third of the time, on instructional program problems about one-half of the time, and on race relations and other social or political issues about one-fourth of the time.[2]

Breakdowns of the causes of secondary school disruptions—such as the Trump and Hunt and the House of Representatives surveys (also supported by Shaffer, 1969)—coincide with this book's analysis of the progression of disruptions within the 1968-1971 period. Additionally, they support Larson's differentiation between secondary school and college disruptions. If most secondary school disruptions were not politically motivated and were different from post-secondary school disruptions, what were their rallying issues? As Larson noted, and as confirmed by the two surveys just discussed, by far the greater proportion of disruptions resulted from students seeking fair play from the administration in disciplinary cases or from students trying to better their day-to-day living conditions within schools. This point is very important, for the kinds of acts that developed into protests ultimately spoke to issues of fairness and equality under the law, and not to the feared randomness of Abbie Hoffman's "revolution for the hell of it."

In the same way Jones (1973:32) observed that unacceptable classroom behavior often indicated that content or methods used by teachers were inappropriate to the needs of students, this study feels that disruptions in secondary schools—particularly over such issues as personal freedoms of expression and dress—indicated that existing rules and regulations were inappropriate for the students. Evidently the U.S. courts felt this way also, for beginning in the 1960s and continuing to the end of 1975, this study found numerous cases which were instructive in relation to its premise. As shown below, the subjects of these legal rulings often paralleled issues fomenting unrest in the secondary schools.

Though not all the cases resulting in court decisions grew from disruptions, ample evidence exists that precisely these issues often became the focal points precipitating disruptions. It is this book's contention that an examination of landmark court cases from 1961 to 1975[3] provides a good understanding of the areas in which pupils felt so strongly that school rules were inappropriate to their needs that they were willing to disrupt the educational process to establish their points of contention. With respect to secondary school disruptions, three general groups of legal actions are of interest: issues relating to procedural due process, issues relating to freedoms of expression, and issues concerned with dress codes.

Pupils' Views of Disruption: Court Cases

Procedural Due Process. "Angered by the expulsion of a Negro girl from the high school cheerleading squad, about 100 black students sat down in the lobby of the school at the beginning of morning classes. Their beef: the cheerleader's expulsion was 'too severe' for the offense. (Out of uniform, she had cheered for Xenia's all-black wrestling opponents during a match. She said her action was prompted by 'derogatory comments' she heard about blacks from Xenia fans.)" (*School Management,* 1969:47).

Court cases growing out of disruptions such as this sit-in challenging the principal's decision to expel the cheerleader ultimately led to more general questions regarding the nature and extent of the principal's *in loco parentis* powers of discipline. As *in loco parentis* powers were increasingly limited by the courts, procedural guidelines were provided for local school administrators when disciplining students. The landmark cases that affected the power of the school to administer discipline began with the 1961 case of *Dixon v. Alabama State Board of Education,* where the court held for the first time that "due process requires notice and some opportunity for hearing before a student...is expelled for misconduct" (*Dixon v. Alabama State Board of Education,* 1961:157). Further, in the nonschool criminal case of *Gault* (1965), the court declared that juveniles are covered by the rights extended to adults under the Constitution. The court specified that juveniles arrested by police must be accorded at least the (1) right to notice of the charges in time to prepare for trial; (2) right to counsel; (3) right to confrontation and cross-examination; and (4) privilege against self-incrimination (*Gault,* 1967:13).

The *Dixon* and *Gault* cases had several important consequences. By the early 1970s, concepts spelled out in these rulings had successfully been applied to public high school expulsions and suspensions (see *Voight v. Van Buren Public Schools,* 1969, for expulsions, and *Williams v. Dade County School Board,* 1971, for suspensions). Further applications of the landmark *Dixon* and *Gault* cases came at the end of 1975, as *Goss v. Lopez* struck a fatal blow at the sixty-year-old concept of *in loco parentis*. In *Goss*, the court held that "when a state provides education for its children, that education cannot be taken away for disciplinary reasons, even temporarily, without due process of the law" (Children Defense Fund, 1975:84). As noted in chapter 3, this ruling will probably result in many fewer suspensions and in principals refusing to handle borderline discipline cases coming from teachers. *Baker v. Owen* is the last major due process ruling that used *Dixon/Gault* reasoning. Also settled in 1975, *Baker* established that though corporal punishment can be legally administered by schools even if the punished child's parents are opposed to it, strict adherence to due process must be followed. Due process guidelines are stipulated by the court.

Freedoms of Expression. St. Louis, Mo.–"Two teachers at Northwest High School were hurt Thursday in a scuffle with a group of demonstrators who attempted to break into the school building at 5140 Riverview Blvd. The demonstration was one of several at city high schools, apparently in abortive efforts to encourage walk-outs by students in support of the Vietnam moratorium.

"Leaders of a militant civil rights group, ACTION, had been distributing leaflets urging high school students to stay out of school Thursday and Friday as part of the anti-war moratorium. School and police officials said the ACTION leaders apparently were trying to link the suspension of a number of the Northwest students with the moratorium issue.

"About 200 students reportedly walked out at Vashon High School at 12:50 p.m. and an unknown person telephoned officials at McKinley High School demanding they dismiss class" (*St. Louis Globe Democrat*, November 14, 1969:2).

Court cases produced by students pressing for freedoms of expression in schools are numerous. In the late 1960s, the court found that wearing buttons with slogans (*Burnside v. Byars*, 1966) and armbands (*Blackwell v. Issaquena School District*, 1966)–or any kind of expression of opinion, for that matter (*Tinker v. Des Moines Independent Community School District*, 1969)–cannot be proscribed by the school as long as the student is not, in the words of the *Tinker* ruling, "interfering with appropriate discipline in the operation of the school, and is not colliding with the rights of others." Further, students may express themselves "even if such expression is offensive to the ear of the administrator, is not traditional, or is potentially disruptive" (Benton, 1971:7). The *Sullivan v. Houston Independent School District* ruling of 1969 exhibited a further test of freedom of expression: the court established guidelines regarding the legal rights of high school students to distribute underground newspapers on or near school grounds.

Dress Codes. "Another major cause of high school student protest in 1968-1969 was that hardy perennial—dress and grooming regulations. One-third of all schools reporting to NASSP [National Association of Secondary School Principals] noted that unrest had erupted over dress requirements; one-fourth had experienced hassles over hair styles. The mini-skirted girl and the long-haired boy were usually at the center of these episodes" (Gudridge, 1969:2).

Court cases testing the power of the school administrator to suspend pupils for violations of dress codes were prevalent from 1967 to 1975. Whereas early court cases on hair length (*Leonard v. School Committee in Attleboro*, 1965) and cleanliness (*Davis v. Firment*, 1967) ruled in favor of the schools' power to determine regulations, by 1966, the *Richards v. Thurston* case applied *Tinker*-like reasoning to hair-length regulations. This case determined that unless facts are presented demonstrating health or sanitary risks, or demonstrating the ways in which long hair interfered with other pupils' performance of schoolwork or that hair length would "create disciplinary problems of a kind reasonably thought to be a concern of public officials," it cannot be proscribed (Gaddy, 1971:32). The definitive case involving freedom of expression in relation to clothing also relies on *Tinker*, and is similar in wording and intent to *Davis*. *Scott v. Board of Education* held that "Board regulation of dress is valid only to the extent necessary to protect the safety of the wearer, male or female, or to control disturbances or distractions which interfere with the education of other students" (*Scott v. Board of Education*, 1969:603).

In summary, findings from studies of diverse groups confirm that the raison d'être of student disruptions and demonstrations most often were pupils' quests for administrative or practical reform rather than protests over some form of American political activity. Secondary school disruptions were frequently seen to develop from some pupils' feelings of lack of certain basic freedoms which they felt should fairly be theirs. In this light, it is more understandable why the vast majority of secondary school disruptions had rallying points either on the status of students as individuals or on the *in loco parentis* authority of the school to administer discipline. This study observes, also, by reading about incidents that precipitated court cases, that many cases relating to procedural due process began as suspensions or expulsions over some form of pupil demonstration relating to student freedoms of expression. Further supporting this contention that court cases can be viewed as expressions of student views about the inappropriateness of the then existing school rules and regulations is the observation that school disruptions end in the early 1970s, just after the majority of landmark court cases sided in favor of the students.

Whether or not school personnel shared the disrupting pupils' basic premises concerning the inappropriateness of the then existing school rules and regulations, of course, affected whether or not school personnel viewed student walk-outs, sit-ins, boycotts, and riots as constructive. Clearly, if school personnel did not share the root assumptions about the unfairness of the schools' positions on dress codes and *in loco parentis* rights of the school administrator, one could expect to see school resistance to conceding the students' points of contention. And, not surprisingly, that is what the study saw—as explained in the following subsection.

School Personnel Views of Disruptions

As disruptions first began to affect high schools, educators and the public began to develop theories about the causes of such troubles. Larson (1972) discussed a number of popular theories[4] and then extracted the essence of them all.[5] The ability to make sense out of a multifaceted problem, however, depends on successful hindsight: post hoc analysis of this sort is invariably 100 percent accurate. The concern here, however, is to understand the views held by school personnel in the mid-to-late 1960s to understand adequately the reactions of that period representing countermoves to student actions.

Until 1968, research and public concern over student disruption was primarily focused on colleges and universities. Early articles anticipating secondary schools as the new locus of disruptions are seen in journals expressing the views of professional educators. Brammer (1968) demonstrated principals' concerns about disruptions in secondary schools in his article, "The Coming Revolt of High School Students." In September 1968, *Nation's Schools* (which reflects the views of state and local boards of education) published the results of their "Opinion Poll," titling the article "Student Unrest Will Spread to High Schools, Many Fear." Both these articles presented the idea that school personnel should "expect student unrest in colleges to filter down to high school this fall" (*Nation's Schools*, 1968:14).

It appears that as disruptions actually began to affect high schools, the initial reactions of school administrators were to consider the disruptions to be externally guided, probably by the Students for a Democratic Society (SDS).[6] This conclusion was based on the established evidence that many post-secondary school disruptions in the early and mid-1960s were indeed externally guided by the SDS, and that this group of activists avowed publicly, in 1968, to make an attempt to recruit new members at the secondary school level.[7] Since college disruptions were often punctuated by riots and takeovers of buildings, school personnel projected that these same kinds of events could be anticipated in secondary schools. That the disruptions would mirror university events was given further credence by the publication of such works as *High School Student Unrest: How to Anticipate Protest, Channel Activism, and Protect Student Rights* (Gudridge, 1969), and *Dissent and Disruption in the Schools: A Handbook for School Administrators* (Benton, 1971).

As mentioned earlier, Larson pointed out what most educators overlooked in 1967-1969: that high school and college disruptions differed fundamentally, and these differences led secondary school pupils to be much more likely to demonstrate for smoking areas or for long hair than for an ending of ROTC on the high school campus or for an ending of the war in Vietnam (Larson, 1972:38). Perhaps the most significant result of overlooking the differences between college and high school disruptions was that school administrators began relying on police and school security officers to help quell disruptions (Vestermark, 1971:69; Fish, 1970:2, 152). These administrative actions had curious effects. First, in an almost classic case of "law of the instrument,"[8] high school pupils suddenly had a new toy. Once given the knowledge that with a little bit of disruption pupils could not only get a lot of attention, but could also get police to come on campus and cause adults to be intimidated by masses of students—and with a little luck, even get the school shut down—students often did just that. The youths had discovered an effective way to aggravate adults when they would not listen to what were felt to be fair student requests.

Second, the hard stand of hiring school district staff (school security officers, often ex-police juvenile officers) trained to orchestrate tactical aspects of paramilitary counteroffensives directed against disrupting mobs institutionalized a certain amount of violence. School districts henceforth expected a certain amount of crime and violence each year, once there was an administrative artifact called an Office of School Security.[9]

Third, disruptions tapered off sharply by 1971,[10] leaving in their wake a change in the bureaucratic structure of many school district offices. Assuming high school disruptions would be similar in content and tactics to post-secondary school disruptions, secondary schools became mirrors of the larger community. Since the larger community used a police force to deal with criminal activity, school districts developed counterparts in the form of an Office of School Security to help deal with the criminal aspects of disruptions as well as with the increasing emergence of actual student crime. The development of Offices of School Security[11] from about 1968 to 1973 marked a basic change in the ways school districts and individual schools dealt with disruptions. The change was most important with respect to crimes in schools. The importance of the security offices (in relation to crimes in the next chapter and, to a certain extent, respecting disruptions further in this chapter) involved their specific interest in the collecting and reporting of statistics on the nature and extent of student misbehaviors.

Summary and Conclusions about Differing Views of Disruptions

In retrospect, there does seem to have been a difference between issues which actually caused students to be disruptive and issues school personnel had expected would cause disruptions. Whereas students seemed concerned with practical issues of school rules and regulations, freedom of press, and whether or not a favored teacher would be fired, the school administrators—probably supported by public opinion—expected disruptions to be over ideological/political issues such as the Vietnam war, the draft, or social inequality.

This point of view on behalf of administrators often led to technological responses, the creation of a system of negotiations, and a kind of school police force.[12] The forming of school security offices, however, represented a change in the bureaucratic structure of school district offices and plays a vital role in the chapter on crime.

Major Trends in Student Disruptions

Major trends in student disruptions, 1967-1975,[13] will be examined in this section. However, let us first look at two caveats: the initial caveat concerns the time period covered; the second, this section's content.

Caveats

Time Periods: Though it may be possible to document occasional high school disruptions from 1950 to 1967, doing so would be very difficult for many reasons. First, the infrequency of disruptive behavior in 1950 to 1967 makes it difficult, if not impossible, to draw reliable conclusions about trends. Second, the only block of disruptions this study can find—resulting in the closing of schools outside the 1967-1975 period—were race-related and occurred immediately after the 1954 Supreme Court desegregation decision of *Brown v. Board of Education of Topeka*. Third, news articles reporting disturbances of the mid-1950s pictured these events as parental protests on school grounds, not as student-led disruptions. In summary, because the mid-1950s actions do not fit this study's definition of disruptions, and because the literature does not yield information indicating even the existence of high school disruptions before 1967, the study restricts its investigation of secondary school disruptions to the period from about 1967 to 1975.[14]

Content of This Section: Because the various studies do not scale the intensity of the reported disruptions and fail to differentiate between legitimate and illegitimate disruptions, it is very difficult to discuss issues of intensity. Whenever possible, however, the study presents hints about the intensity of disruptions over time. Since the kinds of disruptions have been discussed in the "pupils' views" subsection above and extensive material on the intensity issue will not be presented, the primary focus of this section must be on the frequency of pupil disruptions. This section presents a picture of the rise and fall of the student protest movement in public secondary schools across the country.

Rise and Fall of Secondary School Disruptions

"Violence Hits Schools, Colleges: What's Causing It?" was the headline of a *U.S. News and World Report* article. "Violence disruptions of the educational process in the U.S. intensifying. Orderly procedures are being overturned—not just in colleges and universities but in elementary schools and high schools. Student uprisings often are marked by physical intimidation of authorities" (*U.S. News and World Report*, 1968:36).

As chart 4-2 clearly shows, 1968 was a year when media interest in school disruptions climbed sharply.[15] Public concern over this new form of student protest could be seen coming from many different directions. The titles and the content of articles appearing in *U.S. News and World Report* between 1967 and 1975 provide good examples of the intensification in public feelings about disruptions in secondary schools.[16] The list in chart 4-3 capsulizes the articles written by *U.S. News* on this topic.

Within these articles, some special issues should be pointed out. First, the September 2, 1968, article was not clearly responding to public concern about

Chart 4-2
Numbers of Articles in the *New York Times* from 1960 to 1975 on Riots and Disruptions in the Nation's Public Secondary Schools

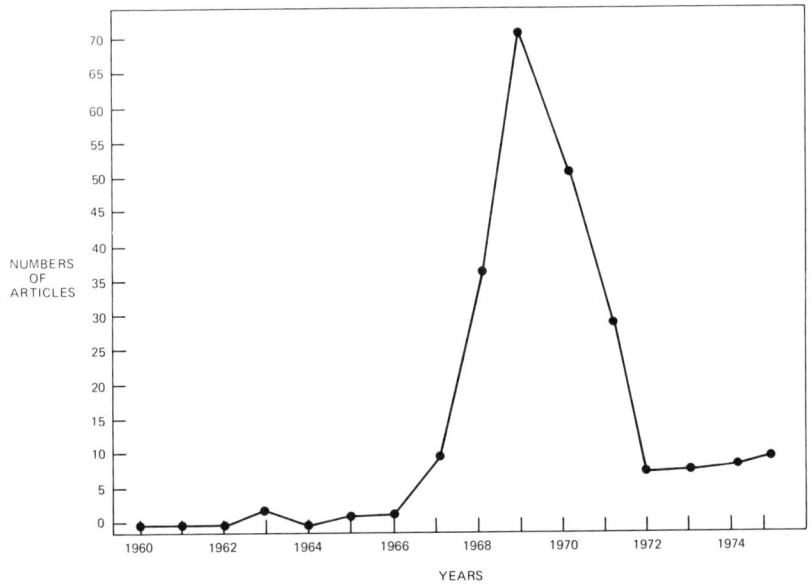

Source: *New York Times Index* 1960 to 1975.

Chart 4-3
Articles on Student Disruptions in *U.S. News and World Report*

Date	Article Title	Content Summary
Sept. 2, 1968	"Violence in Schools— The Outlook Now"	Reflecting attention on the issue of secondary school disruptions by a report by the Lemburg Center for the Study of Violence, the article concluded that most disruptions were racial, but even so, there were not many of them.
Dec. 2, 1968	"More Breakdowns in Public Schools"	Disruptions were still minor, and it looked as though they were a fad, not a movement. Educators' views presented here downplayed the seriousness of the issues.
Mar. 24, 1969	"Now It's High-School Students on a Rampage"	The issue now was clearly one of riots and group violence on a national scale. The article presented cases of disruption from all over the country.
Sept. 22, 1969	"High Schools: Next Target for Unrest"	Disruptions were now more of an issue in secondary schools than in colleges. This article carried "Two warnings [about the serious consequences of school disruptions] to state and local school officials" from the U.S. Commissioner of Education.
Apr. 27, 1970	"Youth Rebellion—Why"	The piece consisted of an interview with Dr. William Glasser, who explored possible causes of school disruptions.
Feb. 21, 1972	"An Uneasy Truce in Troubled High Schools"	"So far, it's been a quieter year in teen-age classrooms. Officials hope the back of student revolt has been broken. But they aren't sure yet" (p. 48). Walter Degnan, president of New York's Council of Supervisors and Administrators noted that "The wave of demonstrations has subsided. But the problem of individual acts of violence is . . . growing in magnitude."

school disruptions, as was the March 24, 1969, article. Rather, the earlier piece repeated findings of a research study on violence which only tangentially touched on secondary schools. Not only is it unclear whether the September 2 article differentiated between secondary and post-secondary schools, but it is also unclear whether disruptions were defined as anything other than riots—the most extreme and uncommon form of disruption. The December 2, 1968, article represented a tentative feeler sent out to "test the public water," as it were. The piece was *probing* to see if there was a problem that would become a public issue, rather than *stating* that the issue of disruption in high schools was clearly at hand. The third article on the chart (March 24, 1969) was of a different genre.

Appearing as the highlighted "March of the News: Front Page of the Week" article, it stated there certainly were problems and the problems were national in scope. This was the first article in this series decisively to assert that as of the spring of 1969, "student violence [had] spread from college campuses to secondary schools across the country" (1969:8). The next article came just after the opening of schools in the fall of the 1969-1970 school year. This piece observed that disruptions were now more of an issue in secondary schools than in colleges and that unless something could be done about such problems, they would pose a real threat to the viability of American education. The September 22, 1969, article was the last to cry out that there was a problem of school disruption. The remaining two articles listed in chart 4-3 were of a more cautious genre, and clearly reflected the turning of public interest away from disruptions and toward crime in the schools.[17]

The 1969-1970 school year was a period of a great deal of activity, both by pupils, in terms of disruptive actions, and by school administrators, in terms of countermeasures to student actions. Studies demonstrating this high level of pupil activity fell into two generic types: statistical studies and opinion polls.

Pupil Activity—Statistical Studies: Chart 4-4 lists the major statistical studies in the area of secondary school disruptions. Though this study cannot develop meaningful conclusions from these data,[18] it can make a number of points: first, data-gathering studies researching the frequency of pupil disruptions ceased after 1970. Even the Bailey work (1971) asked questions only relating to the correlates of disruptions, rather than to the issues of the frequency or intensity of disruptions. Second, because most studies (except tc a limited extent, the Pucinski work) did not scale the intensity of disruptions, address differences between legitimate versus illegitimate disruptions, or uniformly define disruptions, the data presented by these studies—even that relating merely to the frequency of disruptions—are not comparable.

Pupil Activity—Opinion Polls: Perhaps the most helpful research data on the extent of secondary school disruptions came from the National Education Association's research division. Consistently since the 1968-1969 school year, and even occasionally before that, this organization had conducted polls on the attitudes of the nation's teachers. Chart 4-5 presents answers to the "Poll's" question, "students have demonstrated against school policies this year."[19] Though the low incidence levels of disruption are important (and tend to confirm the Pucinski study's 18 percent disruption findings, rather than the more common mid-50 percent figures of other studies), the interesting point is that the peaking of teacher reports of disruptive pupils occurred in the 1969-1970 school year. Still another confirmation that disruptions were a highly localized phenomenon with a definite beginning and end is that 1971-1972 was the last period during which NEA's "Teacher Opinion Poll" asked about student

Chart 4-4
Major Statistical Studies on Student Disruptions

RESEARCHER AND TITLE	PERIOD SURVEYED	DATE OF PUBLICATION	TARGET AUDIENCE
NATIONAL ASSOCIATION OF SECONDARY SCHOOL PRINCIPALS: RESEARCH DIVISION -- "STUDENT ACTIVISM AND CONFLICT"	1967-1969 SCHOOL YEARS	JANUARY, 1971	SECONDARY SCHOOL PRINCIPALS
NATION'S SCHOOLS: "OPINION POLL"	FALL, 1968	SEPTEMBER, 1968	SCHOOL ADMINISTRATORS
LLOYD TRUMP AND JANE HUNT: "THE NATURE AND EXTENT OF STUDENT ACTIVISM"	WINTER, 1969	MAY, 1969	SECONDARY SCHOOL PRINCIPALS
ALAN WESTIN: "RESPONDING TO REBELS WITH A CAUSE"	NOVEMBER, 1968 TO FEBRUARY, 1969	1970	BOOK: FORD FOUNDATION CONFERENCE ON SCHOOLS AND THE DEMOCRATIC PROCESS
U.S. CONGRESS: REP. PUCINSKI; "SURVEY OF UNREST IN THE NATION'S HIGH SCHOOLS"	1968-1969 SCHOOL YEAR	FEBRUARY, 1970	FORMAL REPORT NOT RELEASED; AUDIENCE IS THEREFORE ONLY THOSE WHO READ THE CONGRESSIONAL RECORD
U.S. OFFICE OF EDUCATION: OFFICE OF STUDENTS AND YOUTH -- UNPUBLISHED BY HEW. (SEE I/D/E/A/ REPORTER, SUMMER, 1970)	NOVEMBER, 1969 TO FEBRUARY, 1970	SUMMER, 1970	HEW POLICY LEVEL
STEPHEN K. BAILEY: "DISRUPTION IN URBAN PUBLIC SECONDARY SCHOOLS"	MARCH-JUNE, 1970	1971	U.S. OFFICE OF EDUCATION (THIS REPORT WAS CONDUCTED AT THE REQUEST OF THE U.S. COMMISSIONER OF EDUCATION.)
ROBERT HAVIGHURST: "PROFILE OF THE LARGE-CITY HIGH SCHOOL"	SCHOOL YEARS 1968-1969 AND 1969-1970	NOVEMBER, 1970	SECONDARY SCHOOL PRINCIPALS

FINDINGS	OVERVIEW OF SAMPLE	PROBLEMS
43% (288 SCHOOLS) REPORTED DISRUPTIONS LASTING OVER ONE-HALF DAY.	670 RESPONDENTS (67%) TO 1,000 SURVEYS	NO MEASURES OF SCHOOL VIOLENCE ARE TAKEN. INCIDENCE RATES ARE NOT CALCULATED. LEGITIMATE VERSUS ILLEGITIMATE VIOLENCE IS NOT DISCUSSED.
IN ANSWER TO THE QUESTION "DO YOU EXPECT THE CURRENT STUDENT UNREST IN COLLEGES TO FILTER DOWN TO HIGH SCHOOLS THIS FALL?" THE ANSWERS ARE: 45% YES AND 55% NO.	40% RESPONSE TO A 4% PROPORTIONAL SAMPLE OF 16,000 SCHOOL ADMINISTRATORS IN 50 STATES	QUESTIONS ABOUT THE EXTENT OF DISRUPTIONS ARE NOT ASKED. THERE ARE NO DEFINITIONS EXPLAINING WHAT "DISRUPTIONS" ARE
67% URBAN AND SUBURBAN SCHOOLS EXPERIENCED DISRUPTION. 53% RURAL SCHOOLS HAD DISRUPTIONS.	EVERY 15TH PRINCIPAL THROUGHOUT THE U.S. (1,982) WERE SURVEYED. RESPONSE RATE WAS 52% (1,026)	ALL COMMENTS FOR THE TWO STUDIES LISTED ABOVE ALSO APPLY HERE.
348 SCHOOLS IN 48 STATES HAD SOME KIND OF DISRUPTION. OF THE 348 SCHOOLS, 239 SUFFERED "SERIOUS INCIDENTS."	DATA COLLECTED BY SUBSCRIBING TO A NEWSPAPER CLIPPING SERVICE FOR FOUR MONTHS.	THIS SURVEY WAS DESIGNED ONLY AS AN INFORMAL CONFIRMATION OF OTHER PUBLISHED STUDIES. METHODOLOGICAL PROBLEMS HAVE BEEN DISCUSSED IN CHAPTER II.
18% (2,710) OF THE RESPONDING SCHOOLS INDICATED SOME FORM OF "DISRUPTION AS PROTEST ACTIVITY." 1% (148) OF THE RESPONDING SCHOOLS REPORTED RIOTS AS PROTEST ACTIVITY.	55% RESPONSE TO 29,000 SURVEYS (15,086 RETURNED)	CLOSE ANALYSIS OF THE PERCENTAGES DEVELOPED FOR SOME INCIDENCE CATEGORIES REVEALS THAT THE WRONG POPULATION BASE NUMBER WAS USED; THIS RESULTS IN THE PUBLICATION OF ERRONEOUS PERCENTAGES. SEE, ALSO, ERRORS INDICATED IN NUMBER ONE, ABOVE.
LOCATION OF DISRUPTIONS: 63% URBAN, 33% SUBURBAN, 4% RURAL. SIZE OF CITY: 55% OVER 1 MILLION, 26% LESS THAN 100,000, 11% 100–500,000, 8% 500,000 - 1 MILLION.	NEWSPAPER CLIPPING SERVICE FOR FOUR MONTHS: ANALYSIS OF 130 "MOST SERIOUS" DISRUPTIVE CASES	THE PROBLEMS WITH USING NEWSPAPER CLIPPINGS, ESPECIALLY FOR WINTER MONTHS, IS DISCUSSED IN CHAPTER II AS PART OF BAILEY'S USE OF THE WESTIN MATERIALS.
LARGER SCHOOLS HAVE MORE PROBLEMS. DISRUPTION IS POSITIVELY RELATED TO INTEGRATION: ALL-BLACK OR ALL-WHITE SCHOOLS ARE LESS LIKELY TO SUFFER DISRUPTION. SCHOOLS WITH HIGH PERCENTAGES OF BLACK STUDENTS ARE LESS LIKELY TO BE DISRUPTIVE IF THEY HAVE HIGH PERCENTAGES OF BLACK STAFF.	RETURN RATE WAS ABOUT 35%: 683 OUT OF 2,000	POOR TIMING FOR THE MAILING OF THE QUESTIONNAIRES (EARLY SUMMER, 1970) RESULTED IN LOW RESPONSE RATES.
CONFLICT AMONG STUDENTS AND BETWEEN STUDENTS AND FACULTY IS THE MOST STRIKING ASPECT OF LARGE CITY HIGH SCHOOLS TODAY. CONFLICT IS MOST LIKELY IN SCHOOLS IN A HIGH SOCIOECONOMIC STATUS AREA AND WITH LARGE NUMBERS OF BLACK STUDENTS. 31% OF THE SCHOOLS EXPERIENCED STUDENT STRIKES. 27% OF THE SCHOOLS HAD PICKETING OR PROTEST MARCHES.	THE RETURN RATE WAS 96%: 670 OUT OF 700 HIGH SCHOOLS IN 45 CITIES. POPULATIONS WERE 100% OF THE SCHOOLS IN EACH CITY.	BROAD TIME BAND (TWO YEARS) HINDERS CLEAR MEMORY OF SPECIFIC EVENTS. HIGHLY FOCUSED SCOPE OF THE PROJECT HINDERS GENERALIZABILITY.

Chart 4-5
The National Education Association's Teacher Opinion Poll Asking Questions about the Extent of School Disruptions

	1968-1969	1969-1970	1970-1971	1971-1972
Percent teachers reporting that students in their schools have demonstrated	4.1	6.3	5.3	4.7

Source: Research Division of the National Education Association.

unrest. Beginning in the 1972 academic year, questions focused on student assault and violence. This study now discusses the range of countermeasures available to administrators to reduce student disruptions. The countermeasures covered a continuum from "do nothing" to "occupy the school with riot police." Though solutions were largely left up to local school administrators, polar viewpoints relating to the most appropriate administrative countermeasure to pupil disruptions are interesting to note, since they represented the range of options available to principals and their staffs.

Countermeasures—Don't Escalate Approach: As Mager and Pipe (1970) pointed out in their book about analyzing performance problems in respect to interpersonal relations, a common answer to the question "What would happen if you left it alone?" is that nothing would happen; the problem—whatever the problem—would simply go away. This point is relevant here, for the issue of making the pupils' complaints legitimate by paying attention to them is presented in the *National Association of Secondary School Principals' Bulletin* by Robert Sullivan (1969). Sullivan suggested that high school unrest would flourish under excessive attention, and that the best way to respond to a disruptive situation was to be reasonable, adult, and as detached as possible from the more outlandish demands of the pupils.[20] Similarly vague and general points about reasonableness, straightforwardness, and openness to communication were made by Gudridge (1969) in *High School Student Unrest: How to Anticipate Protest, Channel Activism, and Protect Student Rights*. Ashbaugh (1969) wrote "Nine Tested Approaches for Coping with Conflict Situations"; these approaches were entirely of the "let's-talk-this-over-and-be-reasonable" genre.

Countermeasures—You Had Better Not Try That in My School Approach: Three no-nonsense publications covered the range of options available at this end of the spectrum. First was Erickson's "Activism in the Secondary Schools: Analysis and Recommendations" (1969). He urged the school staff to clearly understand the students' problems before acting, and he stipulated important actions to be taken, including securing the school and photographing the participants. Second, Benton's 1971 *Dissent and Disruption in the Schools: A*

Handbook for School Administrators outlined the rights and privileges of students and provided the proper wording for school administrators when using a megaphone to inform pupils they were unlawfully assembled and would become subject to arrest. This work's recommendations ended at the point at which the disruptive situation was turned over to the police.

Vestermark's 1971 research report (*Responses to Collective Violence in Threat or Act. Vol. 1: Collective Violence in Educational Institutions:* Part II: "The Police Role in Violent Incidents," pp. 25-53) dealt extensively and comprehensively with subjects of *when* police should become involved in terms of the type of disruption (situational or guided), and *how* the police should become involved (preplanning and year-round communication with school authorities as well as crisis intervention). The crux of Vestermark's paper with respect to this subsection was its statement that the use of an intelligence network to warn of impending trouble combined with good tactical intelligence during the disruption based on a general understanding of the nature of disruptions made the difference between being overcome by the event of disruption and overcoming the event of disruption.

In 1967, as many of these reports were being developed and expression of public concern was peaking, Congress decided to conduct its own study (see chart 4-4 for the time placement of the Pucinski study). Though the results are suspect (in ways that have been mentioned in this chapter and chapter 2), Pucinski's survey nonetheless pointed to the indisputable conclusion that in the 1968-1969 school year (a year that is confirmed by NEA's "Teacher Opinion Poll" and other sources as the most active year for secondary school disruptions) there were very few such disturbances. Indeed, the Pucinski study found that only 18 percent of the respondents reported some kind of disruption as protest activity, and virtually no respondents reported riots as a form of protest. This finding, combined with the NEA conclusions, stand in stark comparison to the media presentation of high school disruptions in 1967-1971.[21]

As such findings (see chart 4-4) began to be appreciated by researchers, what small interest there had been in conducting further research into school disruptions faded away. By 1972, as the results of the only Law Enforcement Assistance Administration-funded project researching disruptions became known, and the results indeed indicated that disruptions were no longer a problem (Meyer et al., 1971:10), there was federal, congressional, and public agreement that disruptions in public secondary schools had become a thing of the past. An article in *U.S. News and World Report* expressed the opinion that the "back of student revolt [had] been broken" (*U.S. News and World Report*, February 21, 1972:48). Corroborating evidence that public concern had shifted was demonstrated in chart 4-2, in which the numbers of articles in the *New York Times* written about disruptions had fallen almost to the pre-1967 level.

Summary and Conclusions

This chapter has been concerned with answering three major questions: to what extent can court cases relating to pupil rights be used as indications of the kinds of issues causing pupil unrest; did differences in the points of view of students and school administrators affect an understanding of actions and counteractions relating to disruptions; how many local school administrators have responded to disruptions?

Regarding the first question, this study found that, unlike college students, secondary school students tended to disrupt over issues of school organization and basic constitutional rights of dress and speech. This finding was borne out by a number of research surveys and was reflected by the dozens of highly relevant court cases that appeared from the late 1960s to 1975. In relation to the second and third questions, this study found that differences between reasons for pupil disruption and expectations of educators as to what would cause pupil disruptions (especially 1967 to 1969) often led to administrative overreaction to pupil demonstrations. This overreaction probably resulted from the media-fed anticipation on the part of many school administrators that high school disruptions would parallel political disruptions in colleges. Many administrators became blinded to the actual fairness of the pupil requests. Often, it seemed, requests solidified into demands, and demands required formal negotiation. The original issues became problems, problems became crises, and crises became disruptions.

This chapter also addressed issues of the intensity and frequency of student disruptions. In relation to establishing trends in the intensity of secondary school disruptions, there were a number of barriers. Among other things, failure of research surveys to address such issues as legitimate versus illegitimate disruptions, situational versus externally guided disruptions, or the size or duration of the disruptions made it difficult to draw conclusions. The book concludes, however, that disruptions were never very common, were fairly easily co-opted, and were not sustained for many years after courts repeatedly ruled in the students' favor (thus forcing schools to change many of their administrative practices relating to students' rights in ways that met many of the demands of student protests).

As a result of studying the trends in student disruptions in secondary schools, the book has additionally developed some tentative explanations concerning the reasons for the very brief rise and fall of secondary school disruptions. Though it is unlikely that any single one of the following issues made much difference in the nature, extent, or frequency of disruptions, it is quite likely that taken together they did account for some change in the overall pattern of this form of student misbehavior. Though ignorance of actual causes is enormous, the book suggests that the following four issues do address possible reasons for changes in the frequency of secondary school disruptions. First, by the time disruptions really became an issue, school districts were alert and had already begun planning intervention strategies—and thus were able quickly to co-opt many budding disturbances. Second, as secondary school disruptions often exploded over pragmatic issues of the administrative functioning of schools or of student rights, the resolution of such issues—often with civil court intervention—removed rallying points for further disruptions. Third, by the early 1970s, college and community disruptions had tapered off, so secondary school disruptions were no longer supported by a common movement. Fourth, by the early 1970s, public expression of concern had shifted firmly away from disruptions and onto crime.

Notes

1. Though there were only 2,710 schools reporting disruptions, schools often had more than one disruption. Recorded according to the latter fact, the total exceeded 2,710.

2. As in note 1, some schools had more than one disruption, so the total count of percentages of the reasons for disruptions can and does exceed 100 percent of the schools.

3. Though the study's period for disruptions is 1967 to 1975, it must reach out of that period in this instance. By going back to 1961, it can annotate landmark cases that establish base precedents for later cases falling within the study period.

4. Larson mentioned the following theories about the causes of student disruptions: the outside agitator theory; the generation at war theory; the liberalism has failed theory; the man versus machine theory; and the participatory democracy theory (Larson, 1972:22).

5. Larson's extraction about disruptions was: (1) We have taught students well about freedom, justice, and equality. They took us seriously. (2) We failed to teach them that we did not always mean what we said. They have recognized our hypocrisy but have failed to adopt it as a way of life (Larson, 1972:22).

6. The concept of *situational* versus *guided* violence was the product of Vestermark (1971:86). The idea that disruptions are SDS-fomented occurred frequently. See, for example, *U.S. News and World Report*, May 20, 1968:40; Larson, 1972:21; Erickson, 1969:25; and Westin, 1970:66.

7. The timing of events which convinced educators that the SDS was moving into the secondary schools, and that the results were likely to be riotous were clearly visible. Mid-1960 publications of the SDS (for example, Kleiman, 1967) seemed to point toward radicalization of high schools. At the SDS national conference in 1968, the Interorganizational Secretary was quoted as saying, "Our high schools will be the new thrust. They are used as babysitting

jails ... they are oppressive" (Weinraub, 1968:29). Hearing this quote, Graves (1969) wrote an article in the *National Association of Secondary School Principals' Bulletin* stating that he felt that the SDS was nurturing high school unrest by, among other things, encouraging and sponsoring high school SDS chapters. Further national public concern was voiced by Senator Robert Byrd (D-West Virginia) who suggested that the fourteen-page 1968 SDS publication, titled "High School Reform," proposed nothing less than a "blueprint for the destruction of the entire American educational system" (*U.S. News and World Report*, March 24, 1969:8).

8. The "law of the instrument" states: "Give a small boy a hammer, and suddenly everything needs hammering" (Caplin, 1973:200).

9. The reasoning behind the theory that school districts now developed for expectation of crime and violence is as follows: the Offices of School Security, being staff offices, required budgets which in turn required budget justifications. Budget justifications required reasons and statistics. If there were neither disruptions nor crimes, then there was no justification for an Office of School Security. Since budgets are drawn up in advance of the funding year, the school district must, indeed, develop an expectation of crime for that coming year.

10. As mentioned in chapter 2, Meyer et al. (1971) had to realign their Stanford Research Institute study (funded by the Law Enforcement Assistance Administration) of the nature and extent of student disruptions because school administrators indicated that the disruptions of the previous years were no longer a major concern to them. The Meyer study found that in the 1971 school year, principals were most concerned about apathy or crime: the two ends of the continuum of misbehaviors. Principals, it turned out, had developed the concept of "externalization" insofar as the viewing of disruptions were concerned. The theory of externalization is that the school is only a microcosm of the community at large, and insofar as there were riots and disruptions in the urban city core as well as on the college campuses, clearly the problems were not to be blamed on the secondary schools, but on society as a whole. This concept paved the way for the establishment of school security offices.

Due to the methodological care taken to produce this report, such a wholly unexpected finding carries particular weight. That the researchers were surprised with the discovery of the externalization of the concern over disruptions, and that they had to refocus their research effort, adds circumstantial credence to their findings' objectivity. Additional evidence of a decrease in the educator's concern over disruptions between 1969 and 1972 can be seen in changes in the wording of the National Education Association's "Teacher Opinion Poll of Pupil Behavior" from the 1968-1969 school year to the 1975-1976 school year. (The author thanks Charles Stalford of HEW's National Institute of Education for pointing out these wording changes.)

11. "Office of School Security" is a generic phrase. Many of these offices developed out of the long-established custodial (plant security) divisions of the school district offices. Examples of actual names of the security offices are: Office of Internal Affairs, Special Investigations Department, Property Security Department, Office of School Security.

12. The size and capability of an Office of School Security varies considerably with the needs of school districts. Whereas Los Angeles Unified School District in 1975 was the third largest police force in Los Angeles county (about 300 sworn, armed officers), that was as extreme as the few remaining urban school districts which did not support the concept of school security and never developed a security office.

13. An excellent study of the history and development of post-secondary disruptions appeared in Douglas' *Youth in Turmoil: America's Changing Youth Culture and Student Protest Movements* (1970).

14. Again, as previously noted, the literature suggests that disruptions ceased to be topical after 1971. This study extends the time period from 1971 to 1975 because many articles about secondary school disruptions were published as post hoc analyses.

15. The idea of using the *New York Times Index* to develop an indication of public concern over an issue came from Metzner (1968), who used this technique in relation to school unrest and violence for the period 1940 to 1968. There is one important caveat concerning the use of the *Times Index*. There is a natural inclination for newspapers to overreport the unusual and to disregard the common. To the extent that disruptions were a new phenomenon in 1968-1969 and became common by 1972, chart 4-2 may be biased by primarily reflecting the period of time when school disruptions could reasonably be said to be controversial and newsworthy. The defense for the use of these article counts on disruptions, however, is that these particular years of high interest are confirmed by numerous other sources far removed from any need to sell newspapers.

16. Of the three major weekly news magazines, only *U.S. News and World Report* carried enough articles on school disruptions to enable the study to make patterns out of changes in the titles and content.

17. Other articles on student misbehavior appearing during this time period were concerned with the growing problems of violence and crime; they are discussed in chapter 5.

18. Note that the Trump-Hunt study in the winter of 1969 found 67 percent of the urban and 67 percent of the suburban schools had experienced disruptions, whereas the Pucinski study out of Congress returned the percentage of disruptions as only 18. Some hypothetical explanations for the differences in these findings purportedly studying the same topic in the same time period are: first, the Principals' Association study may have suffered from sample bias in

relation to prejudicial, subjective viewpoints of the respondents; second, the two studies might have asked slightly different questions, resulting in noncomparable conclusions; third, since neither study defines disruption, respondents may have answered in a more or less random manner, with each respondent's answer reflecting his subjective interpretation of the question; and fourth, any combination of the explanations previously mentioned or other contaminations of the sample that are not suggested here.

19. Concerning NEA's "Teacher Opinion Polls," there is the following caveat: though the "Polls" are conducted by using a stratified random probability sample of the nation's schoolteachers—sample size 2,000 teachers, return rate 95 percent—this question is subject to multiple response contamination. If more than one teacher in a school received this NEA "Opinion Poll" questionnaire, then there will be multiple reporting of the same incident of disruption. After discussing this issue with the Director of Research for the National Education Association, the author decided that these data may be used with this caveat. Further, if this bias does exist, it exists on the side of overreporting, rather than underreporting. Since the point stressed in this chapter is that disruptions were never a very common phenomenon, NEA's relatively low figures become all the more supportive with the addition of this caveat.

20. When the concept that principals cannot seem to leave the issues alone is combined with some of the Bailey findings (especially that less experienced principals endorse more active responses to disruptions [Bailey, 1971:12]), one can see a general profile of the principals most interested in the "don't escalate" side of the continuum of responses. The results of a 1971 NASSP research study support this profile that experienced principals were the ones most willing to "talk out" student problems. Among the results of that study were that the five most commonly used "disruption de-escalation techniques" included: (1) formal meetings of principal with student representatives; (2) small-group discussions between faculty members and students; (3) discussions between school persons and adults in the community; (4) creation of new channels for student-faculty communication; and (5) significant curriculum changes (*National Association of Secondary School Principals' Bulletin*, 1971:83). Note that four of the five findings contributed in one way or another to the talk-it-out approach.

21. Only the Pucinski study made an effort to scale the intensity of disruptions experienced by schools. Other studies merely recorded uncategorized incident counts of disturbances in schools. Basing one's thought on information provided by the Pucinski work, one must conclude that most protest activity was mild and easily dealt with by school administrations.

References

Ashbaugh, Carl R.
    1969   "High School Student Activism: Nine Tested Approaches for Coping with Conflict Situations." *Nation's Schools* 83(February):94-96.

Bailey, Stephen K.
- 1971 *Disruption in Urban Public Secondary Schools*. Washington, D.C.: National Association of Secondary School Principals.

Benton, A. Edgar
- 1971 *Dissent and Disruption in the Schools: A Handbook for School Administrators*. Dayton, Ohio: Institute for Development of Educational Activities, Inc.

Brammer, Lawrence M.
- 1968 "The Coming Revolt of High Schools." *Bulletin of the National Association of Secondary School Principals* 399(September):13-22.

Caplin, Nathan, and Morgan, Stephen D.
- 1973 "On Being Useful: The Nature and Consequences of Psychological Research on Social Problems." *American Psychologist* 28:199-211.

Children's Defense Fund (Cambridge: Mass.)
- 1975 *School Suspensions: Are They Helping Children?*

Douglas, Jack D.
- 1970 *Youth in Turmoil: America's Changing Youth Cultures and Student Protest Movements*. Crime and Delinquency Monograph Series. Rockville, Md.: National Institutes of Mental Health.

Erickson, Kenneth; Benson, George; and Huff, Robert
- 1969 "Activism in the Secondary Schools: Analysis and Recommendations." Eugene, Oreg.: Bureau of Educational Research.

Fish, Kenneth L.
- 1970 *Conflict and Dissent in the High School*. New York: Bruce Publishing Company.

Gaddy, Dale
- 1971 *Rights and Freedoms of Public School Students: Directions from the 1960s*. Topeka, Kans.: NOLPE Monograph Series, No. 2.

Graves, Samuel
- 1969 "A Description of Student Unrest." *Bulletin of the National Association of Secondary School Principals* 53(May):191-197.

Gudridge, Beatrice
- 1969 *High School Student Unrest: How to Anticipate Protest, Channel Activism, and Protect Student Rights*. Washington, D.C.: A special report by Education U.S.A., available through National School Public Relations Association.

Havighurst, Robert J.
- 1970 *A Profile of the Large-City High School*. Washington, D.C.: National Association of Secondary School Principals.

Institute for Development of Educational Ideas, Inc.
- 1970 "Disruption in the Nation's High Schools: A Special Report."

Jones, J. William.
- 1973 *Discipline Crisis in Schools*. Washington, D.C.: National Association of Secondary School Principals.

Kleiman, Mark
    1967   "Student Freedom, Conformity, and School Policies." Chicago: Students for a Democratic Society.

Larson, Knute
    1972   *School Discipline in an Age of Rebellion*. New York: Parker Publishing Company, Inc.

Mager, Robert, and Pipe, Peter
    1970   *Analyzing Performance Problems*. Belmont, California: Fearon Publishers.

Metzner, Seymour
    1968   "School Violence in Historical Perspective." A paper presented to the American Educational Research Association, meeting in Los Angeles on February 5-8.

Meyer, John; Chase-Dunn, Chris; and Invarity, James
    1971   "The Expansion of the Autonomy of Youth: Responses of the Secondary School to Problems of Order in the 1960s." Stanford, Calif.: The Laboratory for Social Research, Stanford University.

National Association of Secondary School Principals' Bulletin
    1971   "Student Activism and Conflict." 55(January):70-89.

National Education Association
    1964-   "Teacher Opinion Polls." Washington, D.C.: Research Division of the
    1975   National Education Association.

Nation's Schools
    1968   "Student Unrest Will Spread to High Schools, Many Fear: Opinion Poll." vol. 82, No. 3 (September):14.

New York Times
    1976   *New York Times Index, 1950-1975*.

Pucinski, Roman C.
    1970   "Results of a Survey on Students' Unrest in the Nation's High Schools." *Congressional Record* (February 23):E1178-E1180.

School Management
    1969   "Strategies for Coping with Student Disruption." *School Management* (June):45-58.

Shaffer, Helen B.
    1969   "Discipline in Public Schools," *Educational Research Reports* 2 Number 8 (August 27):635-652.

Sullivan, Robert J.
    1969   "The Overrated Threat." *Bulletin of the National Association of Secondary School Principals* 338(September):36-44.

Trump, J. Lloyd, and Hunt, Jane
    1969   "The Nature and Extent of Student Activism." *Bulletin of the National Association of Secondary School Principals* 337(May):150-158.

U.S. News and World Report
    1968   "Violence Hits Schools, Colleges, as Rebellion Spreads to High Schools." (May 20):36-40.
              "Violence in Schools—The Outlook Now." (September 2):68.
              "More Breakdowns in Public Schools." (December 2):32-34.
    1969   "Now It's High School Students on a Rampage." (March 24):8-10.
              "High Schools: Next Target for Unrest." (September 22):64-66.
    1970   "Youth Rebellion—Why: An Interview with Dr. William Glasser." (April 27):42-45.
    1972   "An Uneasy Truce in Troubled High Schools." (February 21):48-50.

Vestermark, S.D.
    1971   *Responses to Collective Violence in Threat or Act.* Vol. 1: *Collective Violence in Educational Institutions*. Springfield, Va.: National Technical Information Service.

Weinraub, Bernard
    1968   "S.D.S. Maps Drive in High Schools." *New York Times* (December 30):29.

Westin, Alan F.
    1970   "Facing the Issues: Responding to Rebels with a Cause." In *The School and the Democratic Environment*, Danforth Foundation and Ford Foundation (eds.), pp. 65-82. New York: Columbia University Press.

Legal Cases

Baker v. Owen, 441 U.S.L.W. 3235 (U.S. Oct. 20, 1975), aff'd, 395 F. Supp. 294 (M.D.N.C. 1975).
Blackwell v. Issaquena County Board of Education, 363 F. 2d. 749 (Miss., 1966).
Brown v. Board of Education of Topeka, 347 U.S. 483, 74 S. Ct. 686, 98 L. Ed. 873 (Kansas, 1954).
Burnside v. Byars, 363 F. 2d. 744:5th Cir. (1966).
Davis v. Firment, 269 F. Supp. 524 (E.D. La. 1967), aff'd per Curiam, 408 F. 2d. 1085 (1969).
Dixon v. Alabama State Board of Education, 244 F. 2d. 150, 158:5th Cir. (1961), cert. denied, 368 U.S. 930.
Gault v. Arizona, 99 Ariz. 181, 407 P. 2d. 760:(1965), rev'd, 387 U.S., 1:(1967).
Leonard v. School Committee in Attleboro, 349 Mass. 704, 212 N.E. 2d. 468 (1965).
Richards v. Thurston, 304 F. Supp. 499 (Mass. 1966).
Scott v. Board of Education, 305 N.Y.S. 2d. 601 (1969).

Sullivan v. Houston Independent School District, 307 F. Supp. 1328 (Tex., 1969).
Tinker v. Des Moines Independent Community School District, 393 U.S. 503 (1969).
Voight v. Van Buren Public Schools, 306 F. Supp. 1388 (E.D. Mich. 1969).
Williams v. Dade County School Board, 441 F. 2d.:5th Cir. (1971).

5 Crimes

Acts of arson, burglary and malicious mischief cost Los Angeles 2.5 million dollars in 1970-71 school year up from 2.2 million the previous year. The school system can no longer afford to carry insurance since premiums are astronomical with a deductible of $100,000 for each incident.

After 100 Seattle, Washington, parents voluntarily painted the Wedgewood School, young vandals broke in and smeared the unused paint throughout the building.

After breaking into Dana Junior High School in San Pedro, California, four boys turned on a fire hose and flooded classrooms. They then dumped books in the school library and destroyed a number of band instruments.

Vandals did thousands of dollars damage to Tacoma, Washington, schools. The New Whitman School was an ink-stained, equipment-strewn mess. At Stanley High School they ransacked two storerooms leaving the contents in mountains on the floor.

(Grealy, 1973:4)

Introduction

Crimes in public secondary schools are a controversial issue. The aura created by students committing criminal acts against each other or the school staff is unwholesome and is the basis for a great deal of concern on the part of the public, Congress, and elements of the federal government such as the Department of Justice, and the Department of Health, Education and Welfare. Criminal acts in secondary schools differ in two obvious ways from noncriminal disorders: perpetrators are subject to arrest and prosecution; and the violence which often accompanies criminal acts often contributes to schoolwide fear for personal safety. Unlike the disorderly violations of school rules or the often self-righteous-seeming causes of disruptions, criminal acts are generally much more clearly defined by those involved. Though there may be mitigating circumstances surrounding an assault, which ultimately lead the school administration not to press charges, both the offending pupil and the school staff know that an aggravated assault is a criminal act and prosecution will cause the youth a great deal of trouble and inconvenience.[1]

This chapter looks first at crimes from the point of view of pupils and school personnel, and then at trends in school crimes over the years. The trends section is quite detailed, since there are more statistics available for analysis and more controversial topics to consider. It might be useful to review the definition of the term "crime," as discussed in chapter 1, and to stipulate the major questions addressed in this chapter.

Definition of Crime

A crime is an act which is forbidden by public law and which, if committed, can cause an adult to be arrested. With respect to offenses falling in this category, two points are crucial. First, the study concerns itself with an act the moment it is committed, rather than only after a court of law has rendered a criminal conviction; second, it is not concerned with juvenile status offenses such as truancy, curfew violation, and stubborn-child complaints. However, it is particularly interested in including in the criminal-acts category any offense which has the potential or causing a school administrator to involve police or school district security officers.

Major Questions about Crimes

To assist in understanding changes both in the public's perceptions of school crimes and in the possible intensification of criminal acts among pupils, the following questions are addressed.

1. To what extent did crime or the fear of crime in schools affect both student and staff attitudes toward the school and school responses to acts of criminality?

   Studies (especially Lalli and Savitz, 1972) provided compelling evidence to support the thesis that student and staff fear of crime was a major concern in urban schools throughout the nation in 1970-1975. This study examines the issue from various points of view.

2. To what extent can the study establish that the public perception of increased criminal behavior in secondary schools from the late 1960s to 1975 was due in great part to the development of more thorough reporting methods within school district offices of school security?

   One of the primary caveats frequently mentioned when dealing with crime statistics, such as those gathered by the FBI, is that changes in reporting formats or reporting conditions over time distort the real picture of the frequency of incidents of a given crime. In the case of school crimes, there are examples of such distortions. From 1950 to about 1968, no nationally comparable records of aggregate student crimes were kept by school districts, whereas from early 1971 to 1975, extensive nationally comparable records were kept. Comparisons between these periods, therefore, are very risky, and simple comparisons of percentages of crime increases—seen in many unsophisticated surveys—produce biased figures.

Changes in the kinds of data reported within school districts occurred primarily because Offices of School Security were formed (late 1960s) to deal with acts of crime and disruption in schools. In the process of determining the nature and extent of the problems with which security offices had to deal, fresh data were collected and new reports prepared. This chapter discusses later how data-gathering changes brought on by the advent of school security offices in the early 1970s might have affected the public's perceptions of crimes in schools.

3. What information on trends in school crimes from 1950 to 1975 can be developed from available statistics?

Though many of the available statistics are not comparable for various reasons that the study explores, one can still make some general statements about changes in the kinds, frequency, and intensity of school crimes from 1950 to 1975. The study examines the data and develops such conclusions as are possible under these circumstances.

Differing Views of School Crimes

Before discussing actual changes in incidents of crimes in schools, let us first understand possible differences in the nature, extent, or impact crimes have on the overall school population. Whereas pupils and school personnel are undoubtedly concerned about personal safety on the school campus, it is not clear whether two schools with similar crime-incident counts experienced the same degree of fear of crime among students and staff. Evidence from many sources, for example, supports the thesis that in numerous cases both the perpetrators and victims of many repeated offenses were concentrated in a small and well-known group of "friends"—or at least "friendly enemies." As such, high crime incidents alone are not adequate indicators of the level of the fear of crime throughout the school. Well-known and well-controlled groups in one school may result in high crime statistics and low fear levels, whereas in another school the fear of crime may be much greater, with fewer reported incidents of crime.

Another issue to keep in mind is that repeated evidence indicated that schools and security personnel classified certain offenses as crimes, but pupils did not see them as crimes. Though a fight is technically an assault, it is not unusual for adolescents to fight one day and to socialize the next, even as security officers arrive to conduct investigations. Because of such possible differences in interpretation, the following subsections explore the respective views of pupils and school personnel in relation to crimes committed in secondary schools.

Pupils' Views of School Crimes

Writings in sociology and criminology discussing subcultures of violence and peer pressures to engage in deviant behavior are so extensive and accessible as to preclude citing them here. Furthermore, many of the theoretical/sociological issues—such as subcultural deviancy—diverge from the specific focus of this subsection. Such theories are not particularly applicable to this study because the reality of the social organization of the school is such that any pockets of "bad actors" who constantly engage in borderline or outright illegal activity are very likely to be the group of pupils best known to teachers, administrators, and school security officers precisely because they are constantly in trouble.

Rather than any sociological theory explaining the ways youths look at their behavior vis-à-vis the ways in which adults look at students' behavior, this study considers a more pervasive phenomenon: how adolescents in the subculture of school defined criminal acts in relation to how school personnel might have defined such acts. Though practically no literature discusses pupils' views of crimes, it is obvious that students would not look at an instance of playground shoving, for example, as a criminal assault. Thus it was likely that as a cafeteria brawl developed, youths did not anticipate being charged with assault and battery and removed from the school grounds in handcuffs. Does the idea of confusing traditional adolescent behavior with criminal activity sound ridiculous? The reality is not so farfetched. Reporting of instances such as shoving actually once resulted in an inundation of incident reports of assault being filled out and sent to a major security office. In cases where undesirable but legal behavior was confusedly considered by teachers and administrators as falling within the category of offenses to be reported to the security office, the director of security had to redefine the actions which his office considered to be criminal.

Student definitions of extortion and robbery may not be the same as adult definitions. If you, as an adult, were approached by someone who suggested he wanted a "loan" of whatever money you were carrying, you would probably have little doubt that a robbery was taking place. But what of an adolescent on his way to the cafeteria, confronted by one or more youths who ask to "borrow" some change. Is this robbery? Is this extortion? Will he report this kind of offense? Concerning the issue of reporting, the chief variable seemed to be whether or not an adult witnessed the exchange. If no older people were around, such incidents probably remained unnoticed and uncounted. This study is uncertain whether the nonreporting without adult intervention results from differences in the youths' conceptualization of the offense or in the youths' fear of the repercussions of "telling on" a fellow pupil. This study leans toward the theory that young persons often do not consider many of these offenses to be criminal enough to involve the adult community, as the following story illustrates. Peter Blauvelt, the Security Director for Maryland's Prince George's

County Schools, related that his eldest son one day mentioned in passing that though he carried some money in his pocket, he hid the bulk of it in his shoes, since he needed lunch money after "giving" away some of his cash. This kind of accepted extortion undoubtedly occurs in any period—but it increased dramatically from 1970 to 1975. By 1975, mild extortion was probably epidemic in the nation's urban schools.

To be sure, the "weapon" that turns a supposed "gift" into a robbery or an extortion is fear of the consequences of resisting an assailant. This fear-of-crime concept has appeared occasionally in the literature relating to student acts in schools. "There is a degree of fear," admitted one high school senior. "If you see a bunch of guys in the hall, you get nervous. You might get held up" (*Time*, June 2, 1975:39). Indeed, the only survey this study found on student fear of schools was in Lalli and Savitz's *Delinquency and City Life*. Lalli and Savitz's interviews with about 390 youths showed that 44 percent of both delinquents and nondelinquents considered school yards to be unsafe places, and 31 percent felt school halls were unsafe. As the authors noted, "The perception of the school environment as being dangerous could very well influence the students' ability to do well in school. A student who feels that he is in danger of being beaten up or robbed in the school room is not likely to devote full attention to the teacher. Also, the perception of the school yard and halls as dangerous may account somewhat for the high truancy rates which are recorded by the inner city schools" (Lalli and Savitz, 1972:41). This study found two diverse references to student fear of other students. First, Dukiet quoted Dr. Frank Brown, Chairman of the National Committee for Reform of Secondary Education, as saying that "The major concern confronting secondary schools today is the climate of fear where the majority of students are afraid for their safety" (Dukiet, 1973:16); second, the President's Commission on School Finance (1972:46) insisted that schoolchildren must "be free from physical violence and extortion while attending schools."

Three issues interact with respect to varying perceptions of crimes in schools: first, possible nonalignment of definitions of those acts which the adult world considers criminal; second, student unwillingness to involve the adult world in their problems, even while realizing that they are victims of crimes; and third—particularly in urban schools—as the frequency and intensity of acts of violence increase, student fear of crime can become so pervasive that it threatens the very viability of the school as an educational institution. The problems involved with fear can only be resolved through a clearer understanding on the part of pupils and staff as to what constitutes a criminal, reportable act, and what does not.

School Personnel's Views of Crimes

For a number of reasons, some previously discussed and some discussed below, this study proposes that the fear of student crime on the part of school personnel may well be more acute than on the part of pupils. Though there have been no previous studies on this particular issue, tangential studies and journal articles provide compelling indications that the phenomenon does indeed exist. In discussing this proposition, and for clarity of presentation as well, this subsection is divided into three parts, each concerning a different staff level. The first division concerns teachers' views of school-based crime; the second focuses on problems as seen by school administrators; and the third considers the points of view of school district Officers of School Security.

Teachers: Since teachers are exposed to a more general cross section of the school than are pupils, staff members are likely to have a greater fear of student crime than students have. This is so, as previously mentioned, because adults have a better idea of which offenses are criminal, the student/staff grapevine permits the staff to become aware of the entire range of unsavory pupil acts,[2] and the population of teachers in the school is so small, the likelihood that teachers will know of other teachers who have been criminally violated is greater than the likelihood that students will directly know of other students who have been violated.[3]

Teachers' fear of crime in schools has been well documented and seemed to manifest itself in fearful, if cowering, tolerance of the problem or in angry aggression. The tone of the attitude of fearful tolerance was expressed, for example, in Cavan (1969:286), who portrayed teachers as feeling as much prisoners in schools as did pupils.[4] This is so, according to Albert Shanker's (president of the American Federation of Teachers, AFL-CIO, in New York) testimony before Senator Birch Bayh's Subcommittee to Investigate Juvenile Delinquency, in part because of the invidious "stratagem of shifting the blame from the assailant to the victim himself.... Teacher victims may be accused of having provoked assault by demanding, for example, that a student return to his classroom rather than cut class and loiter in the cafeteria" (Subcommittee to Investigate Juvenile Delinquency, 1975:6). Expanding on Shanker's point, Wells referred to one observer of the school crime scene who noted that "unless a teacher is really hurt or scared by a threat, the incident often is not reported. The teacher is fearful of adverse criticism. He or she might be blamed as the cause of the attack, either by superiors or parents, called a 'troublemaker,' or accused of not being able to maintain discipline. Also, teachers often think they can handle the situation without outside help" (Wells, 1971:9). But the teacher was often unable to maintain discipline.

Though the concept of negotiating for classroom control in relation to disorders has been covered in chapter 3, the observations of Werthman relating to normless gang members are applicable here. In "Delinquents in Schools," Werthman described teacher-testing procedures whereby a nucleus of severely troublesome youths suspended conferral of legitimacy to the teacher as class leader until confirming that authority was being exercised on suitable grounds and in a suitable way. The burden of proving that the deacher deserved to be granted a position of authority lay with the teacher (Werthman, 1971:39, 40). McGowan (1973:46) wrote that if there were not too many gang members or other severe disrupters in the class, the teacher may sometimes negotiate with troublesome students and induce them simply to leave the classroom altogether— in exchange for a passing grade. Miller noted that when a school or a class contained too many gang members, the group may "claim control over the school itself or over various rooms and facilities, with such control involving the right to set disciplinary policy . . . and the right to forbid teachers and other school staff from reporting their illegal activities to authorities" (Miller, 1975:203).[5]

These actions noted by Miller and McGowan clearly caused teachers to be frightened. Discussing worried teachers in an article titled "Terror in Schools," a *U.S. News and World Report* writer observed that: "Surveys show that 25 percent of Chicago's teachers consider discipline a constant problem, while 18 percent are worried about their physical safety. According to John Kotsakis, a spokesman for the Chicago Teachers' Union, it isn't uncommon for teachers to refuse to work in certain areas of school buildings for fear of assault from students carrying guns and knives" (Copyright: *U.S. News and World Report*, January 26, 1976:53. Reprinted with permission.)

Expressing concern over almost the identical issue, Jones quoted Lee Dolson, past president of San Francisco's Classroom Teachers Association, as descrying that "teachers are in a state of fear. Hardly a day goes by that I don't talk to a teacher or two phoning from home, using sick leave to stay because they are too sick with fear to go to school and teach" (Jones, 1973:1).

Though the three choices facing teachers troubled by fear of crime were to quit teaching altogether, to manage to live with the fear, or to take some kind of demonstrative action, this study seldom heard about any demonstrative action. In a series of articles in the *Saint Louis Post-Dispatch* (January 18 and February 5 and 6, 1969) an interesting episode about demonstrative action was described. One article reported that "75 percent of all teachers in the East St. Louis school system [675 out of 900 teachers] carry guns, not in order to enforce discipline in their schools, but to protect themselves against the constant possibility of assaults within and outside their classrooms" (Franklin, January 18, 1969:1). In the public uproar about armed public school teachers which followed this admission, the best statement of retraction that the school board could issue was that "the number of teachers [carrying guns to protect themselves] is probably lower now than a year ago" (Ibid.). The part of the episode especially interesting for this study is that when Norval Hickman, the Deputy Coroner for St. Clair County, read about the gun issue and went to police headquarters to demand that all the teachers at one of the high schools be searched, the police refused, and added that as deputy coroner, Hickman himself had police powers and "suggested that he go [to the school] and correct the situation himself" (Franklin, February 5, 1969:1). This study emphasizes that the police are as upset about crimes of secondary school youths as the teachers are, and are not overly anxious to intervene in a situation in which a good tough action (albeit quite illegal) has been taken.

School Administrators: Chapter 3 discussed the phenomenon wherein local school administrators resisted acknowledging the nature and extent of student misbehaviors in relation to disorders. The same general observations hold true for crimes. Whenever possible, principals tried to underplay incidents of misbehavior to avoid presenting to the public an image of either their own lack of control of the school climate or of a more general lack of safety on school grounds. Public mention of this situation was common enough to make belaboring the point superfluous here; thus this study notes only a few authorities who commented on the situation.

By 1970, Congress had become suspicious that school administrators were being less than candid when reporting instances of serious misbehavior and crime. Senator Thomas Dodd, in a draft copy of an unreleased statement intended as the introduction to a proposed 1970 Juvenile Delinquency Subcommittee hearing, stated that "The school systems, through their frequent unwillingness to report violence which they must clearly encounter, through their readiness to give up all semblance of order, may well contribute to the very problems they want to solve" (Dodd, 1970:9). Consistent with this notion that administrators generally resisted reporting offenses fully, Albert Shanker explained the repercussions for well-intentioned teachers of principals' attitudes: "Teachers find that if they report to the principal an assault, the principal who feels that his own reputation or the school's reputation is at stake here, will very frequently turn around and start harassing the teacher by saying 'Well, if you had three assaults, how come you are the one always complaining. You must have more observation or better planning, or this or that.' So the teacher soon finds out that bringing these reports to the attention of the principal is something that is not wanted and tends to suppress that information" (Bayh, 1975:6).

Considering, then, the administrator's desire to underrepresent almost all kinds of pupil misbehaviors, some possible ramifications of such actions can be seen. As discussed in relation to disruptions in chapter 4, the range of choices available to the administrator extended from leaving the problem alone (to wit, making the teacher handle the problem—as expressed in the Shanker quote) to supporting the development of security offices in the school district with security agents in the school. An exceptionally profound insight of the problems of adolescent criminal behavior in schools and administrative responses appeared in Larson's *School Discipline in an Age of Rebellion*. He noted that: "The problem differs significantly from the discipline problems of yesterday and requires different preventive and corrective measures. A single acceleration of force will not work unless we are prepared to go all the way and confront students with loaded guns" (Larson, 1972:35).[6]

In 1972 no obvious national direction for combating crimes in schools existed. By 1975, however, there was a national direction, the one that Larson had feared. In 1975 Chicago had over 700 armed, uniformed, off-duty police in its schools (Brady, 1976); Los Angeles had its own armed police force of 300 officers with an additional 100 support personnel (Subcommittee on Elementary, Secondary and Vocational Education, 1975:107); and New York City Schools had approximately 2,400 guards and security aides in their schools (Marvin, 1976:35). Certainly, these are the largest urban centers and their problems are proportionally more extensive than in Denver, Colorado, or Fresno, California; nonetheless, trends toward escalating the intensity of school responses to pupil misbehaviors—and the inclination to use security forces—were found in hundreds of cities across the nation.

Security Officers: Because Offices of School Security were administratively headquartered in the school district offices and not in individual schools, the views of their staffs merit separate treatment. The views of security officers had an impact on crime in schools in three areas. First, those views affected crimes that were reported; second, security officers could control to a certain extent who found out that crimes had been committed; and third, they influenced future preventive measures schools employed to reduce and control youthful crime.

The first area concerning the nature of crimes reported, operated on two levels. Clearly, the in-school security officers had a certain legitimate amount of leeway in working with the students concerning whether they would use a counsel-and-release approach or arrest the youths or turn them over to the local police. On a more general level, however, the director of school security set school district policy defining many nuances of criminality within broad categories. This means that clear stipulation of such issues as the amount of force and the intention of the act in a student-student assault situation was necessary before judging individual incidents for extenuating circumstances. These guidelines varied between school districts, and to the extent of their variation, the profile of the nature and scope of student crimes also varied.

The development by the school security office of definitions of acts recorded and reported by school districts as criminal extended to all forms of serious pupil misbehavior. The public image of the nature and extent of crime in local school districts was a function of the ways these data were released by the school district and reported by the media. Questions such as whether ash-can fires were recorded as arson, vandalism, or possibly not at all, ultimately became political issues settled by the director of security. Similarly, whether the theft of a student's pocketbook containing $2 was a theft or disregarded, whether it was counted only if it contained over $10, whether it was counted only if it belonged to a staff member, and so forth, were all local decisions. And to the extent that decisions differed, data on the nature and scope of school crimes were not comparable across school district boundaries.

The second issue raised by security officers' views related both to the quality and use of crime-incident data collected by the security office. As security offices were located at different bureaucratic levels in different school district offices, it would be natural to assume that the greater the bureaucratic distance between the director of school security and the superintendent of schools, the less closely the security operation was guided by the superintendent's office. As there was undoubtedly some correlation (not yet studied) between close ties to the school administration and high quality of crime rate data, it is probably fair to surmise that crime-incident data collected and summarized in close cooperation with the district superintendent played an important role in his public relations program.

The third area in which the views of security personnel were critical was that of the development of a comprehensive crime-prevention program for the school district. Ranging from social programs to the installation of closed-circuit TV monitors, the security director's concept of the scope of security dictated the range of tasks undertaken by his office. Good examples of the varying ranges in tasks and responsibilities could be seen in descriptions of Denver's operation (Burton, 1976) and in the operations of Baltimore, Detroit, Los Angeles, Chicago, and Houston, as presented by Grealy (1972).

Since security programs varied as a function of differences in areas where security officers' and directors' views affected the identification and reporting of criminally misbehaving youths, it is necessary to realize that areas of subjectivity existed. Whereas an analysis of the data will establish changes in the kinds, frequency and intensity of crimes in secondary schools, the points discussed above serve as parts of the overall caveat relating to noncomparability of data.

Summary and Conclusions about Differing Views of Student Crimes

The most important concept to keep in mind when considering many types of crimes is that from the students' perspective, offenses may not have been considered crimes at all. One student fighting another student over a classroom or social issue may not have considered the act a violation of a criminal code. However, extortion, robbery, and student-teacher assaults were more likely to have been seen as crimes by students. To the extent that schools had problems of serious crime, students' fear of crime became an issue.

From the teacher's perspective, it is proposed that fear of crime was more pervasive than it was for students. Not only were teachers exposed to a greater cross section of the school's youths than were most students, but student-teacher assaults were likely to be more intense than typical student-student assaults. This was so in part because youths knew they were going to get into a lot of trouble over the incident and were likely to be motivated to make the fight more serious than it would have been were the opponent just another student. This study also suggested that due to different size populations of school teachers and students, fear was likely to be more acute among the staff. Occasionally, cases of staff fear of crime led to the carrying of weapons for self-defense.

School administrators—finding themselves caught between frightened teachers, a politically sensitive school board, and a critical public—tried to play down as many incidents as possible, from crimes to disorders, while turning over as many crimes as possible to the district Offices of School Security. The administrator seemed to be in the most vulnerable position, for if he admitted to his district office of security the total nature and extent of his problems, he feared the district office would demand his removal. If he selectively suppressed reports of crimes in his schools, however, Murphy's laws provided that when he did get sued for mishandling a criminal act in his school, it would be for the very incident he failed to report to the security office.[7]

Security officers had a critical role in determining which students would be reported for criminal acts, both through their abilities to counsel and release and their more general powers to define acts which were prosecutable. Additionally, power varied among school security directors since it was a function of their placement in the bureaucratic maze of school district offices. The closer security directors worked with superintendents, the greater their support for trying new approaches to crime reduction. Finally, the school security office was responsible for designing the crime-prevention program for the school district, and therefore influenced to a great extent the climate within individual schools as well as the tenor of education in the entire city.

Major Trends in Student Crimes

This section considers issues which are both topical and controversial. There is currently much federal and local activity in this field, and the Senate Subcommittee to Investigate Juvenile Delinquency has been focusing specifically on crimes in schools since about 1968. This study has found that data quoted extensively by researchers, the media, and in Senate testimony have roots in few basic documents. Further, whereas a few findings were used extensively in Senate Subcommittee reports and by the media, others have gone almost wholly unnoticed. This section shows changes in student crimes in secondary schools in relation to national data. Much of the data were collected by federal sources. This section also endeavors to develop common and comparable bases for some important nonfederal data. In the following subsections, the first lists available data relating to changes in the kinds, frequency, and intensity of student crime, and the second discusses the data.[8]

Kinds, Frequency, and Intensity of School Crimes (1950-1975)

For easy presentation, this study divides the data in three parts: the first part notes changes in public opinion and public concern about crimes in schools; the second part presents basic data relating to adolescents, schools, and crimes; the third part presents national data on specific crime trends in schools.

Public Concern, as Seen Through Magazine Articles: Though there has always been some crime in schools, the number and extent of crimes threatening the educational climate of the school did not begin until the late 1960s. Chart 5-1 shows changes in one magazine's concern over (and presentation of) student crimes committed in schools. The *U.S. News and World Report* articles began with the September 2, 1968, piece and ended with the January 1976 story on "Terror in Schools."[9] Some of these articles deserve discussion, for they were a product of their time and reflected the views of a period when public concern shifted from disruptions to crimes in public schools.

The September 2, 1968, article was discussed in chapter 4, since the Lemburg study on which it reported was primarily concerned with bombings and group violence such as riots. While it was not clear that the article's discussions of violence were meant to include secondary schools, neither were those schools clearly excluded. The November 17, 1969, article was really only a small blurb, serving to notify the public that the Senate was becoming sensitive to problems of crimes in schools. In 1969 only the vaguest hints existed that violence would be a serious issue for the next six years. The January 26, 1970, story represented the magazine's reaction to the release of the Senate study comparing school crimes in 1964 and 1968. (Chapter 2 discussed the problems involved in this study. It was not officially released by the Juvenile Delinquency Subcommittee.) The important point was that this article was not an independent one on school crime and violence by *U.S. News*. The January 4, 1971, article surveyed violence in general and only briefly touched on high schools. The November 22, 1971, report directly dealt with violence in schools.

The November 22, 1971, article represented a new direction in *U.S. News'* coverage of schools with problems of crime and violence. For the first time, the staff of the magazine had become involved in investigatory reporting. It was the first article of the series that exhibited serious alarm over the extent of school violence; however, it treated the subject as a problem of large-city schools exclusively, disregarding growing problems of school crimes in suburban communities. This article marked the start of a transition between merely repeating findings of other surveys and seriously treating the problems of crime and violence in public schools as worthy of investigative reporting.

Chart 5-1
Articles on Student Crime in *U.S. News and World Report*

Date	Article Title	Content Summary
Sept. 2, 1968	"Violence in Schools—The Outlook Now"	Reflecting public attention on riots and other forms of violence, this was a half-page article reporting on a study by the Lemburg Center for the Study of Violence. "Schools" seemed to include both secondary and post-secondary institutions.
Nov. 17, 1969	"U.S. Teachers—Targets of Violence"	Becoming increasingly aware that there was a problem of assaults and physical violence in secondary schools, this piece noted that the Senate was beginning to investigate secondary school violence. It reported Los Angeles as having 181 assaults in the 1968-1969 school year.
Jan. 26, 1970	"In Public Schools, A Crime Invasion"	This was one of the "informal" releases of the findings of the Senate's "1970 Survey of 155 School Districts" and was one of the earliest articles to begin asking school districts about the nature and extent of their problems. The pattern of expanding the text by using Senate-generated or Senate-repeated figures on crime and violence in schools was used here.
Jan. 4, 1971	"New Pattern of Violence"	"It's terrorism, not riots that experts on violence fear most in 1971. . . . High schools, however, are scenes of expanding racial strife and violence—a trend to which most observers see no end in sight" (p. 23).
Nov. 22, 1971	"High Schools, too, Have a Crime Problem"	The article sketched the nature and extent of crime in schools in five major cities. It reported Los Angeles as having experienced 8,300 crimes on school grounds in the 1970-1971 school year.
Apr. 16, 1973	"More Muscle in the Fight to Stop Violence in Schools"	This article was devoted to a discussion of the range of security measures utilized nationally to combat school crime. It cited Los Angeles as having a $2.75 million budget for security purposes, and employing 235 armed security agents.
June 24, 1974	"Vandalism—A Billion Dollars a Year and Getting Worse"	Using figures developed by Dukiet's 1973 article that the national estimated cost of vandalism, arson, and theft in public schools was $260 million and the cost of security services was about $240 million, this piece outlined the problems across the country.
Apr. 14, 1975	"Violence in Schools: Now a Crackdown"	"Under growing public pressure, communities across the U.S. are mounting a fresh attack against disorders that are disrupting classrooms or threatening life and limb in thousands of public schools" (p. 37). Also in this issue was a small piece on "School-Age Drunks—A Fresh Worry." Both articles outlined the nature and extent of the problems and the current intervention strategies.
Jan. 26, 1976	"Terror in Schools"	For four pages, this article both summarized the Bayh report findings (1975) and reported on a survey of twenty cities by *U.S. News* staff. The outlook, the article concluded, was "officials crack down . . . nothing seems to work" (p. 52). This article served well to present the problems at the very end of 1975.

On April 16, 1973, a background article astutely surveyed the wide variety of types of school security devices and approaches available for counteracting school crime and violence. The reporter noted that the problem of crime in Los Angeles was so severe that the security budget had grown to $2.75 million and that the school district had to hire 235 security agents to control crimes in the schools. On June 24, 1974, *U.S. News* reported estimates of the cost of crime on a national basis. Though not credited to him, these cost estimates had been developed by Dukiet (1973). In addition to the cost data, the article outlined the problem of serious student misbehaviors on a national level.

One way to envision the progression of these articles is: whereas the April 16, 1973, piece said, in effect, "This is how school security is going to handle the problem," and the June 24, 1974, work said, "OK—here's who security should focus on controlling," the April 14, 1975, article said, "Here we go: We're gonna crack down now." It is fitting to end with the January 26, 1976, piece, which lamented, though "officials crack down... nothing seems to work." Certainly it is stretching a point to suggest that the editors of *U.S. News and World Report* intentionally serialized this way; however, changes in the magazine staff's perceptions—and possibly the general public's—of problems of school crime and violence stand out most clearly when presented in such a fashion.

Public Opinion: To supplement the indications of trends in public concern that these articles provided, two surveys of public opinion deserve note: the National Education Association's "Teacher Opinion Polls," and the "Gallup Polls of Attitudes toward Education." For this study, the "Teacher Opinion Polls" served only one purpose—to reinforce the year in which teachers' concerns clearly shifted from disruptions to crimes. According to the "Teacher Opinion Polls," this shift took place in 1971. From the 1968 academic year through and including 1971, the statement for which the NEA "Poll" sought response of a stratified random probability sample of the nation's teachers ($N = 2,000$: return rate fluctuated 85-90 percent) was whether "students have demonstrated against school policies this year." Beginning in the 1971 academic year and continuing to the end of 1975, those receiving surveys were asked to respond to the statement, "I was attacked this year by a student." The year in which this change occurred is important for an historical analysis of the trends in school crime.

The "Gallup Polls of Attitudes toward Education" begin in 1969 and appeared annually thereafter.[10] According to Gallup, in every year except 1971, discipline was the public's foremost concern. Discipline, however, had been an elusive term, and the "Polls" seemed to use it when referring to pupil misbehaviors. As the public became more specific in its concerns, the "Polls" reflected that specificity. Vandalism and apathy appeared in the 1971 survey as issues independent of discipline, for example. Also, problems of integration and desegregation—very likely violence-related issues—were separated out of the general discipline-problems category. Indeed, while in 1971 and 1973 three out of the top five public concerns focused on pupil misbehaviors, not until 1974 were there clear indications that public attitudes about obviously reflecting Gallup's quest for clarification of the kinds of in-school misbehaviors that upset the public. One query was about gang activity and the other, stealing. The "Poll" 's findings were that in relation to stealing, the distribution was remarkably even between regions of the United States (though stealing prevailed slightly more in the West) and was easily anticipated in relation to community size (the larger the community, the more concern over stealing in schools). In relation to gangs, the results held few surprises; concern about gang occurrence was greater in large urban centers than in suburban or rural areas (Gallup, 1974:21). Not until the 1975 "Poll" did the public clearly separate concern over discipline from concern over crime. In the 1975 "Poll," 4 percent of the sample considered crime/vandalism/stealing to be among the "biggest problems with which the public schools in this country must deal" (Gallup, 1975:236).

This study is not absolutely certain why the Gallup "Polls" did not provide a more precise indication of changes in public attitudes about pupil misbehaviors in schools. It theorizes, however, that as changes from disorders to disruptions to crimes were gradual and overlapped, the general public (having scant exposure to or interest in the subtleties of these shifts) responded to the "Polls" in only the most general terms. Discipline, from the first "Poll" in 1969 to the last one considered in 1975, took on any number of meanings and did not have the same precise meaning in any two years. The "Polls," then, did not surrender specific year-of-change information in relation to shifts in the public's attitudes toward student crimes in public schools, though in a general sense they supported this study's position.

The most valuable point to be understood through this review of media coverage and public opinion on this topic is that such coverage probably encouraged closer inspection of local school problems, which in turn logically contributed to greater media coverage, which was ultimately translated to greater public concern. Though this study would not suggest that the media overstated or overplayed the problem of crime in secondary schools, the reader must recognize that this contaminating variable does strongly affect comparisons made about the topic between the pre- and post-1970 periods.

Basic Data Relevant to Student Crime: A number of statistics bear particularly on this study of changes in the kinds of frequency of student crimes. Chart 5-2, for example, notes that the U.S. population of fourteen to seventeen year olds increased 2.0 times between 1950 and 1975, whereas the number of pupils enrolled in grades nine to twelve increased more then 2.3 times. This difference is reflected in column 5, where there is a 14 percent increase in pupil enrollment. Column 6, indicating the average daily attendance (ADA) of all school-aged

Chart 5-2
Basic Data Concerning Pupils, Teachers, and Schools

Year	U.S. Population[1] Total 1[a]	14-17 2[a]	Pupils, Grades 9-12[1] 3[a]	Percent Change 4	Percent Enrolled 5	ADA K-12[2] 6[a]	Number of Schools[2] 7	Teachers, Grades 7-12[2] 8[b]	Consumer Price Index[3] 9
1950	150	8.4	6.1	—	72.6	22.3	24,542	324	72.1
1951	152	8.5	6.2	1.64	72.9			na	77.8
1952	155	8.7	6.5	4.84	74.7	23.3	23,746	343	79.5
1953	158	8.8	6.6	1.54	75.0			na	80.1
1954	160	9.0	7.1	7.58	78.8	25.7	25,637	377	80.5
1955	163	9.2	7.2	1.41	78.3			408	80.2
1956	166	9.6	7.7	6.94	80.2	27.7	26,046	447	81.4
1957	169	10.3	8.1	5.19	78.6			473	84.3
1958	172	10.8	8.5	4.94	78.7	29.7	25,507	491	86.6
1959	175	11.1	8.6	1.18	77.5			524	87.3
1960	178	11.2	9.2	6.97	82.1	32.5	25,784	550	88.7
1961	181	12.1	9.8	6.52	81.0			592	89.6
1962	184	12.8	10.4	6.12	81.3	34.7	25,350	621	90.6
1963	187	13.5	11.2	7.69	83.0			669	91.7
1964	189	14.3	11.6	3.57	81.1	37.4	26,431	709	92.4
1965	192	14.2	11.7	0.86	82.4			746	94.5
1966	194	14.4	12.1	5.13	84.0	39.2	26,597	783	97.2

1967	197	14.7	12.6	4.13	85.7		27,011	815	100.0
1968	199	15.2	12.9	2.38	84.9	40.8		860	104.2
1969	200	15.6	13.3	3.10	85.3			906	109.8
1970	203	15.9	13.6	2.26	85.5	41.9	26,282	927	116.3
1971	205	16.3	14.1	3.68	86.5		25,352	952	121.3
1972	207	16.6	14.2	0.71	85.5	42.3	23,572	963	125.3
1973	209	16.7	14.4	0.70	86.2		23,919	986	133.1
1974	210	16.9	14.4	0.00	85.2	41.4	25,906	998	147.1
1975	213	16.9	14.6	1.39	86.4		25,697	1,019	161.2

Sources: 1. U.S. Department of Commerce: Bureau of the Census. 2. U.S. Department of Health, Education and Welfare: National Center for Education Statistics. 3. U.S. Department of Labor: Bureau of Labor Statistics.
[a]Numbers are in millions. [b]Numbers are in thousands.

children, shows an increase in the numbers of enrolled pupils as the years advanced. This happened, furthermore, as the numbers of schools shrank, after peaking about 1966. It is clear from column 7 that by 1975 and despite a 139 percent increase in enrolled pupils, there was only about a 5 percent increase in secondary schools; clearly, the average school size had increased greatly. The data in column 8 are useful when considering rates of assaults on teachers, for the number of teachers working in any one year obviously affected the size of the "target group" of assaultees. Column 9 provides the Consumer Price Index data which must be considered when comparing crime cost data over time.

Charts 5-3 and 5-4 show official arrest data exclusively for highschool age youths. Chart 5-3 indicates changes in Part I crimes. Part I offenses are those used by the FBI to develop their monthly Crime Index and include arrests for criminal homicide, forcible rape, robbery, aggravated assault, burglary, larceny-theft, and auto theft. Chart 5-4 shows changes in Part II crimes. Part II offenses are all those not covered by Part I, and include other assaults, arson, fraud, vandalism, stolen property, weapons charges, drugs, drunkenness, and miscellaneous others. Chart 5-5 provides an indication of gross changes in arrest rates for certain specific criminal offenses in which youths were often involved. This chart reduces all offenses to incident rates per 100,000 population; crimes most frequently engaged in by fifteen to seventeen year olds clearly stand out. It is particularly important to note that despite some common beliefs to the contrary, the data—when presented in this fashion—clearly show that crimes against property grew at a faster rate than crimes against persons.

Chart 5-6 pictures the growth of the National Association of School Security directors from its creation in 1969 by Joseph I. Grealy, to its 345 members in 1975. Since this association consists almost exclusively of directors of school security and was begun as security offices first began to appear within school districts, its growth importantly indicates the increased national use of Offices of School Security in the battle to reduce and control serious student misbehaviors in schools.

National Figures on School Crimes: The only previously published works which purport to show changes in the frequency of crimes in schools over time were developed by the Senate Subcommittee to Investigate Juvenile Delinquency, chaired (from November 1970 through 1975) by Senator Birch Bayh. The first study, conducted under the previous chairman, Senator Thomas Dodd, attempted to compare school crimes in 1964 and 1968. The data supplied to the Subcommittee by school districts were incomplete, however, and little reliance has ever been placed on that study's findings. Interestingly, this early congressional study (discussed in chapter 2 and popularly—though inaccurately—called the "Study of 110 School Districts") entered the public domain by a devious path. Representative Johnathan Bingham read the results into the *Congressional Record* as an introduction to his proposed Safe Schools Act, and the national

Chart 5-3
Total Part I Arrest Rates of Youths Fifteen to Seventeen Years Old

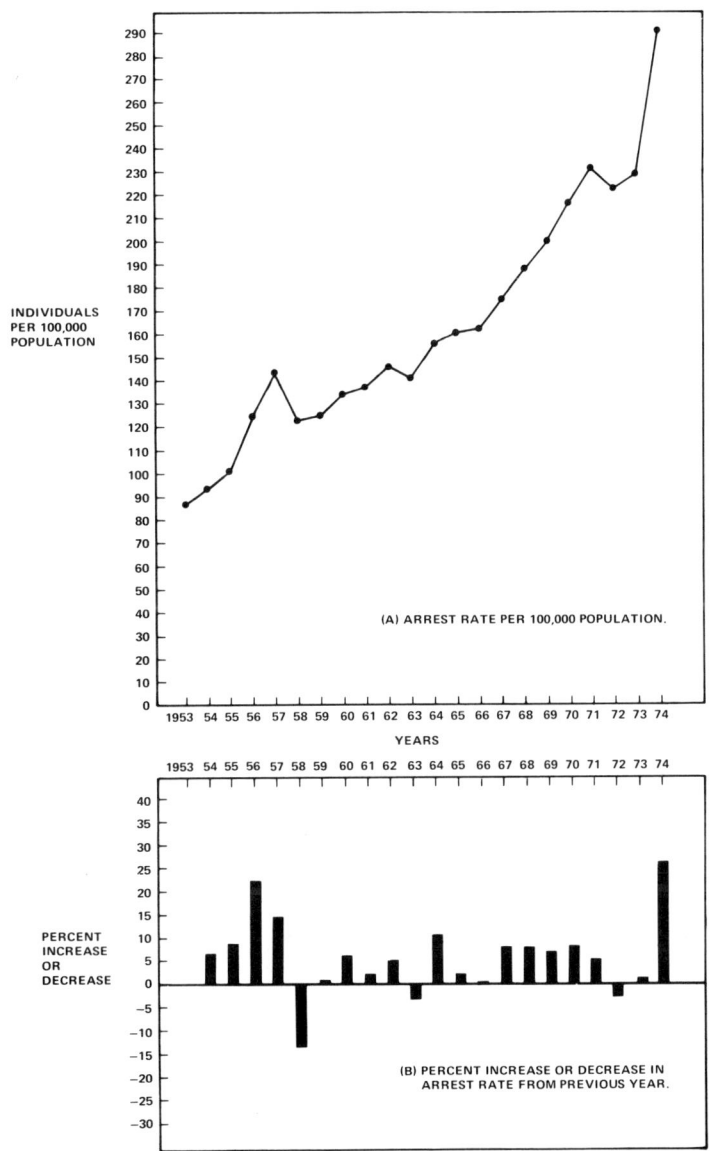

Source: Statistics Branch, Uniform Crime Reporting Division, U.S. Department of Justice.

Chart 5-4
Total Part II Arrest Rates of Youths Fifteen to Seventeen Years Old

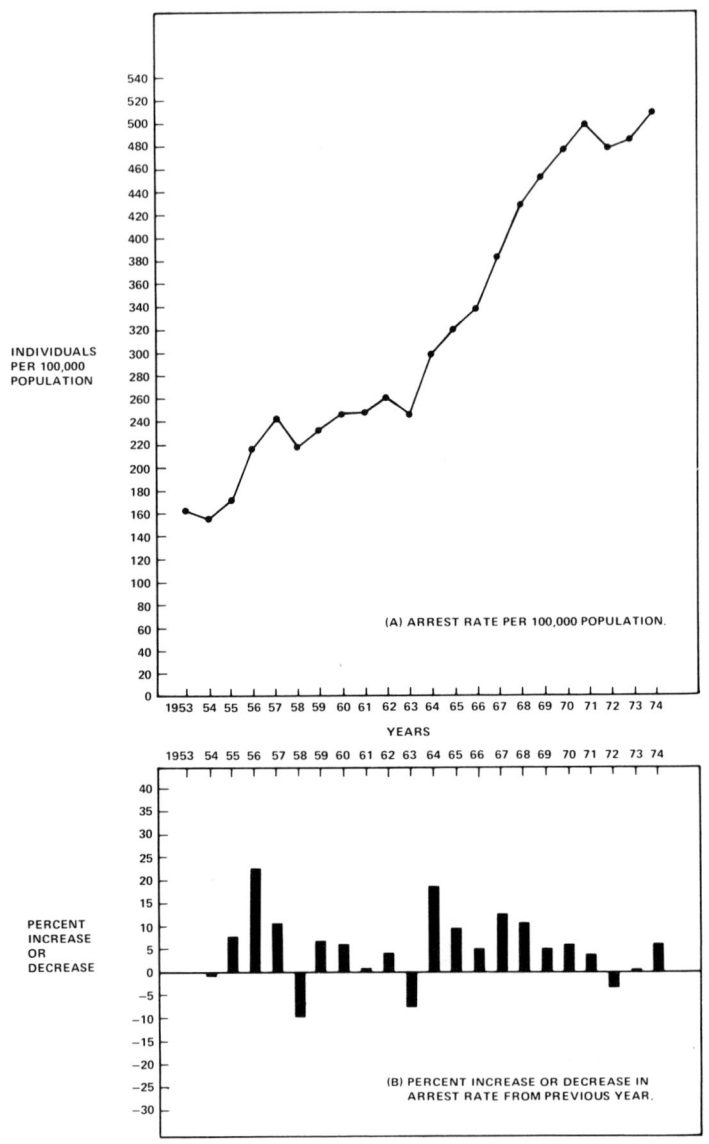

Source: Statistics Branch, Uniform Crime Reporting Division, U.S. Department of Justice.

Chart 5-5
Gross Changes in Arrest Rates of Fifteen to Seventeen Year Olds Per 100,000 Population from 1953 to 1974

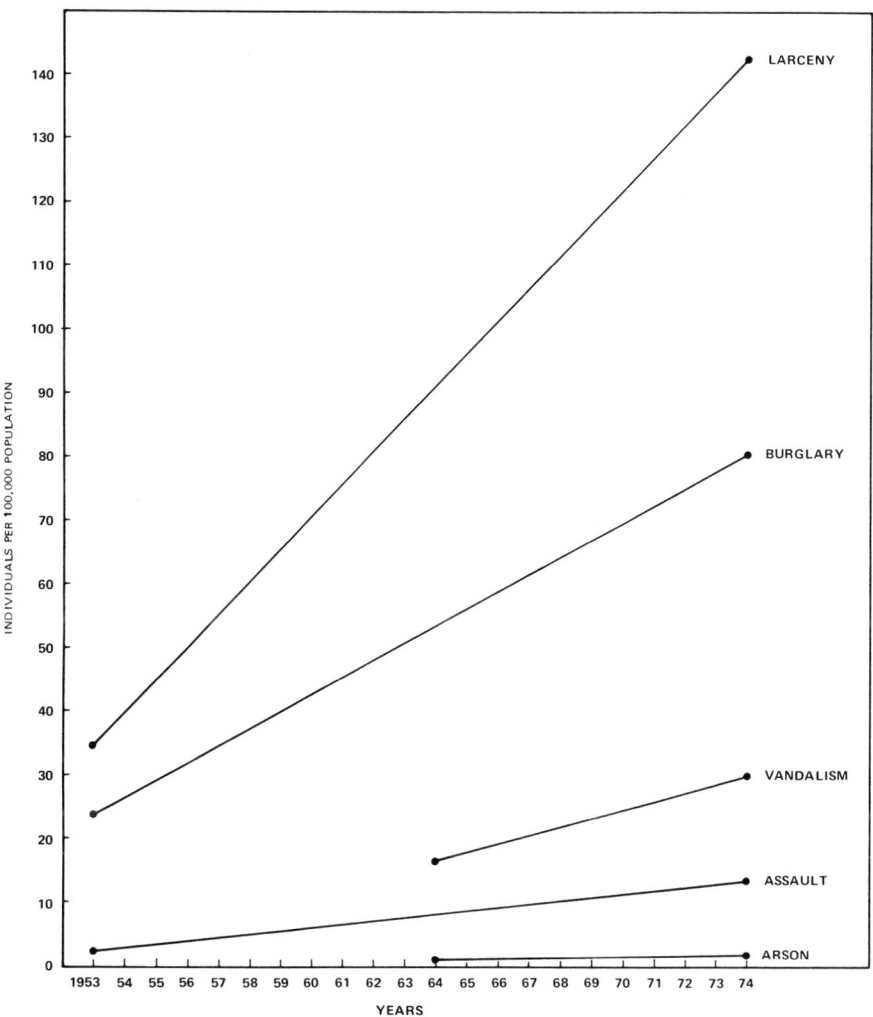

Source: Statistics Branch, Uniform Crime Reporting Division, U.S. Department of Justice.

media picked up the statistics and quoted them as if they were hard facts. The next Juvenile Delinquency Subcommittee study to try to determine the nature and extent of school crime compared 1973 to 1970; this study (Bayh, 1975) is commonly called the "Schools' Report Card."

As pointed out in chapter 2, neither of these studies was intended as a

Chart 5-6
Growth of Membership in the National Association of School Security Directors

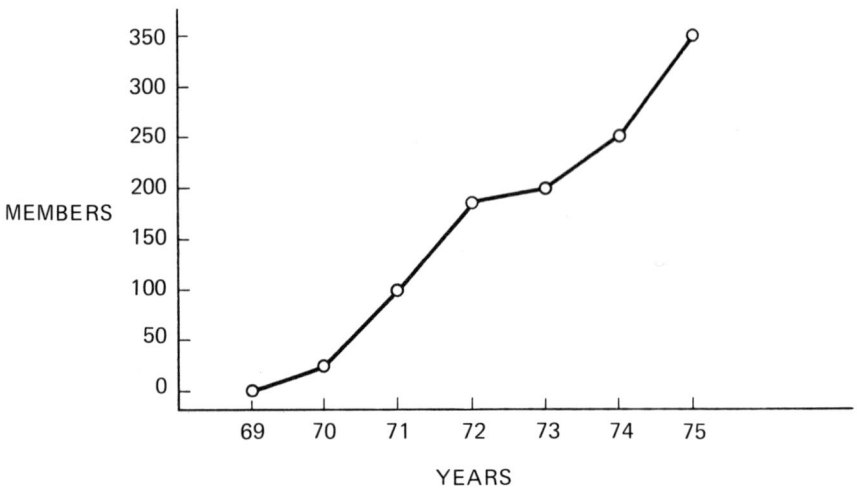

Source: Joseph I. Grealy, President, National Association of School Security Directors. Letter, dated March 4, 1976 (information used with permission).

research report, but rather as a rough gauge of changes in the nature and extent of problems of crime and violence in schools. As opposed to formal studies for academic audiences, these works intended to warn the public about a growing issue. In that respect they succeed admirably, and new legislation was drafted and proposed, based on the perceived need. In relation to the usefulness of these Senate studies for this study, there is no argument with the ultimate findings of either report (that the nature and extent of school-based crime and violence increased dramatically over time), but they were not statistical research studies and are therefore of no value for this book. Indeed, in this study, our approaches used to achieve an understanding of the extent of crime in schools were twofold: first, noting changes in absolute numbers of offenses committed by pupils in schools; and second, observing reported changes in overall costs of crime in schools.

Numbers of Crimes in Schools: The difficulties involved in presenting data reflecting trends in the numbers of crimes committed in schools were endemic. In summary, the problems were that:

1. Definitions of those acts considered criminal varied between school districts.
2. Reporting procedures, even for those acts considered criminal in different districts, varied between schools within one district as well as between districts.
3. Until the 1970s, very few districts kept comprehensive data on student criminality, and until about 1973 no effort was made to develop uniform definitions in different school districts and to collect, aggregate, and publish these data.
4. Local school administrators traditionally played down their problems to preserve the impression that they were in control of their school situation.

It was sometimes possible to avoid many of these problems by citing readily available and comparable single-city data on a few select crime types, but such data were generally of little help in developing a picture of national trends.[11] Rather than risk regional anomalies, however, this study presents available national data that have been developed. These data cover some of the most troublesome types of school crimes: assault, fire, and vandalism.

Assault data which were national in scope and covered a major part of the 1950-1975 period were available from two sources: the FBI's *Uniform Crime Reports* (*UCR*) and the National Education Association's "Teacher Opinion Poll of Pupil Behavior." The FBI data, which have been reduced to rate per 100,000 population of juveniles aged fifteen to seventeen, showed that between 1953 and 1974 a dramatic increase in assaults took place (chart 5-7). For effective use of these rate data, one must consider caveats previously discussed. In brief, the relevant restrictions on the use of these data are as follows. First, the numbers of law enforcement districts reporting to the *UCR* varied annually; second, police policies relating to when to counsel and release, and when to arrest the juvenile, differed between years and among jurisdictions; third, the number of assaults reported to the *UCR* that specifically occur on school grounds were unknown;[12] and fourth, the intensity of in-school actions which precipitated police arrest for assault were ill-defined and inconsistent between school districts. Chart 5-7, therefore, is primarily useful for visualizing the increased police activity vis-à-vis assault arrests of high school age youths, and really is not an indication of assaults in schools.

To focus more exactly on assaults on teachers, this study turned to the National Education Association's "Teacher Opinion Polls" (chart 5-8). As previously mentioned, assaults on teachers were more of an issue than student-student assaults, partly because of the shock value associated with the former offenses. The "Teacher Opinion Polls" question of whether "I was attacked this year by a student" appeared in 1956 as well as in later years, and thus is particularly relevant to this study. In interesting opposition to what might have

Chart 5-7
Assault Arrests Rates of Youths Fifteen to Seventeen Years Old

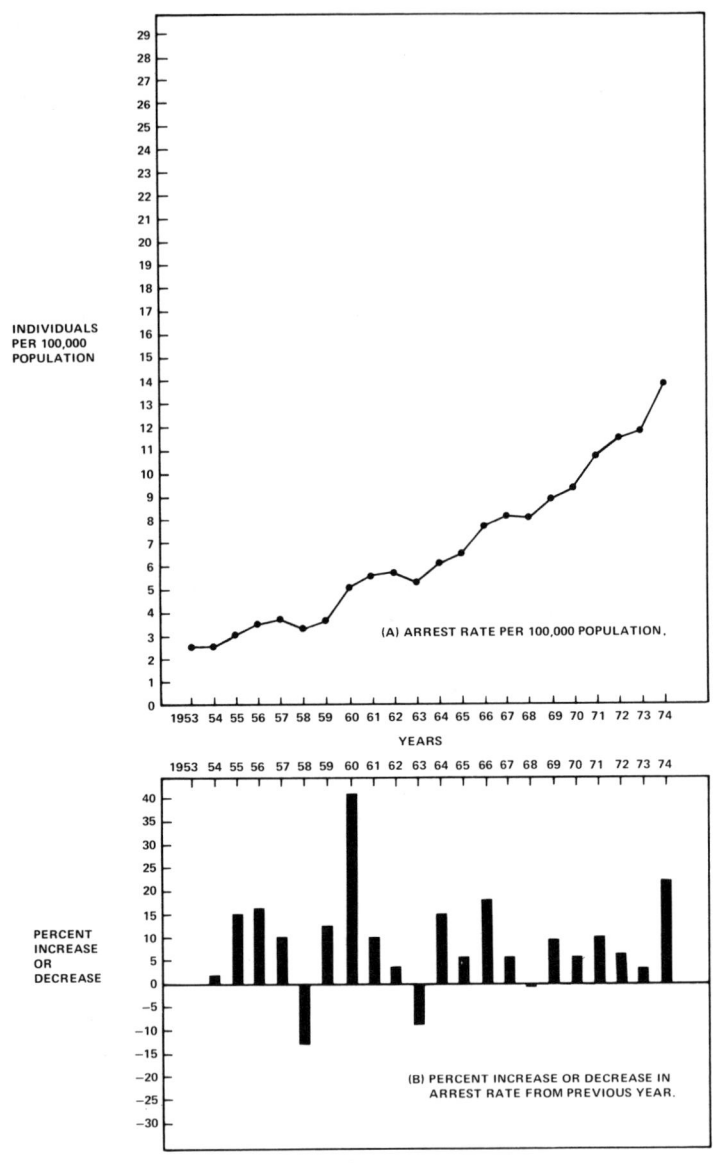

Source: Statistics Branch, Uniform Crime Reporting Division, U.S. Department of Justice.

Chart 5-8
Teacher Assaults from 1956 to 1975[a]

Year	Percent Assaulted[b]	Total Number of Teachers[b]	Number of Teachers Assaulted (est.)
1955-1956	1.6	1,141	18.3
1971-1972	2.0	2,063	41.3
1972-1973	2.2	2,103	46.3
1973-1974	3.0	2,138	64.1
1974-1975	2.4	2,165	52.0

Sources: National Education Association: Research Division, Teacher Opinion Polls, and U.S. Department of Health, Education and Welfare: National Center for Education Statistics.
[a]The actual question asked each year was: "I was personally attacked this year by a pupil."
[b]Numbers in these columns are in thousands.

been expected, there have been almost no changes in the percent of teachers assaulted over the period 1956-1975.[13] Considering that the "Polls" were conducted by developing a probability sample of the nation's schools and then selecting one of every 1,000 teachers, the results shown on chart 5-8 are a fair representation of the extent of pupil-teacher assaults in the country. Further, chart 5-9 puts these figures in context. As the chart shows, though a change from 1.6 percent assaults in 1956 to 2.4 percent assaults in 1975 is a 75 percent increase, the overall picture is better seen against a backdrop clearly showing the percentage of teachers assaulted in relation to 100 percent of the teachers. The potential analytical errors resulting from drawing conclusions based on percent-change data were discussed in detail in chapter 1. The issue is that conclusions based on percentage changes in low-number populations overemphasizes the extent of any problem under consideration.

This study draws the following conclusions about assaults from these data and from a review of numerous articles on teacher assaults:

1. Assault was loosely defined, and included many cases of "hands-on" in some form or other.
2. An unknown, but presumably significant number of assaults against teachers were committed by outsiders, notably parents with some grievance or older pupils who had previously attended the school.
3. Pupils did not often assault teachers, and when they did, it was often judged objectively to be the result of some kind of provocation by the teacher.
4. Junior high schools (grades seven to nine) reported by far the majority of assaults against teachers.[14]

Chart 5-9
Percent U.S. Teachers Reporting to Have Been Personally Assaulted

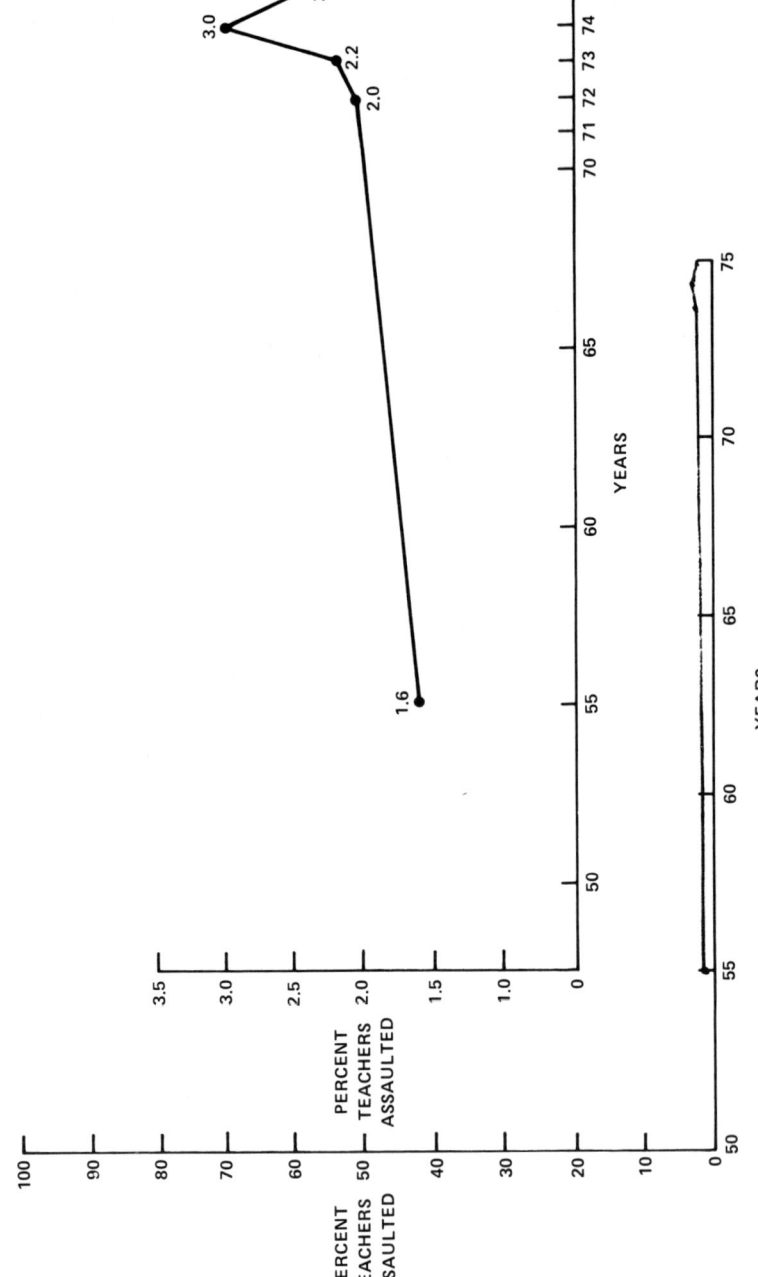

Source: National Education Association's "Teacher Opinion Polls of Pupil Behavior."

Fire data that were national in scope and focused on schools were available through the National Fire Protection Association (NFPA) in Boston (see chart 5-10).[15] That association developed national estimates showing the relative order of magnitude of fire losses from each of a number of causes and indicating year-to-year trends. While these data were reasonable approximations based on experiences in typical states, the association cautioned that specific figures should not be taken as exact records of occurrences in any category. The figures serve only to indicate gross trends.[16]

One can learn a great deal from the data provided by the association. As chart 5-11 shows, the annual costs of school fires[17] climbed 525 percent in terms of actual recorded costs (from $17 million in 1950 to $106.2 million in 1974). If one uses the Consumer Price Index (chart 5-2), however, the increase in terms of 1967 constant-dollars for that period was a mere 179 percent ($23.5 million in 1950 to $65.88 million in 1974). Also relevant here, the value of all school property increased from 1950 to 1974. The actual dollar increase in property value from 13.4 billion to $102.1 billion was 662 percent, while even the adjusted increase from $18.6 billion to $63.3 billion showed an increase of 240 percent (chart 5-12). This study concludes, then, that the adjusted value of schools over time increased more rapidly than the adjusted value of costs of fires over the same period (see chart 5-13 for a graphic display of this last phenomenon).

In chart 5-11B, there are changes in the numbers of fires reported between 1950 and 1975. The gross increase of 859 percent was essentially ten times greater than the 86 percent increase in the average daily attendance (ADA) of all enrolled pupils of the same period. Thus it cannot be suggested that increases in fires correlated with increases in pupils, and the study must conclude that students were undertaking a greater intensity of activity. Furthermore, chart 5-13 confirms this notion.

Data collected by the NFPA were grouped into two categories: fires resulting from faulty wiring/misused equipment, and fires of an incendiary nature resulting from willful or accidental acts of people. The shift over time away from electrical toward incendiary fires (Strom, 1974:20) further suggested increased student involvement in the origin of the blazes (arson). Chart 5-14 shows the changing percent of school fires exclusively of incendiary origin and also displays the concurrent decrease in the number of the nation's schools.[18] The study concludes from these data that unlike some other types of crimes, school fires seemed to be increasing in absolute numbers and absolute dollar costs throughout 1950-1975. Further, in a later comparison of fire costs to overall crime costs, fires account for the single greatest percentage of the latter cost.

Vandalism was the most common school offense and, after fires, often the most costly.[19] The FBI's *Uniform Crime Reports* defines vandalism as the "willful or malicious destruction, injury, disfigurement or defacement of

Chart 5-10
Arson Arrest Rates of Youths Fifteen to Seventeen Years Old

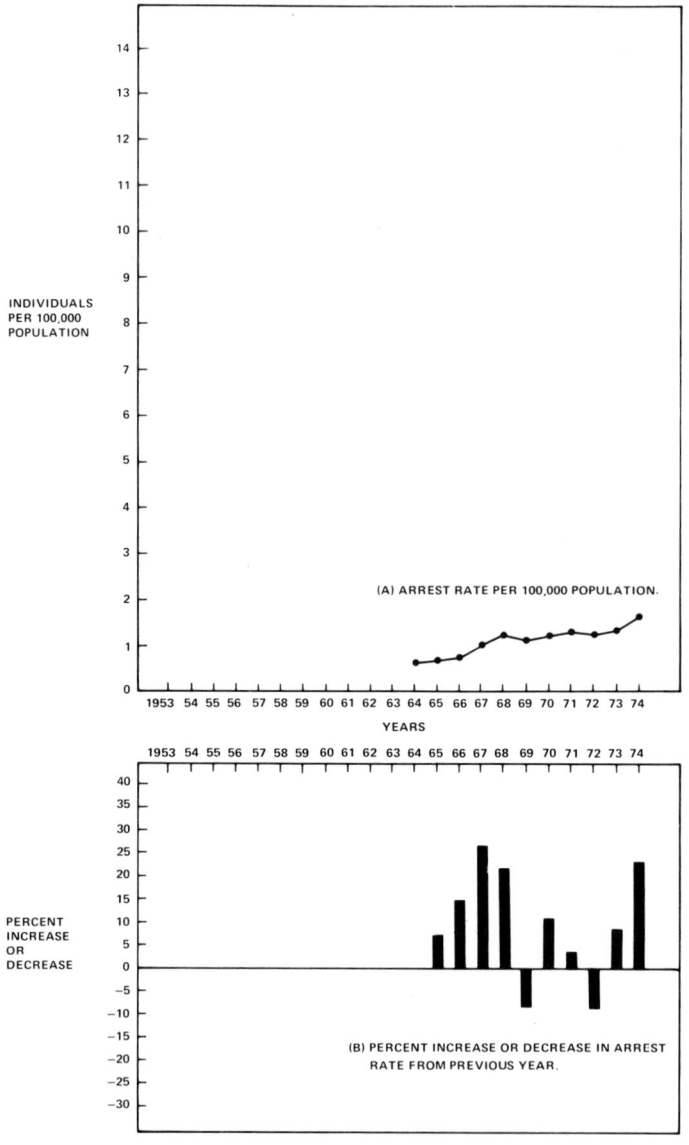

Source: Statistics Branch, Uniform Crime Reporting Division, U.S. Department of Justice.
Note: Data on arson was first collected in 1964.

**Chart 5-11
School Fires: Costs and Numbers**

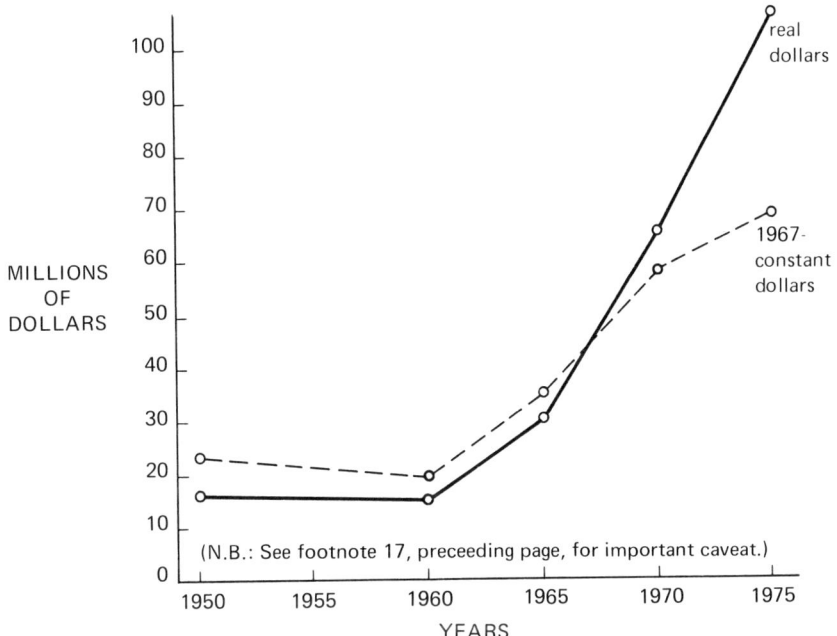

A. *Costs of Fires*

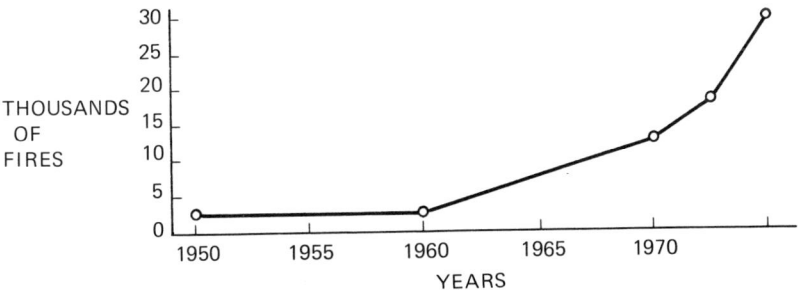

B. *Numbers of Fires*

Sources: All figures were provided by the National Fire Protection Association. Adjustments for constant dollars are made by using the Consumer Price Index for 1967 constant-dollars.

Chart 5-12
Value of All School Property—in Real Dollars and in Constant Dollars—from 1950 to 1974

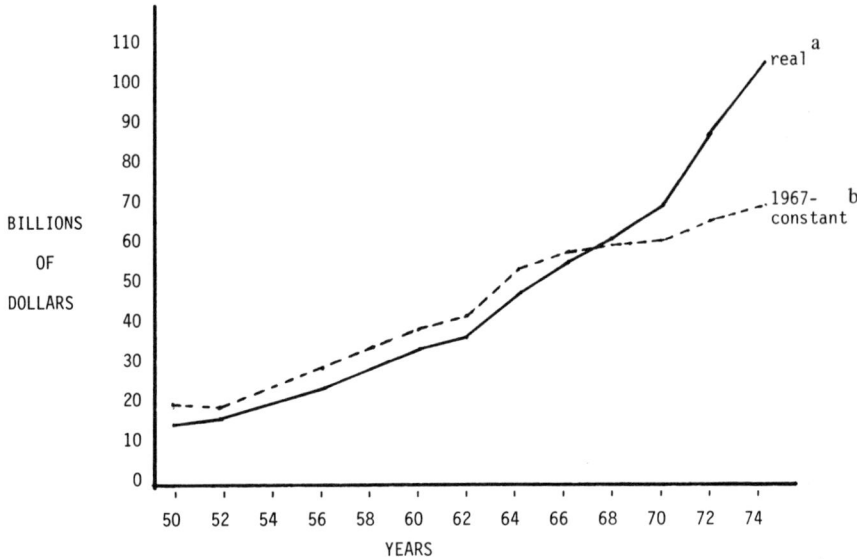

Note: Figures for 1954 are unavailable.

[a]U.S. Department of Health, Education and Welfare: National Center for Education Statistics.

[b]U.S. Department of Labor: Bureau of Labor Statistics, Consumer Price Index 1967-constant dollars.

property without consent of the owner or person having custody or control" (U.S. Department of Justice, 1971:58), but data on school vandalism—either local or national—was seldom so clearly defined. It has been unclear, for example, whether acts of vandalism recorded by individual schools, school districts, or formal research studies represented willful or accidental vandalism. In many cases, things were merely broken (Forer, 1970:263), but no merely broken category ever existed for recording crime costs. Furthermore, there was nationwide—and sometimes schoolwide—lack of agreement as to the acts included in the category of vandalism. Additionally, school administrators to some extent may have resisted being wholly candid about the nature and extent of their vandalism losses, for, as in the case of many crimes, exposure might have led to censure by district officials or the public (Dukiet, 1973:16).

As a caveat to further discussion about vandalism, this study points out that

Chart 5-13
Percentage Increases in School Values, Student Attendance, and School Fires

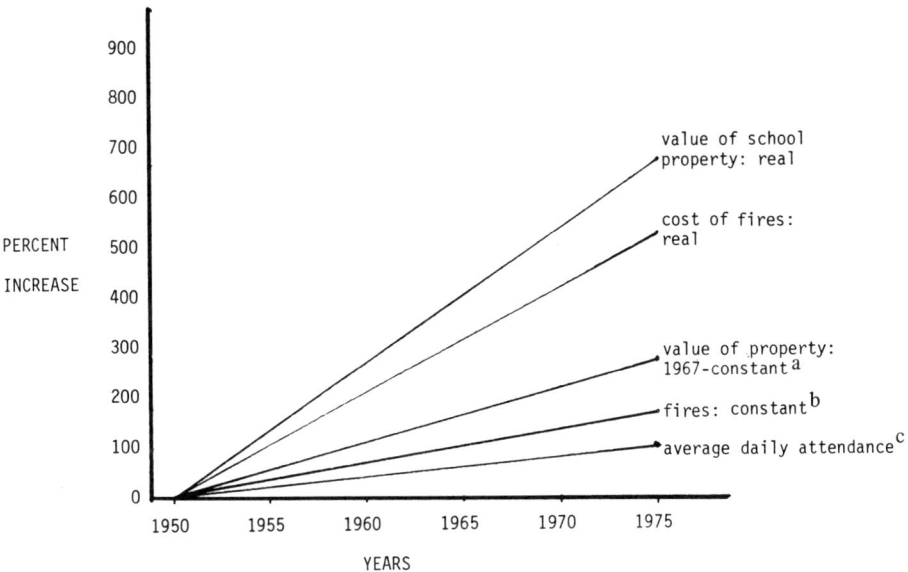

[a] Derived by applying Consumer Price Index to school value data provided from the Department of Health, Education and Welfare: Center for Educational Statistics.

[b] Derived by applying the Consumer Price Index to the costs of school fires provided by the National Fire Protection Association.

[c] Information provided by the Department of Health, Education and Welfare: Center for Education Statistics.

the term "vandalism" was used in a number of different ways by a number of different authors. Most dangerously, many works presented summaries of literature on vandalism in which authors using different definitions of the term appeared as if their definitions were comparable. Here, for example, are problems the study found in comparing only some of the best-known works in the area of school vandalism: (1) Neill (1975:10) wrote that "The second most frequent act of vandalism cited by school districts after glass breakage is theft or burglary ..." (2) Baltimore's *Annual Report of Vandalism in Selected Great Cities and Maryland Counties* (every year from 1964) divided vandalism into the categories: windows, larceny, arson, and miscellaneous. (3) Dukiet (1973), used by *U.S. News*, combined the costs of all crimes under the heading "costs of vandalism."

Chart 5-14
Percent of Fires of Incendiary Origin[1] as Compared with Decreasing Numbers of Schools[2]

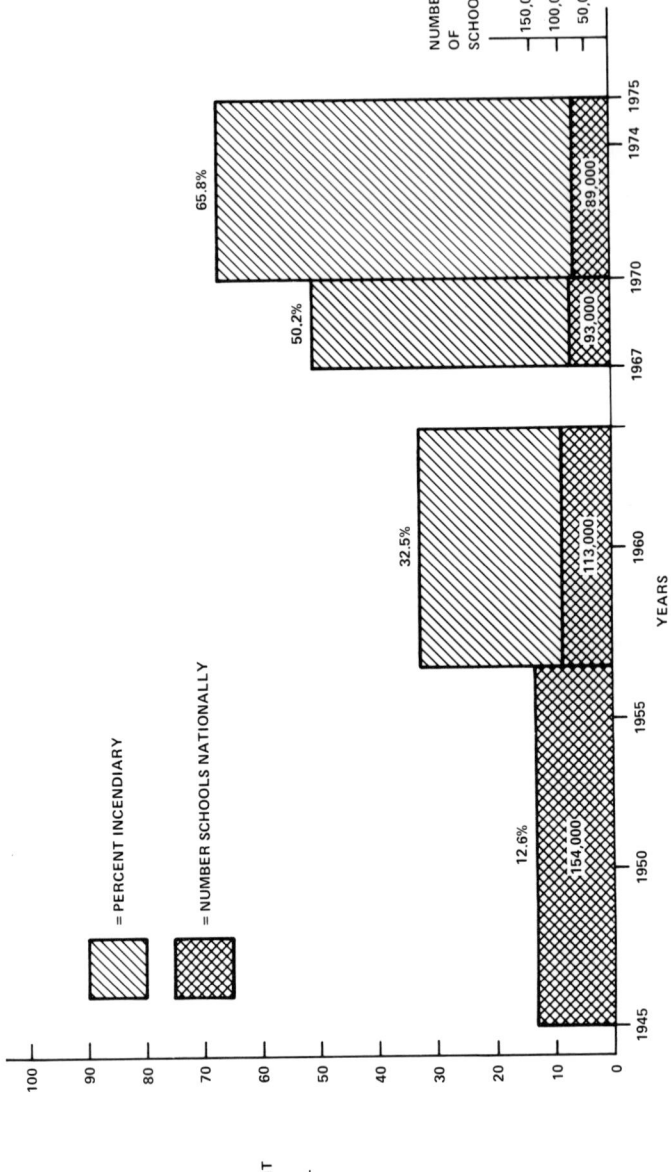

Sources: 1. National Fire Protection Association estimates. 2. U.S. Department of Health, Education and Welfare: National Center for Education Statistics.

Faced with the problematic fact that vandalism is such a generalized category, it is more convenient to speak about glass breakage and equipment damage as they are included in discussions of total dollar costs of crime. This approach is better than spending a great deal of time on specific acts of vandalism, since nationally comparable data on uniformly defined acts of vandalism are not extant.

Before discussing national costs of crime and vandalism, there are some general indications of changes in the nature and extent of such problems. The earliest indication of citywide school vandalism came from Boston in 1952. As a result of Boston's school crime wave in 1952, the following year saw a united campaign mounted by school officials to reduce vandalism in schools. As a product of that city's travail, "the cases of breaking and entering public schools and the resulting vandalism was reduced from 78 cases in 1952 to 22 cases in 1953" (Senate Subcommittee on Juvenile Delinquency, 1957:131). As a more current indication of the problem's extent, the cost of Boston's vandalism was reported to have reached $535,000 by 1967 (Olson and Carpenter, 1971:4). By calendar year 1975, Anthony L. Galeota, Chief Structural Engineer, Department of Planning and Engineering, Boston Public Schools, placed the dollar loss to vandalism, arson, and theft at about $1 million ($620,000 constant 1967).

In Los Angeles, where malicious mischief had been a separate category since the early 1950s, offense counts went from 335 in 1952 down to 100 in the 1958 school year and up to 1,275 in 1973. Also in Los Angeles, the combined vandalism and theft property loss climbed 2,829 percent from $38,431 in the academic year 1950 to $1,112,784 in 1974 (Green, 1976).[20]

Whereas the Boston and Los Angeles examples addressed the overall question of the extent of change in the frequency and cost of school vandalism over time, the Mesa example addresses the often overlooked issue of changes in the nature of acts reported as vandalism. In Mesa, Arizona, as the cost of vandalism rose from $0.58 per pupil in the 1972 academic year to $1.29 in 1973, window replacement and repair became prohibitive. The school system at that point turned first to bullet-proof polycarbon replacements for the glass, but found that the youths soon realized they could burn these windows with cigarettes, ignite them entirely with lighter fluid, or scratch words on them with sharp objects. Mesa's experimental alternative to polycarbons, as reported by Neill (1975:34), was sheet aluminum. As stated above, this study treats this action as a proxy for changes in intensity of acts of vandalism against schools. (Incidentally, this was a suburban school where, according to the literature, problems with vandalism were less severe than in urban-core schools.)

Having cautioned the reader about difficulties associated with analyzing vandalism data and provided general indications of examples of changes in the kinds, frequency, and intensity of acts of vandalism over time, this study now presents the findings of the only two studies in this area that are helpful to further understanding of the phenomenon of vandalism in schools. These studies were by Greenberg (1969) and Olson (1971).

The Greenberg work contained summary findings of a 1966 study by the California Association of School Business Officials (CASBO); these results have been useful for analysis of trends in school vandalism. The CASBO findings were interesting, for they reflected the feelings of the early 1960s in relation to problems of youthful vandals on school grounds and the roles schools played in combating vandalism. The study discovered: though most schools had vandalism problems, in the average district, losses were not large enough to justify the costs of electronic alarm systems; and a system of vandal prevention based on apprehension of the vandal was generally ineffective (Greenberg, 1969:36).

The Olson study was both a thoroughly statistical study (complete with a lengthy discussion of the sample selection, analysis of the representativeness of the returns, and findings listed with a chart showing confidence levels) and a representation of the extent of knowledge of school vandalism in the late 1960s. Among Olson's extensive findings were:

1. Large staff size and high vandalism rates were positively correlated.
2. Money recovered from previous incidents of vandalism and continued high rates of vandalism were positively correlated.
3. Ladders to the roofs of buildings and vandalism were positively correlated.
4. General orderliness of the school and vandalism were negatively correlated.
5. Vandal apprehension and vandalism rates were negatively correlated. (Olson and Carpenter, 1971:58).

Studies and editorials on incidents of vandalism ultimately led to studies and editorials on costs of vandalism and crime. Since the definition of vandalism was anything but clear when national data were combined and changes in the cost of crime were logically separate from this discussion of assaults, arson, and vandalism acts, this study treats cost data as a separate subsection.

National Figures on the Costs of School Crimes: Surprisingly, few groups during 1950-1975 developed estimates of the costs of school crime on a national basis. This is odd, considering the extraordinary press coverage usually accorded these figures when they were released. Therefore, all references of cost estimates have been traced to a few sources. In 1969 the U.S. Office of Education estimated that vandalism accounted for about $100 million in losses nationally. (In this case, as in a number of the following references, vandalism included arson and theft.) In 1970 the National Education Association raised the estimate of national losses to $200 million, and the National School Public Relations Association used these figures in their reports (see Wells, 1971).

Two conflicting findings appeared in 1973. That the higher figures were invariably quoted by the media and in Senate testimony is perhaps a commentary on American sensationalism. The best known of these reports was Dukiet's 1973 study prepared for Market Data Retrieval, Inc. Solely on the basis of telephone conversations with administrators in twenty-five school districts, Dukiet projected the cost of school vandalism, arson, and theft to be $260 million, and the cost of school security services to be another $240 million. The sensational total of $500 million was amply cited (see *U.S. News*' June 24, 1974, article; or Neill, 1975). However, another 1973 study, conducted by Educational Research Service, Inc., of a stratified random sample of the nation's 11,693 public school systems with 300 or more pupils enrolled (the sample represented 70 percent of all operating school districts) estimated the cost of crimes to be $86.2 million. This report went on to break down the cost data on a per pupil basis, not only for all schools, but also for the four categories surveyed: large schools, medium-sized schools, small and very small schools. This breakdown clearly allowed readers to develop analytical conclusions in ways that the Dukiet article precluded.

Two other groups that made estimates of the national costs of crime and violence were the National Association of School Security Directors and the publication *School Product News*. The findings of these two groups were quite different and are discussed briefly here.

In the case of the NASSD, Lucius Burton, Public Affairs Chairman of the Association, received an unspecified number of returns from NASSD's annual questionnaire to its members (which represented only a portion of the nation's school districts). This questionnaire (see Appendix B) asked the nature, extent, and costs of all kinds of criminal activity in schools. Burton then grouped returns according to the type of communities from which they came (urban, suburban, rural) and to the communities' sizes. From these data, he developed averages of the nature, extent, and cost of crime for districts which returned questionnaires. The final step was a simple extrapolation to produce national estimates. The NASSD released these figures with the caveat that they were only estimates. The 1974 estimate was that school crime cost the nation about $594 million for that year alone, excluding costs of repair, clean-up, and security services (Grealy, 1975:51).

In the case of *School Product News*' study, the editor, David Slaybaugh, directed a mailing of his questionnaire to a random sample of school districts across the nation. Slaybaugh did not give sample selection or other information about the research methodology; however, the return rate fluctuated closely around 16 percent (see chart 5-15). Though Slaybaugh analyzed these surveys extensively and used a consistent format for every year, the low response rate may have contributed to a large positive bias due to respondents' self-selection. With this caveat, the study presents extrapolated national crime costs from his data. This extrapolation is made possible by combining information provided from HEW's National Center for Education Statistics (in the fall of 1974 there were 1,894 school districts in the country with enrollments of 5,000 or more pupils) and Slaybaugh's finding that the average cost of crime per school district was about $53,000 (Slaybaugh, 1975:10). The resulting projected national cost

Chart 5-15
School Product News' Annual Survey into the Costs of Vandalism Nationally

	1970-1971	1971-1972	1972-1973	1973-1974	1974-1975
Average costs of vandalism, arson, and theft per school district	$55,000	$63,031	$28,631	$62,991[a] ($38,226)	$52,652[a] ($33,227)
Sample data (all samples were random; randomness is not explained)	Information not available	17% return (331 out of 2,000 districts enrolling over 5,000 pupils)	16% return (192 out of 1,232 districts enrolling over 5,000 pupils)	15% return (561 out of 3,810 districts enrolling over 2,500 pupils) 314 returns from districts enrolling 5,000 pupils	15% return (581 out of 3,776 districts enrolling over 2,500 pupils) 322 returns from districts enrolling 5,000 pupils

Source: *School Product News'* annual "School Security Survey" for the years indicated.

[a]These figures represent computations based only on school districts with enrollments greater than 5,000. This limitation allows comparability with the first three years of the study, all of which are limited to such school districts. The lower figures show the average costs of vandalism, arson, and theft when the much more numerous smaller districts are added in. It is these lower figures that actually appear in the *School Product News* report as the summary figures. Though this report calculates the higher figure for 1973-1974, it does not do so for 1974-1975.

of vandalism, arson, and theft for 1974 was $100.4 million. This tends to confirm the 1973 findings by the Educational Research Service, Inc., that the national costs were about $82.2 million.[21]

It is not clear why the NASSD figures were ultimately so much higher than those of other studies; however, discrepancies may have been due to the possibility that different divisions of school district offices filled out different questionnaires. Whereas the NASSD surveys were completed by the Office of School Security, other surveys may have been sent there or to custodial or insurance divisions. The custodial or insurance divisions may well have become involved because the non-NASSD forms primarily asked about costs due to vandalism and arson and did not obviously have much to do with crime data. Other divisions, furthermore, probably kept different kinds of cost data than the security offices did. The data would be different in part because security offices' interest in costs of crime would be secondary to their interest in actively reducing and preventing criminal acts on school grounds.

It is necessary to add a note of caution to this discussion of costs of crime and vandalism. Even if the costs of vandalism, arson, and theft did amount to the NASSD estimate of $600 million per year, one must consider that the gross value of all school property as calculated by HEW was about $100 billion (see chart 5-13). Thus the damage to facilities amounted to only about one-half of 1 percent. Certainly there was a problem—and it may or may not have been a $600 million problem—but even if it were that costly, the percent damage done was miniscule.

A second note of caution is that national figures for arrests of fifteen to seventeen year olds in the categories vandalism, larceny, and burglary rose sharply in the late 1960s. Charts 5-16, 5-17, and 5-18 demonstrate this upswing just as the value of school property also increased. Was there a relationship between these increases? Perhaps there was, but this is primarily a point only to watch, not to analyze in depth. It may be that the absolute rates of vandalism and associated crimes were pulled up by the added temptation of high-value property within easy access. In addition, the numbers of pupils attending schools constantly increased in this period, whereas the numbers of schools decreased, as they consolidated into larger units. These issues must be considered when speaking about trends in crimes and violence in schools.

Shifts in the Kinds, Frequency, and Intensity of School Crimes

This study has now identified four critical variables that affected its ability to interpret these data. In relation to crime trends in schools, these issues conspired especially to thwart trend interpretation. The four points are: (1) changes in the methods of reporting crimes in schools; (2) changes in the school's and

Chart 5-16
Vandalism Arrest Rates of Youths Fifteen to Seventeen Years Old

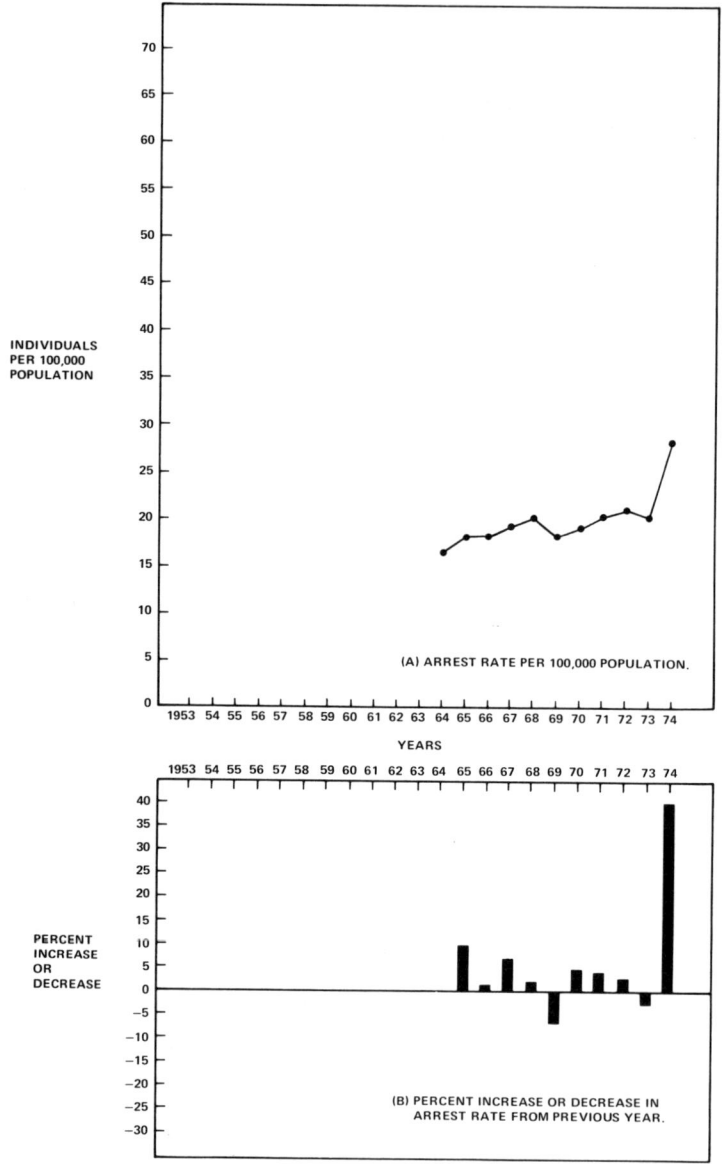

Source: Statistics Branch, Uniform Crime Reporting Division, U.S. Department of Justice.
Note: Data on vandalism was first collected in 1964.

Chart 5-17
Larceny/Theft Arrest Rates of Youths Fifteen to Seventeen Years Old

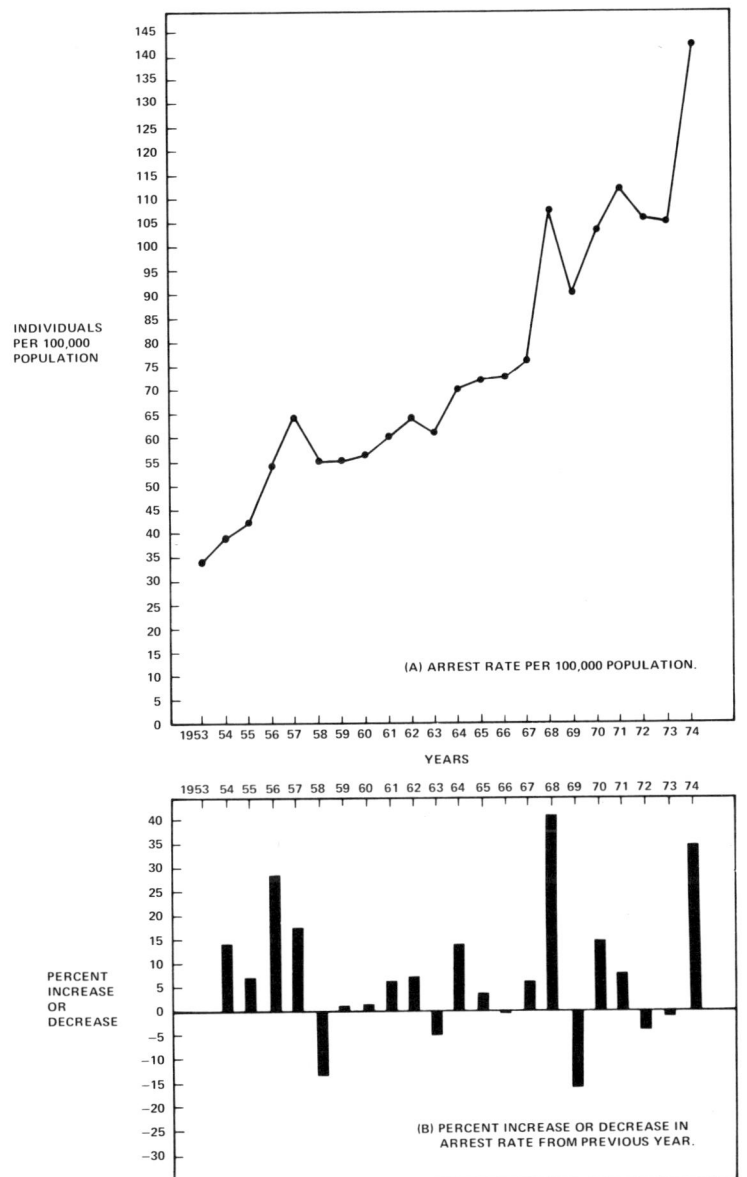

Source: Statistics Branch, Uniform Crime Reporting Division, U.S. Department of Justice.

Chart 5-18
Burglary Arrest Rates of Youths Fifteen to Seventeen Years Old

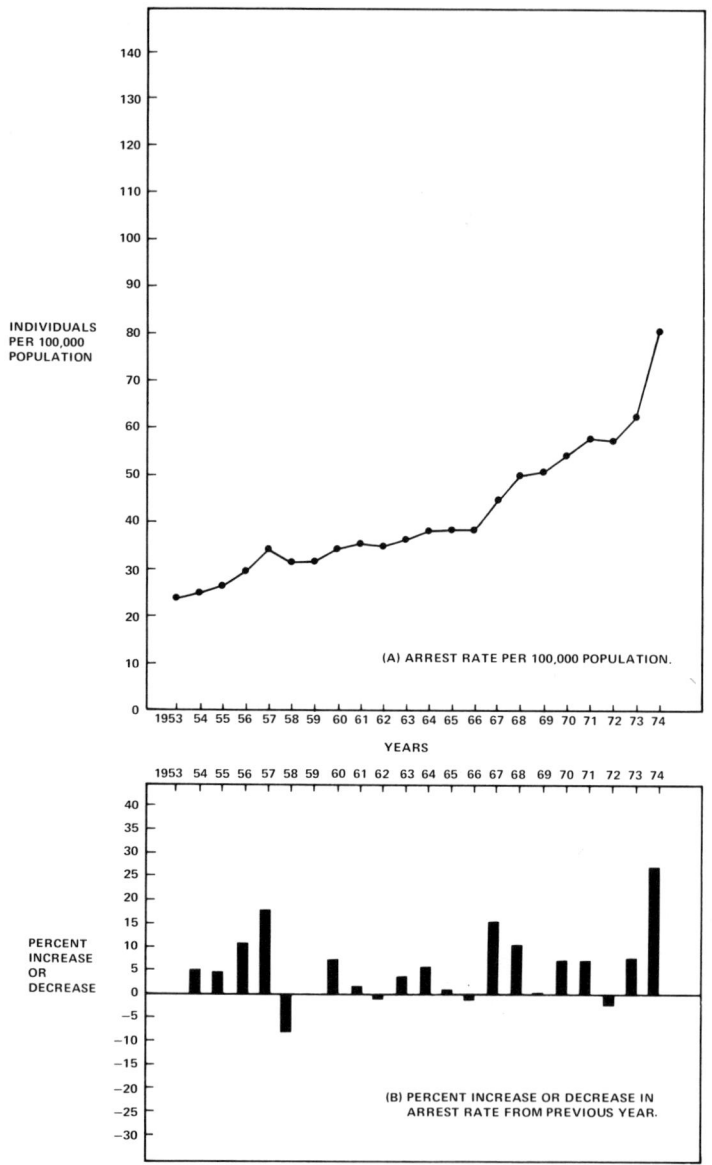

Source: Statistics Branch, Uniform Crime Reporting Division, U.S. Department of Justice.

community's definitions of acceptable behavior; (3) changes in behaviors the school and the community considered acceptable; and (4) changes in concepts of *in loco parentis* coupled with increases in the numbers of youths in schools.

Changes in Reporting Methods: This problem had three aspects: inconsistent definitions, involvement of the school security office in the record-keeping chain, and the increasing tendency away from telephone-type surveys toward formal, scientifically developed studies. The problem of inconsistent definitions was itself relevant on two levels: intraschool and interdistrict. Within the school itself, problems of subjectivity in relation to noncriminal disorders make a case-study approach necessary for developing valid trend data. Lacking such exactitude in this study, general incident counts collected under district-defined categories only allowed approximate conclusions. Between districts, as stated before, definitions of seemingly common crime categories were inconsistent. In 1973 the newly formed National Association of School Security Directors began among its membership a program aimed at unifying and collating definitions of criminal offenses committed by students in schools. From this effort, an annual summary of school crime, using agreed-on definitions, emerged. Though data by 1975 were finally beginning to be representative of national problems of crimes in schools, school crime information collected—from whatever source—before the end of 1975 would have been increasingly noncomparable for the reasons discussed throughout this study.

The involvement of the Office of School Security in keeping records on criminal incidents also strongly affected the interpretation of these data. Not only did individual Offices of School Security develop many definitions of offenses, but also the need for and development of such offices took place in different years for every city in the country. Los Angeles had an office of security since the late 1940s; Washington, D.C., Baltimore, and Denver developed security offices in the late 1960s; and many cities, particularly smaller ones, still did not have security offices by 1975. Due to these staggered start-up times, the stage of development for each district security office affected the quality and quantity of available crime-incident data. A slight variation on this same problem, but closely related, was that directors of security did not have the same authority in all districts. Differences in authority introduced possible inconsistencies in the quality and uniformity of incident reports that individual schools turned in to the security offices (see appendix C).

The increased use of scientific methodology to determine the nature and extent of the crime problem in schools strongly affected the results of these studies. Less formal studies, such as Dukiet's in 1973, began giving way to more elaborate undertakings in which researchers drew probability samples for the populations studied, and employed approved techniques of sampling and data analysis. Such approaches were used in NEA's "Teacher Opinion Polls of Pupil Behavior"; *School Product News*' effort to fix the annual costs of vandalism, arson, and theft; and the National Institute of Education's "Safe Schools Study," which falls outside this study's period. As scientific methods were increasingly used in this area, clarification of the nature and extent of the problems of student crime became increasingly available.

Changes in the Ways Schools Intervened to Reduce Crimes: When Offices of School Security increasingly developed in the early 1970s, their employees first attacked crimes that could be interdicted through the use of target-hardening techniques. The literature (Wells, 1971; *U.S. News* articles from 1973; Neill, 1975; or Marvin, 1976) frequently discussed the more common types of security measures such as school guards, identification cards, emergency call systems, closed-circuit television monitors, perimeter alarms, polycarbon windows, and others. Though this study has not discussed the impact such crime-intervention measures had on school-crime data, introducing these programs clearly adds variables which would compound the difficulty of determining what was actually taking place. It has been unclear, for example, whether absolute rates of offenses slowed as a result of school security office initiatives; whether the absolute numbers of criminal offenses decreased while public awareness of crimes increased (leaving the incorrect public impression that school crimes were increasing); or whether youthful criminality continued unabated in the face of the best efforts of the schools to reduce it.

Changes in Definitions of Acceptable Behavior: As the kinds of secondary school pupil misbehaviors became both more serious and more frequent, acts which would have not been tolerated in previous years became more acceptable both to school personnel and the community. Smoking in the bathroom, for example, remained a suspendible offense throughout the 1950s and well into the 1960s. Marijuana possession, which would undoubtedly have meant expulsion in the 1950s and suspension in the late 1960s, was no longer a clear-cut suspendible offense by 1975. The amount of marijuana and the student's intent (personal consumption or dealing) affected the school's responses. These changes in tolerated behavior altered the types of incidents reported from year to year and contaminated the interpretation of national trends over time.

In Loco Parentis Concepts: As discussed in detail in relation to disruptions (chapter 4), court cases clearly showed changes in the legal authority of school administrators to administer many forms of discipline. As numbers of pupils increased (chart 5-2), frequency of in-school offenses increased, and the power freely to administer discipline decreased, changes occurred in the kinds of offenses which invoked administrative response. These changes—clearly toward tolerating increasingly offensive behavior—resulted in variations from year to year in the numbers of youths referred to the school administrator for any one kind of offense. The study has been unable to avoid presenting some data which were contaminated by counting different intensities of the same generic act over time.[22]

In summary, when dealing with changes in data in relation to the nature or extent of school crimes, the study considers changes over time in reporting methods, school intervention techniques and strategies, behaviors which may change in their acceptability by the community and school, and ramifications of the authority of school personnel to administer discipline.

Summary and Conclusions

This chapter has addressed three broad questions: how did crime or the fear of crime affect pupils, staff, or the school's responses to such serious problems; to what extent could this study link changes in the public's attitudes about crimes in schools to changes in the reporting of crimes that occurred as Offices of School Security were formed throughout the country; what gross trends about the nature and extent of crimes in secondary schools could be developed from the available data, and what did such trends reveal about changes in the nature and extent of various crimes?

Concerning the issues of pupil and staff attitudes toward crime and violence in schools, the study observed that individual perceptions as to whether acts of serious misbehavior were criminal or not sometimes differed. Furthermore, in relation to the educational environment, fear of crime was likely to be more damaging than actual incidents of crime and fear affected teachers more than pupils. The school's responses to crime and violence were consistent with those discussed in previous chapters. Principals concerned with not appearing to have an uncontrolled or unsafe school played down as many offenses as possible, but by the early 1970s, followed procedural due process when administering discipline to offenders who simply could not be overlooked. School districts, while attempting to meet the threat of serious misbehaviors in schools, developed Offices of School Security in the late 1960s and early 1970s. As these offices began to collect, define, and record offense-incident information in relation to serious student misbehaviors, an avalanche of these newly developed data became available.

Concerning the second and third issues under consideration here, whether changes in the reporting of offenses due to the advent of school security offices—plus their development of uniform reporting procedures, combined with changes in nationally reported incidents over time—conspired to leave an incorrect impression of the amount of increase in student crimes in schools, this study found the following. With respect to assaults on teachers, changes in reporting methods gave the public an impression of an increase not substantiated by the data. With respect to vandalism, burglary, larceny, and arson, however, the absolute rates of incidents probably increased.

Vandalism, theft, and burglary began increasing in the same period during which the value of all school property also increased and more and more pupils were in fewer and fewer schools. This study found that dollar loss caused by fires was indeed increasing more rapidly than was the aggregate value of school property, and that fires were often the single most costly loss suffered by a school or a school district.

The overall conclusion, however, is that the hard proof of changes in incidents this study has provided was not necessary to determine that the nature and extent of school crimes had changed over time. It is clear that in the 1950s, cities had virtually no need for school security offices, whereas they did need such offices by 1975. It is clear that damage done to schools by vandalism was not great enough in 1950 to merit the national attention it received in 1975. It is clear that in 1950, teachers and pupils did not fear their schools, as they often did by 1975. That the data are imperfect in no way inhibits this study from pointing out that the kinds, frequency, intensity, and costs of school crimes increased out of proportion to increases in the pupil population in this period, and that the fear of crime—particularly in urban schools—often was of such a magnitude as to prevent learning from taking place.

Notes

1. The point to be made here is that in the case of the commission of a criminal act, the administrator of the school must make a primary decision whether or not to prosecute the offender. In cases involving disciplinary action in response to violations of school rules (disorders), however, school responses may—to a much greater extent—be affected by the particular mood of the school administrator and various socioeconomic and situational variables discussed in chapter 3.

2. In the "trends" section, the study demonstrates how this grapevine effect can result in a subjective feeling of gross lack of safety which exceeds the actual threat as measured by the numbers of acts committed. This point is critical in understanding trend changes, for public perceptions seem to precipitate reactions to problems that are objectively less severe than statistics indicate.

3. The issue is solely one of the size of the "population at risk." Granted more pupils than teachers were assaulted; however, often pupils who repeatedly were assaulted belonged to a small subset of the overall pupil population. Even without making this kind of theoretical speculation, however, *numbers* seem to be the key to this analysis of the impact of assaults. The study proposes that 100 student-student assaults in a semester out of a student population of 2,000 will not get anything like the attention of five student-teacher assaults in the same semester. Among the contributing reasons—in addition to those mentioned in the study—are that teacher assault reflects a breakdown in the traditional

authority structure of the school, and is topical for media coverage; teacher assaults are more likely to end in court action, which will receive media coverage; and teachers, unlike pupils, have unions which will not consider student-teacher assaults to be an inconsequential action.

4. The prison allegory developed by Cavan and others may well have originated with Goffman's *Asylums*. The study found no mention of comparisons of schools with prisons predating the Goffman work.

5. Miller never clearly specified the number of gang members in a class or in a school necessary to develop the critical mass required to take control. Individual personalities of pupils and teachers probably are the key variables here. Whereas in one situation, a particularly tough seventeen year old may be sufficiently unruly to destroy order in a class with an easily frightened instructor, in another situation, it may take four or five gang members sufficiently to intimidate and wrest control from a stronger teacher.

6. "Force," as used by Larson and as intended here, does not exclusively mean an increase from a few police in a school to an entire school security force in the school district. Indeed, in the broader sense, Larson warned against such a transition because the handling of behavioral problems with more intense forms of traditional countermeasures is dangerous. Detention halls, paddling, and suspensions for a few pupils worked to maintain discipline in schools in the 1950s when the numbers of offenders were few. Massive use of these methods was what Larson challenged. The question, then, clearly becomes, Where do we go after these measures to prevent and reduce student misbehaviors fail to produce the desired result? Larson's answer was that if schools increased the intensity of their responses instead of looking for root causes and solutions, the path led irrevocably to "confronting students with loaded guns." This study concurs with the Larson analysis.

7. Murphy's first law states that "If anything can go wrong, it will." The second law states, in effect, that "On a continuum of things that can go wrong, it is the worst possible alternative that invariably does go wrong."

8. The "discussion" subsection addresses the more major caveats and considerations in relation to the analysis of the data.

9. One *U.S. News and World Report* article was in a class by itself. On December 6, 1957, the magazine carried an article about the New York Grand Jury recommendation that police be stationed in school corridors to curtail some 2,100 crime complaints received in one year (presumably the 1956-1957 school year). This suggestion by the Grand Jury was emphatically rejected by the New York School Superintendent. The study could not find any follow-up articles about New York's school crime problem, and therefore considered this article to be in a different category from the series of works listed in chart -51.

10. Note: The first five years of the "Gallup Polls" were collected into one work, cited as Elam, 1973.

11. Particularly available examples of the technique of comparing single-city data over time to demonstrate dramatic changes can be seen in the National School Public Relations Association works of Wells (1971) and Neill (1975) and in the *U.S. News and World Report* articles listed in chart 5-1.

12. As part of the State Schools Study administered by HEW, the National Center for Education Statistics is currently studying this. Data estimating the percentage of assault arrests for offenses occurring on school grounds should be available by late 1977.

13. From readings of this period, the author had been led to believe that tremendous increases in teacher assaults had taken place over the study's time period. By carefully reading the NEA questions cited by the Bayh report and others as showing increases in teacher assaults, and by reading the NEA computer printouts of all the questions and responses developed as a result of the "Teacher Opinion Polls," one can easily see what has happened.

Whereas the first question in each year in the NEA series on assaults asked for a response to the statement, "I was personally attacked . . ." the third item in that same group of questions for each year sought response to the statement, "A teacher in my school was attacked . . ." Clearly this question was subject to hearsay reporting, value judgments, and double answering. It was this question which was usually cited publicly. Dramatic increases in assaulted teachers thus appeared to take place over time (see also chapter 1, note 11). Because of these points, results ultimately developed through close analysis of the NEA "Polls" over time were quite surprising.

14. This fourth item is an area ripe for research. The only available study on assaults was prepared by the security office of a very large school district and is confidential. The data, however, showed that for grades Kindergarten through twelve fully 50 percent of the assaults were by seventh, eighth, and ninth grade pupils: For grades seven to twelve, about 70 percent were committed by the junior high school youths. Both the sample size and the time period were adequate to ensure statistical reliability and validity of the findings: generalizability is unknown.

15. For purposes of information, the data available from the FBI's *Uniform Crime Reports* concerning the arson arrests of fifteen to seventeen year olds are included in chart 5-10. These data, which were not collected until 1964, represent arrests for fires started by youths irrespective of location. Therefore it cannot possibly be determined from the *Uniform Crime Reports* whether or not trends in school arsons have changed.

16. This caveat, and permission to use the data, were given in a letter dated April 29, 1976, from John Ottoson, Director of the Fire Analysis Department in the National Fire Protection Association. Data presented either in the text or in the charts which came from the NFPA may not be reused without correct citation and a letter of authorization from them. The NFPA has been particu-

larly helpful and cooperative in providing counsel and information, and the author thanks them.

17. Until 1965, school fires included fires in post-secondary institutions as well as in schools offering grades Kindergarten through twelve. This de-emphasized current high costs of fires which were specifically for elementary and secondary schools, for the base figures up to 1965 really should be lower when compared with the data after that date. This information also provided insight into the period (the mid-1960s) when public school fires became enough of an issue in their own right to warrant separate counting.

18. One caveat goes with data relating to decreases in the number of the nation's schools. "Schools" were entities made up of one or more buildings, the HEW's National Center for Education Statistics retrieved information only relating to the number of such institutions. Therefore it could not be determined whether the gross numbers of the nation's school buildings had changed. That information would have been helpful in refining conclusions made about increases in the number of fires in relation to decreases in the number of schools.

19. The prevalence of vandalism was due in part to the vagueness of the word itself. Broken windows at a school were often considered vandalism even if the offender gained entry through them and stole property. Technically, once a building was entered, the authorities should have lodged a complaint of breaking and entering or burglary, rather than vandalism. If the security report read "vandalism," however, ensuring cost data relating to the given offense were listed as damage resulting from vandalism, rather than damage associated with burglary.

20. From 1950 to 1975, Los Angeles' student enrollment increased at roughly the same rate as the national student enrollment. The increase in L.A. was from 367,474 pupils in 1950 to 731,828 in 1975. This 99 percent increase compares favorably with the 86 percent increase in the average daily attendance of the nation's students as a whole (chart 5-2, column 6). Note: If these dollar figures are adjusted using the Consumer Price Index, the percent change will decrease. Using 1967 constant dollars for the 1950 and 1974 vandalism cost data, the increase was 1,311 percent—from $53,376 in 1950 to $753,481 in 1974.

21. The Consumer Price Index value difference between 1973 and 1974 is 0.09885. To compare the two studies' figures on national costs of crime, multiply 100.4 times 0.09885 and subtract the results from 100.4. The resulting number—90.5—closely approximates the 82.2 estimate by Educational Research Service, Inc., as to the 1973 costs of crime. One can readily attribute the difference between 82.2 and 90.5 to absolute changes in the costs of crime from 1973 to 1974, or to small differences in the sample selection. (The analytical caveat here is that the 1973 study was for all school districts enrolling over 300 pupils, whereas the 1974 study was for all school districts having more than

5,000 pupils.) There is no *prima facie* reason not to compare these figures, for close analysis of crime cost data indicates that while larger districts had much more vandalism, smaller districts had higher fire loss—possibly due to slower rural response time by fire companies—and so the sample population variable may cancel out.

22. Since this point is somewhat confusing, here is an example: Using the marijuana example from the previous subtopic, the study supposes that suspension rates for drug use would be much different if the compared periods were the 1950s, the late 1960s, and the mid-1970s. This is so, in part, due not only to changes in public tolerance of the use of marijuana, but also to the fact that by the mid-1970s, legal procedures schools had to follow to guarantee students' rights under the Constitution precluded schools from administering severe discipline to any but the most severe offenders.

References

Bayh, Birch
    1975   "Our Nation's Schools—A Report Card: 'A' in School Violence and Vandalism." Washington, D.C.: Preliminary Report of the Subcommittee to Investigate Juvenile Delinquency, Judiciary Committee, U.S. Senate (April).

Brady, Ed
    1976   "Numbers of Armed Off-Duty Police in Chicago's Public Schools from 1966 to 1975." Compiled by special request by Mr. Brady.

Burton, Charles L.
    1976   "The Denver Experience." *School Security Journal*, no. 3, 3 (March):47, 48.

Cavan, Ruth S.
    1969   *Juvenile Delinquency: Development, Treatment, Control*. New York: J.B. Lippincott Company.

Dodd, Thomas J.
    1970   "Violence in Schools: Hearing Statement." Washington, D.C.: Subcommittee on Juvenile Delinquency (unreleased second draft).

Dukiet, Kenneth H.
    1973   "Spotlight on School Security." *School Management* (November/December):16-18.

Educational Research Service, Inc.
    1974   "Losses Due to Vandalism, Arson, and Theft in Public School Systems, 1972-1973." Arlington, Va.: Educational Research Service, Inc.

Elam, Stanley (ed.)
    1973   *The Gallup Polls of Attitudes toward Education 1969-1973*. Bloomington, Ind.: Phi Delta Kappa, Inc.

Forer, Lois G.
　1970　*No One will Lissen*, New York: John Day, pp. 259-268.
Franklin, Donald E.
　1969　"In East St. Louis Schools, 3 out of 4 Teachers Carry Guns." *St. Louis Post-Dispatch* (February 5):front page.
Gallup, George
　1974　"Sixth Annual Gallup Poll of Public Attitudes toward Education." *Phi Delta Kappan* (September):20:32.
　1975　"Seventh Annual Gallup Poll of Public Attitudes toward Education." *Phi Delta Kappan* (December):227-240.
Goffman, Erving
　1961　*Asylums* New York: Anchor-Doubleday.
Grealy, Joseph I.
　1972　"Summary of Paper on Descriptive Analysis of Five School Security Forces." This summary was utilized in a report to the New York School Board and is unpublished.
　1973　"Terrifying Increases in Violent Crime in the Schools." Press release for the Fourth Annual Conference of the National Association of School Security Directors: Las Vegas, Nev. (July 15).
　1975　"Nature and Extent of School Violence and Vandalism: Testimony before U.S. Senate Subcommittee to Investigate Juvenile Delinquency." *School Security Journal*, no. 5, 2 (May):51-54.
　1976　Data concerning growth of the National Association of School Security Directors. Letter to the author (March 4).
Green, Richard
　1976　Summary Statistics from the Los Angeles School Security Section (unpublished data).
Greenberg, Bernard
　1969　*School Vandalism: A National Dilemma*. Menlo Park, Calif.: Stanford Research Institute (October).
Jones, J. William
　1973　*Discipline Crisis in Schools: The Problem, Causes and Search for Solution*. Washington, D.C.: National School Public Relations Association.
Lalli, Michael, and Savitz, Leonard
　1972　*Delinquency and City Life*. Washington, D.C.: National Institute of Law Enforcement and Criminal Justice, Law Enforcement Assistance Administration, U.S. Department of Justice (January).
Larson, Knute
　1972　*School Discipline in an Age of Rebellion*. New York: Parker Publishing Company, Inc.
McGowan, William N.
　1973　"Crime Control in Public Schools: Space Age Solutions." *National Association of Secondary School Principals Bulletin* (April):43-48.

Marvin, Michael et al.
    1976   *Planning Assistance Programs to Reduce School Violence and Disruption*. Philadelphia, Pa.: Research for Better Schools.

Miller, Walter B.
    1975   *Violence by Youth Gangs and Youth Groups in Major American Cities*. Washington, D.C.: Interim Report of Grant 74 NI-990047 to the Law Enforcement Assistance Administration.

National Education Association
    1956   "Teacher Opinion on Pupil Behavior, 1955-1956." Washington, D.C.: *Research Bulletin of the National Education Association*, vol. 34, no. 2 (April).
    1964- "Teacher Opinion Polls." Washington, D.C.: Research Division of
    1975   the National Education Association.

National Fire Protection Association
    1973   "A Study of School Fires." Boston, Mass.: National Fire Protection Association.

Neill, Shirley B.
    1975   *Violence and Vandalism: Current Trends in School Policies and Programs*. Arlington, Va.: National School Public Relations.

Olson, Howard C., and Carpenter, Jan B.
    1971   "A Survey of Techniques to Reduce Vandalism and Delinquency in Schools." Washington, D.C.: National Technical Information Service, U.S. Department of Commerce.

President's Commission on School Finance
    1972   *Schools, People and Money: The Need for Educational Reform*. Washington, D.C.: Government Printing Office.

Slaybaugh, David J.
    1975   "School Security Survey." *School Product News* (June):10-15.

Strom, Maggie
    1974   "School Fires: Part of Our Overall Crime Problem." *Security World* 11 Number 3 (March):19-23.

Subcommittee to Investigate Juvenile Delinquency
    1957   "Report No. 130." Washington, D.C.: Committee on the Judiciary, 84th Congress, 2nd Session.

Time Magazine
    1975   "Violence in Evanston." (June 2):39.

U.S. Department of Commerce
    1976   "U.S. Population of 15-17 Year Olds from 1950 to 1975." Compiled by special request by the Statistics Division, Bureau of Census.
           "High School Enrollment Figures, 1950-1974." Compiled by special request by the Office of Congressional Liaison, Bureau of Census.

U.S. Department of Justice
    1971   "Uniform Crime Reports of the Federal Bureau of Investigation." Washington, D.C.: Federal Bureau of Investigation.

1976 "Arrests of Youths Ages 15-17 from 1953 to 1974." Prepared by special request by the Statistics Branch, Uniform Crime Reports Division.

U.S. News and World Report
1957 "Policemen in School Corridors?" (December 6):94.
1968 "Violence in Schools—The Outlook Now." (September 2):68.
1969 "U.S. Teachers—Targets of Violence." (November 17):80.
1970 "In Public Schools, A Crime Invasion." (January 26):9.
1971 "New Pattern of Violence." (January 4):23-25.
"High Schools, too, Have a Crime Problem." (November 22):26.
1973 "More Muscle in the Fight to Stop Violence in Schools." (April 16):113-116.
1974 "Vandalism—A Billion Dollars a Year and Getting Worse." (June 24):39-41.
1975 "Violence in Schools: Now a Crackdown." (April 14):37-40.
1976 "Terror in Schools." (January 26):52-55.

Wells, Elmer
1971 *Vandalism and Violence: Innovative Strategies Reduce Cost to Schools*. Washington, D.C.: National School Public Relations Association.

Werthman, Carl
1971 "Delinquents in Schools: A Test for the Legitimacy of Authority." In B.R. Cosin et al. (eds.), *School and Society: A Sociological Reader*. Cambridge, Mass.: MIT Press.

6 Conclusions and Recommendations

This book has consistently analyzed pupil misbehaviors in secondary schools. For an easy approach, it divided misbehaviors into three categories: noncriminal disorders, group disruptions, and crimes. For each of these categories it investigated the literature and developed and analyzed the statistics that bore on the given problem.

The next two sections reflect the organization of the whole thesis. Whereas the book began by asking four basic questions that cut across the three misbehavior types, the chapters took in-depth looks at substantive issues. The following section summarizes the major findings developed through the in-depth approach, whereas the "conclusions" section takes the four original questions proposed in chapter 1 and presents findings provided through analyses of all kinds of misbehaviors over the entire period under study. The third section deals with probable future trends in the areas of student misbehaviors and school responses to such misbehaviors. Though this section only hints at further research, the last section is more explicit, providing recommendations for further study based on the information gained from the study.

Summary

Disorders

In relation to disorders, this study found that the nature and extent of such misbehaviors were distinctly different during three specificable time periods. From 1950 to about 1964 school administrators had rather free use of *in loco parentis* authority to administer in-school discipline and to suspend youths who threatened the educational climate of the school. Also, the numbers of disorderly students were fewer and the kinds of mischievous behavior they engaged in tended more toward pranks than anything else. From about 1950 to 1964,[1] teachers passed to school administrators, youths exhibited intolerable behavior, and administrators passed back out to the community problem students with whom they could not deal. Suspensions and expulsions were the mechanisms used to pass pupils from the schools to the community.

The second period (1964 to 1971) saw extensive problems in student-teacher relationships. These problems most often occurred in the form of teacher-testing: the art of finding a teacher's psychological weakness and repeatedly playing on it. This form of student amusement was particularly effective in cases in which new instructors tried to become friends with pupils, thus destroying the youth-adult distinction that would normally have existed with a teacher in an authority position. Educational theories during this period were rooted in the assumption that control precedes learning. Pupils' testing of this assumption contributed substantially to misbehavior problems in individual classrooms. It is in this period also that court cases challenging the schools' absolute power to administer discipline began to arise—particularly in relation to discipline that resulted in suspensions or expulsions.

From about 1971 to 1975, incidents of classroom disorders seemed to decline, even though there were concurrent indications that pupil crimes were becoming more of an issue. This was a new era for schools, for now riotous disruptions had passed, pupil populations had stabilized, and college graduates were no longer seeking teaching positions in the urban-core schools in attempts to avoid the army draft. By 1975, the power of the school administration freely to administer discipline as if it were a parent had been struck down in courts. As schools historically had suspended disorderly students for highly subjective reasons, such suspensions were increasingly looked on as possible examples of de facto segregation. It seemed that the rate of disorders was unchanged in this period, but that increased school and community tolerance of student violations of school rule infractions, combined with mounting public concern over the more serious acts of crime in schools, conspired to direct public attention away from disorders.

Disruptions

The study's findings indicated that secondary school disruptions occurred within a relatively short time period: from about 1969 to about 1971. Furthermore, disruptions were never very extensive, were generally over issues of school procedures or students' rights, and tapered off sharply both as civil court suits ruled in favor of the youths' claims and protest movements in colleges lost momentum. Because school administrators were often led by public sentiment and educational policymakers to expect riots similar to those occurring in colleges, school administrators throughout the country tended to overreact to early pupil protests. By the time educators realized the nature of the differences between the two genres of protest movements and ceased taking paramilitary counteractions as threats of protests began to surface in individual schools, pupils had largely won their new rights and freedoms. By the early 1970s, disruptions had largely given way to crimes as the most topical nationwide issue in public secondary schools.

Crimes

In-depth study of crimes in schools drew attention to the possibility that some offenses committed entirely within the student community may not have been perceived by pupils as criminal acts. However, some of these acts, when committed by pupils against adults, were most likely perceived by the pupils as illegal.[2] The study also proposed that the fear of crime issue was likely to be more serious among faculty than students. This was true for three reasons: adults were more aware of acts defined as crimes; they were more aware of the potential seriousness of criminal acts; and the staff was forced—through the mechanics of classroom scheduling—to interact with a greater cross section of the total student population than were the pupils, who tended to be insulated by their travel in peer clusters.

The study showed the initial response of school administrators to almost every form of pupil misbehavior played down the seriousness of any single event to avoid giving the appearance of a disorderly or unsafe school. Most importantly, this observation applied to criminal acts in the schools insofar as such acts were likely to result in legal actions against the individual school administration or the entire school district. To the extent school administrators became concerned about possible litigation, the study suggested that school district offices of school security increasingly became involved with various information on possibly criminal offense incidents. This information was used for further investigation of criminal acts, gauging changes in the nature and extent of school crimes throughout the district, and providing court testimony in civil suits brought by students.

As in-school crime offense data became available for the first time in the late 1960s, the public was exposed to misrepresentation of statistics. Changes in reporting methods gave the distorted impression that incidents of student crimes increased horrendously. This study contends that whereas absolute numbers of criminal acts did go up in this period, they did not go up at anything like the rate reported by most popular sources.

The major question of chapter 5 was one of the major questions of the entire book: What could the available statistics reveal about what was really going on in schools? Since this was discussed in great detail previously, suffice it to say here that the percentage of assaults on teachers was relatively unchanged over time, and that fires and vandalism had dramatically increased over time, in relation to all kinds of variables.[3]

Conclusions

This work is predicated on four questions basic to an understanding of the nature and extent of changes in pupil misbehaviors in schools over time: What ways can statistics about pupil misbehaviors help or hinder efforts to reduce misbehaviors in secondary schools; what relationship can be established between student actions, school reactions, and pupil counteractions; what actions can the school develop to help curtail problems of violent misbehavior such as vandalism and assault; how can an understanding of historical trends in the areas of noncriminal disorders, group disruptions, and crimes be helpful in planning intervention programs and techniques to curtail misbehaviors in schools?

Statistics as Aids or Inhibitors

The collection, presentation, and analysis of data have implications primarily in regard to disruptions and crimes. In the case of disruptions, as more and more data became available, researchers became increasingly aware of two facts. They first realized that secondary school protests were basically different from college protests, insofar as younger students focused almost exclusively on school-related and often legitimate issues, whereas college students focused more generally on issues of political and ideological scope. The researchers' second new awareness was that secondary school protests—culminating in the disruption of the operation of the school—were relatively rare even during 1969, when they occurred most frequently. By 1972, as government and academic researchers repeatedly discovered that local schools no longer considered group disruptions to be topical or problematic, crimes rather than disruptions became the new focus of research.

The data available on disruptions had certain vital shortcomings: they did not differentiate between legitimate and illegitimate protests, nor did they develop protest-intensity scales. Differences between secondary and post-secondary school actions therefore remained disguised in the protest-incident counts for years. As such incident counts rose sharply in the late 1960s, local school personnel, fearing the worst, agreed with the public impression that riots were a common form of protest, and that as force might well be required to quell them, advanced preparation was necessary. Offices of School Security were therefore formed in this time period both to make advanced preparation and as a form of such preparation.

Data on crime in schools have been somewhat controversial (see chapter 5). In several studies, investigators used quite primitive methods of survey and analysis in attempts to get a feeling for the breadth of serious student misbehaviors, without fully realizing the errors their research methods introduced in the analysis of data. The most serious of such errors occurred in the categories of sample selection and respondent bias—introduced through telephone interviews—and data collection and analysis errors—introduced through naive research methods. Unfortunately, studies containing these errors invariably developed erroneously inflated data. These data—often given a cloak of respectability because of the ways they were released to the public—were widely disseminated and believed. Release of often weak data unfortunately resulted in the problem that as researchers began challenging earlier works, some public attention shifted away from the original issues of increases in school crimes and focused instead on fights over the legitimacy of previously collected data.

Another example of how desired short-term effects produced by inflated statistics may be accompanied by undesirable long-term effects concerns the development of Offices of School Security. Whereas the public was willing to divert funds from educational programs to security offices when fantastic (if inaccurate) increases in criminal incidents in schools were published, that the public will continue to support these offices as the crime rates become adjusted to more real levels in future years is questionable.

This study's conclusions about crimes in schools drawn from data reviewed are that: though many of the available studies are out-and-out misrepresentations of facts, one cannot possibly disregard the obvious evidence that the nature and extent of school crimes have dramatically increased in seriousness; the fear of crimes and violence, particularly in urban schools, has crippled the ability of many educational institutions to conduct competent educational programs; the measures often taken to reduce crimes and the fear of crimes have left pupils and teachers alike with the feeling of being prisoners of the school; and there are no quick solutions in sight to these problems. Perhaps the most grave possibility for the future is public withdrawal of support from school security operations in an adverse reaction to apparent spectacular decreases in crimes in schools. Such apparent decreases will be likely to result from new and more rigorously scientific studies which, by avoiding contaminating research errors of previous studies, may well produce cleaner—if less spectacular—findings.

Actions, Reactions, and Counteractions

For several reasons, this study has not been able to deal with this issue to the expected extent. Perhaps the lack of intradistrict coordination around single problems—due to the autonomy of local school administrations—may affect this matter. Without intradistrict unity, there can be no purposeful national unity on single problems. Without finding districtwide unity of purpose, this study was largely unable to reach meaningful conclusions about national trends in actions and reactions. Though there must be case-study approaches in individual schools to show specific cases of reactions by schools to actions of pupils, this study proposes some general conclusions of national scope.

First, as suspensions without due process and other potential violations of pupils' rights grew more and more extensive in the late 1960s, pupils increasingly responded by suing the schools for violating their Constitutional rights. By the early 1970s, schools reacted by complying with the legal rulings and developing new due process procedures to safeguard against further court action. An outgrowth of this process, however, was that administrations became more cautious about who was suspended and what offenses required suspensions. Increasingly disruptive behavior became tolerated in schools, since suspension mechanisms were now under the watchful eyes of the courts. This syndrome may very likely lead to increased fear of crime in schools as the cycle crests. The crest should be noticeable through the actions of courts, which should begin modifying their rulings in favor of increased school administration of discipline.

Second, as threats of pupil disruptions and riots swept down from colleges to secondary schools in the late 1960s, school districts—particularly in large urban areas—established Offices of School Security to help cope with the disturbances and increasing instances of student crime. Offices of School Security, which represented bureaucratic responses to behavioral problems, were notably more successful controlling property crimes than personal crimes.[4] After disruptions subsided in the early 1970s, however, the bureaucratically entrenched security offices remained in place. As school personnel saw pupil activity becoming increasingly criminal—especially in the areas of vandalism, arson, and burglary—security offices responded by developing intrusion detection systems with central office monitors designed to reduce incidents of these offenses. As acts of property crime were increasingly reduced, personal crime became more noticeable, and the issue of student and staff fear of crime developed new importance. By 1975, the fear of crime and violence was the leading issue in urban schools.

Third, as the value of all school property increased, the percentage of enrolled pupils increased, and the value of the dollar decreased, both the numbers and the costs of vandalism, arson, and burglary increased. It is not surprising, then, that as property values and exposure to risk increased, schools reported more frequent damage at greater apparent total cost.

School Responses to Violent Misbehavior

This book has occasionally mentioned the range of intervention techniques for reducing incidents of crime and violence in schools. Current cataloging of school and security office strategies—particularly relating to target-hardening programs—was commonly in the public domain and not usefully repeated in this study. A difficulty often encountered, however, was that programs which authors of such summary studies commonly discussed tended to include pupils neither in the process of planning nor in continued involvement and support. Indeed, most programs specifically targeted to the prevention and reduction of student crime and violence were conceived and implemented by adults alone. Such program planning runs counter to this study's findings.

One conclusion which surfaced repeatedly was that decisions made without pupil involvement invited counteractions by pupils. One cannot overemphasize the importance of seeking student input: unless and until school personnel involve students—through whatever means suit the situation—in the development of actions purportedly geared to helping pupils, it is difficult to see how solutions can be found. Stopgap measures do not necessarily require communication between students and staff, and almost all choices for the prevention and control of disruptions and crimes discussed in this book represented no more than stopgaps.

There is some uncertainty as to whether school responses to disruptions would have developed as they did had the needs of pupils been ministered to beginning in the early 1960s. Of course, hindsight is always crystal clear; however, one may regard pupil demands settled by courts in favor of students in the late 1960s as having had their origins in the *in loco parentis* cases concerning college youths in the late 1950s and early 1960s. That the secondary school disruptions also followed this pattern would have been clear to school administrators in 1968 instead of in 1972 had the specter of antiwar and race riots in colleges and cities not prevented their hearing what pupils were saying in their protests.

Intervention Programs and Techniques

This issue was answered in large part when discussing the previous three issues; however, the following conclusions should be noted.

1. Through an understanding of what this study has done with national data, planners should be able to develop similar data for their own school districts to determine whether gross changes in numbers of schools, pupils, or teachers might account for some degree of their local problems relating to school crime and violence.
2. Through an understanding of possible repercussions of incorrectly gathering or presenting data related to student crimes in schools, school district planners may be more cautious when preparing their own reports. The study's specific observation about the ramifications of the presentation of erroneous or misleading data is that school districts are stampeded into responding to a problem that is not as serious as first pictured.
3. Through an understanding of how the interpretation of data changes when other major changeable data are combined with the original figures, planners should better be able to develop and interpret incident trends for specific offense categories in their schools or school districts.
4. Through an understanding of the origins, roles, and needs of school security offices (needs which range from providing clear definitions of terms to anticipating the next year's crime rate in the schools), planners interested in

reducing serious pupil misbehaviors should be able to communicate more openly with local school security directors.

Extrapolations

Though the study ends in 1975, there are probable trends in pupil, school, and security office actions continuing on into the future. Some of these trends have their roots quite early in the study period, while others began to surface only in 1975. This section discusses some of these probable futures. While the study has already touched on most of the following points, there are some new issues and nuances of previously presented issues. Separate subsections address the futures for pupils, local schools, and School Security Offices.

Future Student Actions

The overall trends—both in the school and the community—have for many years been toward redefining the ways youths and adults interact: increasingly, adolescents have had greater autonomy. As social relationships changed within the family unit, the roles of students and schools changed. Because adolescent autonomy will probably accelerate over time and schools will increasingly find it difficult to cope with seriously misbehaving pupils, any number of specific probable future trends are possible.

Gang Activity: For the next several years, gang activity in schools is likely to become an increasing problem in large city schools. Current research literature observes that for the first time in the history of recent documentation of gang activity, school grounds are now considered legitimate turf for the carrying on of gang business as usual. These findings are prophetic. Only the largest American cities are likely to have any serious degree of trouble controlling gang takeovers of schools—in the same way that only the largest cities have gang problems in the first place—but students and school staffs in cities which do end up with such problems are also likely to experience tremendous increases in the fear of crime. Fear of the potential danger of gang activity in schools is likely to be the key factor motivating schools to take counteractions.

Future Shock: As the nation increasingly becomes a technocracy, the population of persons bright enough, agile enough, and clever enough to master the increasingly vast knowledge necessary to be productive members of society will become smaller. Material presented to pupils will of necessity become more and more complex, and pupils unable to see value in the data or unable to master the data will increasingly become burdens to the nation's educational machinery.

Though this is certainly a slow trend, it is nonetheless becoming increasingly clear.

Other probable ramifications of divisiveness resulting from the increasing difficulty of educational demands made on students are questions asked by students about the relevance of curricula to life. Such questioning is likely to be dramatized in the polar behavior patterns of withdrawal/apathy and anger/hostility. In illustration of ways such behaviors are likely to be translated into action, the future holds the following trends: decrease in average daily attendance, increase in absolute rates of crimes of violence, increase in absolute rates of such victimless crimes as alcohol and drug use, and the schools' experiencing increasing difficulty in getting adolescents "turned on" to education.

Future Local School Actions

As outlined in chapter 3 on disorders, the long trend in the erosion of *in loco parentis* powers of schools will have lasting impact on teachers and pupils. The pattern of impact approximately proceeds according to the following structure. First, loss of *in loco parentis* power by local school administrators freely to suspend pupils without observing procedural due process forces principals to suspend fewer pupils, because of the additional bureaucratic headache of following due process guidelines for large numbers of pupils. Second, principals, seeking to reduce the numbers of pupils being thrust on them by teachers, will communicate to the teachers—by word or action—that only the most serious cases of misbehavior should be sent to the office for disciplinary action. Third, teachers, seeing further erosion of central-office support for the disciplining of marginal cases of intolerable student behavior, will increasingly try to reduce incidents that might necessitate sending pupils to the office.

In an attempt to maintain control of classes, teachers are likely—possibly subconsciously—to misuse grades. Instead of using superior grades to reward superior academic performance alone, teachers will increasingly give grades for a mixture of educational achievement and good behavior. This particularly invidious form of grade inflation will be doubly tragic. Not only will graduates be severely let down when they try to get into colleges with their seemingly high marks, but also it will be primarily the nicer, more polite, and considerate pupils who will fall victim to this particular trap. Grade inflation—leading to an inflated sense of a pupil's educational achievement—will be challenged, however, by objective measurement against the national Scholastic Aptitude Tests. When SAT scores are low while secondary school grades are high, pupils and community members will turn on the public educational system with a vengeance, accusing teachers alternatively of grading too high or educating too little. The pupils' anger and tension will increase, challenges to the legitimacy of schools will increase, and so the functional ability of schools will decrease. And the public—recalling wasted tax dollars, wasted youths, wasted warnings by educators, and rampant school crime—will support the students.

This syndrome will constitute the most serious behavior-related problem facing schools in the near future. Unless educators and researchers begin to provide warnings about ramifications such as these to the increases in crimes and the fear of crimes in schools, the American educational system a decade from now will be much different from what it is today.

Future for School Security Offices

Though originally formed primarily to reduce incidents and costs of acts of crime and violence in schools, school security offices will increasingly be used to reduce the fear of crime and to form a liaison with pupils in classroom settings. The fear of crime issue is partly resolved through the mere presence of security agents in schools, though good pupil relations must form the cornerstone of any lasting preventive program targeting the prevention and control of student misbehaviors in schools. Such liaisons may occur in the form of classroom instruction (for example, in classes such as "The Law and You") or in the form of school programs (for example, "Student-Security Advisory Groups").

Another future for Offices of School Security that have developed centrally monitored citywide or countywide intrusion and fire detection systems is that city or county officials will probably ask for certain public buildings and facilities to be added to the school's security network. Facilities such as libraries and city storage buildings would probably be among the first additions.

Recommendations for Further Study

As a result of information obtained through this study, the following suggestions for further study seem appropriate:

1. It would be valuable if a guide to the literature on school crime were available. Researchers could combine annotations of studies prepared by diverse groups with a guide of the ongoing research; current researchers would thus have easy access to a guide in this area. Periodically annotated bibliographies would be very useful.
2. Research which could draw some conclusions about serious student misbehaviors as an almost inevitable by-product of changes in the *in loco parentis* concept, the public attitudes toward compulsory education, the public laws governing the age of employability of adolescents, and the shifts in the juvenile population as a whole, would be a valuable contribution to the field of education.

3. Assembly and annotation of school security programs which involve students in approaches to the reduction and control of serious student misbehaviors could be very helpful to public school personnel throughout the country.
4. Scientific research into the psychological impact on pupils of various technological responses to issues of school crime and violence would be helpful for future planning of crime intervention programs. Pupils—and even teachers—increasingly feel themselves in prisons without (sometimes with) bars, and achievement levels in schools with highly sophisticated and viable security systems may well differ from matched-sample schools without such systems.
5. Research into the kinds of and extent to which serious student misbehaviors are not viewed as criminal actions by a majority of pupils in a school (concurrently viewed as criminal by a majority of the school's staff) would be very significant for further crime-reduction planning. Sociodemographic mixtures of the school and staff would have to be considered.

Ultimately, of course, some solutions will have to be found for those increases in pupil misbehaviors which limit schools' ability to educate youths. The American public cannot—and doubtless will not—long overlook a continuation of the current trends toward greater lawlessness in schools. A technologically based society which requires a continual supply of evermore capable and well-educated citizens to continue national growth will not be able to sit passively, while a relatively small percentage of adolescents brings the entire educational system to its knees.

The author hopes this document has succeeded in contributing to the general awareness of changes in the nature and extent of various kinds of student misbehaviors from 1950 to 1975. Hopefully, too, as readers develop an historical perspective of this problem, alarm over probable consequences that may well result will be channeled into constructive action to reverse the above trends.

Notes

1. By way of stressing that the behaviors noted did not fit precisely into time periods, the study overlaps these year groupings by one year. Thus the first period ended approximately in 1964, and the second one began approximately in 1964. Clearly, some cases of virtually any kind of student behavior can be documented for any of the twenty-five years covered in this paper.

2. The example provided in chapter 5 was of the difference between student-student assault and student-teacher assault. Unlike the student-student assault situation, a student-teacher assault was more likely to be seen by the participating student as a criminal act for which he was likely to get into a great

deal of trouble. Perceiving the probable consequences of his act, the offending student may have increased the intensity of his assault; in such an instance, the student reasons that "As long as I am going to get into trouble over this, I might as well make it good." No known research study investigated this difference in intensity as a function of the perception of wrongdoing; the study proposes in its "recommendations" sections that this is an area ripe for such study.

3. In arriving at these conclusions, the study considered changes in the following basic data: police arrest rates of juveniles for selected crimes, average daily school attendance, national youth populations, numbers of pupils enrolled in schools, numbers of schools, numbers of teachers, value of all school property, and the Consumer Price Index. Other data was provided by professional organizations with specialized interests.

4. The inability of school security offices to solve the basic behavioral problems of youths is a pragmatic issue. The mandate of most security offices is to control behavior deemed either unacceptable or illegal, whereas such behavior—on the part of pupils—may well represent visible manifestations of broader social or educational ills. The difference, then, between attacking the cause of the problem versus attacking the manifestation of the problem will forever be reflected in the inability of the school security office actually to solve behavioral problems of students.

Appendix A
Major Social and Educational Activity Relating to Juveniles between 1950 and 1975

1952	Senator Estes Kefauver (D-Tenn.) proposed the creation of a subcommittee to the Senate Judiciary Committee for the purpose of investigating juvenile delinquency.
1952	The Department of Health, Education and Welfare's Children's Bureau established a Juvenile Delinquency Branch in its Division of Social Services.
1953	The Subcommittee on Juvenile Delinquency was authorized by voice vote in the spring of the year.
1954	*Brown v. Board of Education in Topeka* Supreme Court decision held that "separate educational facilities are inherently unequal."
1954	The Secretary of the Department of Health, Education and Welfare called for a national conference on juvenile delinquency.
1955	President Eisenhower called for federal legislation to assist states in dealing with juvenile delinquency prevention.
1957	*Sputnik 1* was launched by the Soviet Union in October. This marked a turning away from the Deweyian concept of education, and the development of accelerated studies of science and math in public schools.
1955-58	Period of numerous articles in the *New York Times*, the *Chicago Tribune* and the *U.S. News and World Report* on school riots kindled by attempts to desegregate schools in compliance with the 1954 *Brown* decision.
1957	Juvenile delinquency bills were set aside in Congress (in a compromise move) and the National Defense Education Act was passed.
1959	Representative John Fogarty (D-Rhode Island), Chairman of the House Appropriations Subcommittee on Labor and Health, Education and Welfare requested a report on juvenile delinquency from the Children's Bureau and the National Institutes of Mental Health. The joint report was submitted to Congress in February 1960.
1960	The House Appropriations Committee directed the National Institutes of Mental Health to earmark $1 million of supplementary funds (provided for fiscal year 1961) for "new programs and activities aimed at solving the problem of juvenile delinquency." One of the projects developed with particular interest was New York's "Mobilization for Youth" effort. The guiding philosophy for this project was the "differential opportunity structures" theory of Lloyd Ohlin and Richard Cloward.

1961	The Kennedy Administration decided that delinquency prevention was a priority issue. David Hackett, Assistant Attorney General, was selected to lead this effort. After exposure to many professionals in the field of juvenile delinquency prevention, Hackett chose Lloyd Ohlin as a principal administration theorist for delinquency-related issues.
1961	The Juvenile Delinquency and Youth Offenses Control Act of 1961 was signed into law. Administration of the Act was placed with the Department of Health, Education and Welfare. Lloyd Ohlin was made head of the Office of Juvenile Delinquency.
1964	The 1961 Juvenile Delinquency and Youth Offenses Control Act expired. No further congressional action took place until 1968.
1964	Congress passed the Civil Rights Act, which specifically insisted that segregation in all its forms was illegal.
1964	Students at the University of California, Berkeley, rioted over issues of freedom of speech. This was the first of a wave of college riots that swept the country. By 1968, riots had reached secondary schools.
1965	Congress passed the Elementary and Secondary Education Act of 1965. This was HEW's answer to remedying problems of differential opportunity structures in schools—claimed by Ohlin (and the Administration) to be a root cause of delinquency. The HEW word for this kind of selective, supplemental funding was compensatory education.
1966	Coleman Report (HEW) . . . Racial Isolation in the Schools. Despite the 1954 *Brown* decision, schools were still segregated. This report touched off fresh controversy, which continued throughout the period of this study.
1967	*Gault v. Arizona* (387 U.S. 1, 1967) allowed the Supreme Court to establish that juveniles have rights of procedural due process (notice of charges, counsel, confrontation, and cross-examination) that are the same as adults.
1968	The Juvenile Delinquency Prevention and Control Act of 1968 was signed into law. Responsibility for administration of the Act was placed with HEW, which was now responsible for developing a national juvenile delinquency prevention program. The name of the office was significantly broadened from the 1961 title. It was called the Youth Development and Delinquency Prevention Administration.
1968	The Omnibus Crime Control Act of 1968 passed both Houses of Congress and was signed into law. This act, which was administered by the Justice Department, provided for passing federal monies to the states. Both this Act and the HEW Act allowed juvenile delinquency prevention monies to go directly to states. Within the Department of Justice, a new administration was formed to specifically administer this act. It was called the Law Enforcement Assistance Administra-

	tion. There was no specific office of juvenile delinquency within LEAA at that time.
1966-69	Students tested school rules resulting in suspensions, and extensive court activity.
1968-69	Secondary school riots tested rights of freedom of expression; police were brought onto campus.
1969	The U.S. Supreme Court held that school desegregation conducted slowly with "all deliberate speed [is] no longer constitutionally permissible." Desegregation plans must be implemented "at once."
1969-72	Period of extensive drug use by school students.
1970	The National Association of School Security Directors was formed.
1971	The Justice Department's Omnibus Crime Control Act of 1968 (LEAA) was amended to specifically include the prevention, control, and reduction of juvenile delinquency.
1971	The Department of Health, Education and Welfare's Juvenile Delinquency Prevention and Control Act of 1968 was extended. The Interdepartmental Council to Coordinate All Federal Juvenile Delinquency Programs was included at this time. Though riding on HEW legislation, the Juvenile Delinquency Council was placed by the Administration in the Department of Justice, and the Chairman of the Council was the LEAA Administrator. This Juvenile Delinquency Council was an early attempt to coordinate the overall federal juvenile delinquency prevention efforts.
1971	Congress introduced the first bill proposing to control crime in schools. Representative Bingham (D-New York) introduced the Safe School Act. It was not passed.
1972	The National Fire Protection Association noted a shift in the nature of school fires from incendiary to arson, over a twenty-five-year period.
1972	In a study published in *School Management*, researchers estimated that school arson, theft, and vandalism cost the nation's schools on the order of $260 million a year.
1973	The Omnibus Crime Control Act of 1968, as amended in 1971, was again amended in 1973 to require specifically that states add a juvenile delinquency component to their State Plans.
1974	Congress passed the Education Amendments to the Elementary and Secondary Education Act with instructions to HEW to conduct a "Safe School Study" into the nature, extent, and cost of school-based crime and violence. Responsibility for conducting this study was divided between the National Center for Education Statistics and the National Institute of Education.
1974	Congress passed the Juvenile Justice and Delinquency Prevention Act of 1974, creating an Office of Juvenile Justice and Delinquency Prevention within the Law Enforcement Assistance Administration.

	The Act authorized $325 million over a three-year period. "Maintenance of effort" clause required that LEAA could not reduce its previous rate of expenditure, which was fixed at $112 million annually.
1974	The Department of Health, Education and Welfare underwent a reorganization. The Youth Development and Delinquency Prevention Administration was moved out of the Division of Social and Rehabilitation Services and placed in a newly formed Office of Human Development. The YDDPA name was changed to the Office of Youth Development.
1975	*Wood v. Strickland* (420 U.S. 308, 95 S. Ct. 992, 1975) and *Goss v. Lopez* (419 U.S. 565, 95 S. Ct. 729, 1975) established that school personnel must follow procedural due process in suspension cases, even if the suspension were for less than ten days. Also, these rulings held that school personnel can be considered financially responsible for violations of due process that cause mental trauma to the student.
1975	The National Association of School Security Directors developed extrapolated figures placing costs of school arson, theft, and vandalism at $594 million per year.
1975	The Senate Subcommittee on Juvenile Delinquency released its Preliminary Report on crime and violence in schools.
1975	The FBI's *Uniform Crime Report* arrest rate data showed arrests of fifteen to seventeen year olds for total Part I offenses to be 71 percent above the 1953 rate, and total Part II offenses to be 64 percent above the 1953 rate (holding youth population and police reporting anomalies constant).

Appendix B
Uniform Report Format

This form was developed by the National Association of School Security Directors to develop estimates of the nature and extent of costs of school crime nationally.

Uniform Report of School Losses and Offenses

School District: _____ Period Covering: _____

Total Enrollment: _____ Number of Security Personnel: _____

Total No. of Buildings: _____ Prepared by: _____

	I. No. of Offenses	II. Dollar Cost	III. Offenses Cleared	IV. Dollar Recovery
I. Arson—the malicious burning or attempt to burn: a. School Board property b. Personal property c. False fire alarms				
II. Assaults—the unlawful inflicting of or intent to inflict bodily injury upon another: a. On student b. On teachers (administrators) c. On others				
III. Bomb Incidents—the threat or use of an incendiary or explosive devices (simulated or real): a. Threats—total b. Evacuations—required c. Bombings—accomplished				
IV. Burglary—Breaking—Entering—includes burglary, housebreaking, safe cracking, or any unlawful entry to commit a felony or theft. Even though force was not used to gain entry includes attempted burglary (count burglaries here not under larceny): a. Burglary (Loss and number) b. Breaking and entering (damage and number)				
V. Larceny—theft of property not resulting from burglary or breaking and entering: a. School b. Personal				

	I. No. of Offenses	II. Dollar Cost	III. Offenses Cleared	IV. Dollar Recovery

VI. Vandalism—wanton on and/or malicious destruction, defacement, rendering inoperable, unusable property of:
  a. Schools
     1. Facilities/equipment
     2. Windows
  b. Personal				

VII. Robbery—stealing or taking anything of value from a person by force or violence or by putting in fear—includes assault to rob and attempt to rob:
  a. Armed or forcible robbery
  b. "Shakedowns" or extortion
     (by use of fear)				

VIII. Trespassing—the unlawful presence of a person on school property: a. No. of offenses				

IX. Controlled Substances—includes alcohol, coca leaves, opium, cannabis and every other substance neither chemically nor physically distinguishable from them and any other drugs to which the Federal Narcotics Laws may now apply (includes synthetics):
  a. Possession
     2. Marijuana
     3. Other
  b. Sale
     1. Alcohol
     2. Marijuana
     3. Other
  c. Use
     1. Alcohol
     2. Marijuana
     3. Other				

X. Homicides/Manslaughter
  a. School hours—normal
  b. Outside school hours				

XI. Rape
  a. Student
  b. Teacher
  c. Other				

XII. Other Sex Offenses—includes exposure, molestation and all other unnatural sex acts:
  a. Student
  b. Teacher
  c. Other				

	I. No. of Offenses	II. Dollar Cost	III. Offenses Cleared	IV. Dollar Recovery

XIII. Weapons
    a. Possession (on the person)
        1. Guns
        2. Knives
        3. Other
    b. Found (in lockers, etc.)
        1. Guns
        2. Knives
        3. Other				

XIV. Demonstrations–a group action in a school setting that disrupts the officially defined educational process:
    a. Riots (massive collective disturbances)
    b. Disorderly (organized, possibly sanctioned but peaceful)
    c. Orderly
    d. Gang conflict
    e. Students
    f. Nonstudents
    g. Both
    h. Racial (or racial overtones)
    i. No. of days school closed result of student disturbance				

XV. Bus Incidents
    a. Resulting in accidents
    b. Other				

Totals				

Appendix C
Incident Reports

These two incident reports are of interest largely due to the differences in the kinds of data they request. Though both forms are quite thorough in the data they request, difficulties arise when trying to compare such information collected between school districts.

PRINCE GEORGE'S COUNTY PUBLIC SCHOOLS
SECURITY INCIDENT REPORT AND
SELF INSURANCE FORM

Official Use Only

Police Number	
	Security Number

Area: ☐ Northern ☐ Central ☐ Southern

1. Complainant's Name	2. Title	3. Type of Incident
4. Complainant's Address	5. Home Phone	6. Date Occurred	7. Time Occurred
8. City/State		9. Date Reported	10. Time Reported
11. Name of School	12. School Phone	13. Location of Incident
14. Victim's Name	15. Race/Sex/DOB	16. Point of Entry
17. Victim's Address	18. Home Phone	19. Means Used to Enter
20. Victim's Condition	21. Parents Notified ☐ Yes ☐ No	22. Describe Weapon Used

23. Description of Vehicle from which theft occurred. Year/Make/Model/Tag #

24. Suspect/Accused: Name/Address/Race/Sex/DOB/Hgt./Wgt./Hair/Type of haircut/scars/beard/Clothing

| | 25. Was Suspect Charged? ☐ Yes ☐ No | 26. Student ☐ Yes ☐ No ☐ Unk |
| 27. School Property ☐ Yes ☐ No | 28. Total Value of Property $ | 29. Personal Property ☐ Yes ☐ No | 30. Value of Property $ |

| 31. Witness #1 | Name | Address | 32. Home Phone | 33. Business Phone |

#2.

34. Police Notified ☐ Yes ☐ No	35. Officer's Name & Identification Number	36. Date Police Notified	37. Maint. Notified ☐ Yes ☐ No
38. Security Notified ☐ Yes ☐ No	39. Person Notified	40. Date Notified	41. Plant Oper. Not. ☐ Yes ☐ No
42. Bomb Threats/Arson: Bldg. ___ Evac: ☐ Yes ☐ No	43. Fire Board Notification Name:	44. Time/Date	45. Did Fire Dept. Respond ☐ Yes ☐ No

46. NARRATIVE: Describe details of incident, include description of property lost, stolen or damaged, give value of each item, make, model and serial numbers, describe damage to building. (NOTE: if repairs to building are necessary submit a copy of this report to the Maintenance Dept.) Tell what action has been taken. Include in narrative a statement indicating what specific measures were taken to protect property lost or stolen.

(Use reverse side if additional space is required)

Principal's Signature _____ Date: _____

Form 10 M 3/76   **White Copy:** Security   **Yellow Copy:** Investigator   **Pink Copy:** Self Insurance   **Goldenrod Copy:** School

GRAND RAPIDS SCHOOL SYSTEM
GRAND RAPIDS, MICHIGAN

SECURITY OFFICE REPORT

REPORT NO. _____
FILE CLASS _____
BUILDING OR DEPARTMENT CODE _____
TIME REPORTED _____ DATE _____

REPORTED BY _____ ADDRESS _____
POSITION _____ PHONE _____
NATURE OF INCIDENT _____

DATE AND TIME _____ ☐ DAMAGE ☐ MISSING PROPERTY ☐ ALARM
AREA OCCURED _____
REPORT _____
_____
_____
_____
_____
_____
_____
_____
_____
_____
_____
_____
_____
_____

SUSPECTS. ☐ NONE ☐ APPREHENDED ☐ KNOWN

1. _____
2. _____
3. _____

ITEMS MISSING – TYPE	BRAND	MODEL	CODE NO.	SERIAL NO.	VALUE
1.					
2.					
3.					
4.					
5.					
6.					

(USE BACK IF NEEDED)

REMARKS OR RECOM-MENDATIONS: _____
_____
_____

ACTION TAKEN: ☐ POLICE NOTIFIED. THEIR NO. _____ ☐ FILE CARDS MADE OUT _____
☐ OTHER _____ ☐ RECORDED _____

REPORT BY _____ TITLE _____

Author Index

Ackerly, Robert, 69
Ashbaugh, Carl, 98

Bailey, Stephen, 4, 17, 22, 41n, 83, 95, 104n
Baker, Donald, 65
Bayh, Birch, 14n, 33, 54, 116
Beck, Bertram, 52
Benton, A. Edgar, 31, 88, 90, 98
Berger, Michael, 8, 11
Betchkal, James, 11
Bingham, John, 33
Brady, Edward, 156
Brammer, Lawrence, 90
Brodsky, Stanley, 18, 27-28, 15n
Burton, Charles, 118

Calpin, Nathan, 102n
Cavan, Ruth, 67, 72n, 114
Cobb, Marion, 53

Dailey, John, 68
De Cecco, John, 56
Dodd, Thomas, 116
Douglas, Jack, 103n
Dukiet, Kenneth, 113, 138, 139, 142-143

Edgar, Alvin, 53, 67
Elam, Stanley. *See* Gallup
Elliott, Delbert, 75n
Erickson, Kenneth, 4, 17, 21, 41n, 83, 98, 101n

Fish, Kenneth, 91
Forer, Lois, 76n, 138
Franklin, Donald, 115

Gaddy, Dale, 30, 89
Gallup, George, 35, 65, 122-123
Gitchoff, G. Thomas, 73n
Glasser, William, 52
Goldstein, Stephen, 60, 77n

Graubard, Paul, 52
Graves, Samuel, 101n
Grealy, Joseph, 118, 143
Green, Richard, 141
Greenberg, Bernard, 18, 26, 141-142
Guidridge, Beatrice, 31, 32, 85, 89-90

Hagstrom, Warren, 17-18, 21
Harris, Lou, 35
Havighurst, Robert, 17, 21-22, 41n
Herrick, Mary, 55
Hicks, Edward, 55, 68
Holt, John, 72n
Hypps, Irene, 62

Jones, J. William, 32, 86, 115

Kerber, August, 63
Kleiman, Mark, 101n
Kvaraceus, William, 63

Lalli, Michael, 110, 113
Larson, Knute, 9, 50, 85, 90 *passim*, 101n, 116-117
Levy, Gerald, 51 *passim*
Liddle, Gordon, 52
Liebow, Elliot, 72n

McGowan, William, 115
Mackler, Bernard, 71n
Mager, Robert, 72n, 98
Marvin, Michael, 8, 15n, 18, 28, 117, 150
Metzner, Seymour, 103n
Meyer, John, 17, 25, 42n, 64, 99, 102n
Miller, Walter, 18, 29, 52, 115
Morris, Gordon, 65

Neill, Shirley, 6, 139, 141, 143, 150
Nemy, Enid, 16

Olson, Howard, 141-142

Parody, Ovid, 68
Phay, Robert, 30, 77n
Piety, Marilyn, 54, 71n
Polk, Kenneth, 17, 20-21, 47, 50, 52, 72n
Postman, Neil, 75n
Prescott, Arthur, 54, 72n, 55, 67
Pucinski, Roman, 33, 38, 85-86, 95, 99

Roberts, Joan, 54, 68
Rubenstein, Annette, 76n

Satlow, David, 53
Schubert, Delwyn, 66
Shaffer, Helen, 86
Sherman, Stanley, 71n
Slaybaugh, David, 38, 143

Smith, Phillip, 59
Snow, Robert. *See* Kerber
Stullken, Edward, 67
Sullivan, Robert, 98

Trump, J. Lloyd, 85

Vestermark, S.D., 17, 21, 24-25, 91, 98
Vincent, Harold, 67
Vinter, Robert, 54, 72n

Weinraub, Bernard, 101n
Wells, Elmer, 32, 53-54, 114, 142, 150
Werthman, Carl, 114
Westin, Alan, 23, 41n, 101n
Wilkerson, Doxy, 63

Subject Index

Absenteeism, 64-65; crime, fear of, 113; non-readers, 76n. *See also* suspensions; pushouts

Action-reaction cycle. *See* laws and theories

Activism, research on, 22. *See also* disruptions; protests; S.D.S.

Administrators: discipline, management of, 68; disruptions, management of, 104n; pass youths to community, 68; as primary decision makers, 152n; views on crime, 68; views on disorders, 104n

Aggregate response patterns. *See* laws and theories

Alcohol: self-destructive behavior, 64; studies of, 65-66; trends in use, 65

Analytical problems with studies, 131; bias, personal, 71n; counting non-response as non-problem, 33; definitions, changes in, 64; fires, 155n; newspapers, use of, 23; rates, non-use of, 33; reporting periods, 10; in research, 152n; scaling of data, 23; schools, changing numbers of, 155n; terminology, changing, 11; tolerated behavior, changes in, 150; *Uniform Crime Reports* and arson, 154n; vandalism, 155n; variables, major, 145, 149. *See also* inflation; methodological errors in data; presentation errors in studies; statistical data

Apathy, 25, 42n; emerging concern, 121-123; expressed as absenteeism, 76n. *See also* absenteeism; alcohol; withdrawal

Arrest data, 36, 126-129. *See also Uniform Crime Report*

Arrest powers, implications of, 73n

Arson, 43n. *See also* fires

Assaults: against students, 22; against teachers, 14n, 131-134; national data, 131-134; teacher non-report of, 116

Attendance, average daily, 123-124

Authority, pupils' challenge, 18

Baker v. Owen, 88

Blackwell v. Issaquena School District, 88

Boycotts. *See* disruptions

Brown v. Board of Education of Topeka, 92

Burnside v. Byars, 69, 88

Census Bureau, data used, 36

Children's Defense Fund, 17, 19, 30, 39, 50, 65, 68, 70, 77n, 88

Collective violence. *See* disruptions; violence

Community, resistance of suspensions, 69

Congress, interest in disruptions, 99; mandating research, 34

Congressional studies: Bayh, 1975, 33-34; Bingham, 1971, 33-34; Pucinski, 1970, 33. *See also author index by name*

Consumer price index, 124-126, 137-139 (all charts). *See also* inflation

Corporal punishment, 76n; court cases, 87-88

Court cases, 87-90. *See also individual cases*

Crime in school: administrators' views, 116-117, approaches to understanding, 130; data on, problems in developing, 130-131; effect of, 111; expectation of, 102n; security officers' views, 117-118; teachers' views, 114-116; tolerance of, 11, 150

Criminal behavior: defining, 117-118; theories of, 111-112

"Critical mass" theory. *See* laws and theories

Data: national scope, 126; need for, 7; relating to student crime, 223 *passim*. *See also* analytical problems with studies; methodological errors in data; presentation errors in studies; statistical data

Davis v. Firment, 89

Definition of terms: crime, 4, 110; discipline, 72n; disorder, 3, 48; disruption, 4, 21, 83; expulsion, 40n; force, 153n; misbehavior, 1; office of school security, 103n; pushout, 40n; self-destructive behavior, 76n; "serious" offenses, 72n; status offenses, 4; suspension, 40n; target hardening, 15n; tolerated behavior, 13n; troublesome, 75n; vandalism, 135, 138; violence, 3

Definitions, problems with, 24, 41n

Desegregation, as a national concern, 123

Discipline, 66-67; as national concern, 122-123. *See also* Gallup *in author index*

Disorders: administration response, 68; college attendance, 18-19; court cases, 69; "critical mass theory," 51-52; school management of, 47; intensity of, 61 *passim*; pupils' views, 50-53; school administrators' views, 55; school personnel views, 53; school responses, 66; security officers' views, 56-57; biased interpretation, 48; teachers' reaction, 66-67; time periods, 58

Disruptions: collective violence, 24; college, 103n; college versus secondary school, 84-85, 91; conflicting research findings, 99, 103n; Congressional interest in, 99; co-opting of, 31; countermeasures, 98-99; court cases reflecting pupil's views, 87-90; frequency of, 92-100; guided versus situational, 24-25; periods of occurrence, 95, 99, 101n, 103n; pupils' views, 85-87;

research on, 30-32, 85; research problems, 95; school personnel views, 90-91; shift to secondary schools, 90; S.D.S. involvement in, 101n; theories of cause, 101n; trends, 92-100; types of, 85-92

Dixon v. Alabama State Board of Education, 87

Dress codes, court cases, 89-90

Due process, 69-70. *See also Gault v. Arizona; Goss v. Lopez; Wood v. Strickland; Baker v. Owen; Tinker v. Des Moines School District*

Enrollment data, 123-126

Expulsions, 60; court cases, 87; research, 30

Externalization of problems, theory of. *See* laws and theories

Extrapolations: school actions, 169; student actions, 168; security office actions, 170; tighter discipline, 77n

Failing, and misconduct, 52

Fear of crime, 113; teachers' views, 72n

Fear of retaliation by students, 112-113

Fires: national data, 135-137; research, 39; urban versus rural, 42n. *See also* arson

Force: definition of, 153n; effects of greater use, 116-117

Freedom of expression, court cases, 88

Gang activity, 29; national concern, 123; projected problems, 168

Gault v. Arizona, 6, 69, 87

Goss v. Lopez, 6, 69, 87

"Grapevine effect." *See* laws and theories; fear of crime

Group actions. *See* disruptions

Inflation: cost of fires, 137-139 (charts); cost of school crime, 142-143; value of all school property, 138 (chart)

In loco parentis, 69-70, 77n, 87 *passim*, 150-151

Kennedy Memorial, Robert F., 17, 20, 71n

Law of the Instrument. *See* laws and theories
Laws and theories: action-reaction cycle, 8 (chart); aggregate response patterns, 59; "critical mass theory," 55, 62, 153n; externalization of problems, 102n; "grapevine effect," 152n; law of the instrument, 91; Murphy's law, 153n; problem progression, rule of, 60
LEAA studies: Brodsky, 27-28; Marvin, 28; Meyer, 25; Miller, 29; Vestermark, 24-25
Legal issues, indications of student concern, 86-90. *See also specific court cases or subject headings*
Leonard v. School Committee in Attleboro, 89

Media, coverage versus research findings, 27. *See also U.S. News and World Report*; newspapers; *New York Times*
Methodological errors in data: effect on findings, 149-150; alcoholism study, 66; examples of, 38, 92; Teacher Opinion Polls, 104n. *See also* analytical problems with studies; presentation errors in studies; statistical data
Misbehaviors: anticipation of, 7-8; school's role in creating, 20-21
Murphy's Law. *See* laws and theories

National Association of School Security Directors: and Congress, 34; growth of, 126; uniform terminology, 11
National Association of Secondary School Principals *Bulletin*, 104n
National Education Association, 17-18, 60-61. *See also* Teacher Opinion Polls
National Fire Protection Association, 135, 154n. *See also* fires
National Institute of Alcoholism and Alcohol Abuse, 65
National School Public Relations Association, 32
Nation's Schools, 90
Newspapers: articles on disruptions, 93; use of, for research, 42n, 103n
New York Times, 93

Offenders, cliques within school, 111
Offenses, types of, 2 (chart)
Office of School security. *See* school security offices
Outsiders. *See* trespass

Panel on School Safety, 18, 26-27, 65
"Passing" theory. *See* problem progression, rule of, listed under laws and theories
Police and disruptions, 99. *See also* Vestermark *in author index*
Political action in schools, 85-86. *See also* disruptions
Polls: Lou Harris, 35; George Gallup, 35-56. *See also author index*; Teacher Opinion Polls
Populations: data on, 123; shifts affecting research, 33-34
Presentation errors in studies: absolute numbers, 14n; "percent-change," 7, 14n; population base, 7, 14n; terminology, 150. *See also* analytical problems with studies; methodological errors in data; statistical data
Principals. *See* administrators
Problem progression, rule of. *See* laws and theories
Procedural due process, court cases, 87-88
Programs to reduce violence and vandalism: approaches, changes in, 150; Brodsky survey, 27; local

Programs to reduce violence and vandalism (cont.)
   funds affect, 59; Marvin review, 28; New York, recommendations in, 26-27
Projections. *See* extrapolations
Protests: intensity of, 104n; reasons for, 84-90. *See also* disruptions; S.D.S.
Psychiatric model for treating disorderly pupils, 62
Public concern: measures of, 36
Pushouts, research about, 20, 30. *See also* absenteeism; suspensions

Race and violence, 22
Reporting of offenses: methods of, 10-11, 149-150; influenced by security offices, 117; variables in, 112, 114
Research. *See* analytical problems; methodological errors; presentation errors
Richards v. Thruston, 89
Riots, research on, 38. *See also* disruptions

School Management, 87
School Product News, 38. *See* Slaybaugh *in author index*
Schools: "babysitting jails," 101n; data on numbers of, 123-126; "externalizing" problems, 64; offenses, differentiation of, 2 (chart); reflecting community problems, 65; responsible for student's behavior, 70; rules and protest activity, 89-90; students' needs unmet, 86
School security offices: budgeting for, 102n; definition of, 103n; development of, 56; and disruptions, 91; record-keeping, 56, redefine offense categories, 64; reporting methods change, 10-11; varied responsibilities, 73n; views of crimes, 117-118
Scott v. Board of Education, 89
S.D.S. (Students for a Democratic Society), 90; and disruptions, 101n
Senate studies. *See* Congressional studies
Sit-ins. *See* disruptions
Social variables and disorders, 63
Sputnick I, ramifications of, 75n
Stanford Research Institute studies. *See* Greenberg, Meyer, *in author index*
Statistical data: and bureaucracies, 14n; and Congress, 32-34; causes of disruptions, 87; improper use of, 7; suspensions for disorders, 68; value of, 7. *See also* analytic errors; presentation errors; polls
Stealing, as a national concern, 123
Students: behavior, self destructive, 64; "conning," 72n; criminal acts, view of, 112-113; discipline, uneven, 50; failing, fear of, 52; hostility toward school, 63; as inventory, 56; "passed" to the community, 66 *passim*; rights, 69, 87-88; surrenders to school, 63; teachers, loss of respect for, 51, 71n; troubled versus troublesome, 71n; views of themselves, 72n
Students' misbehaviors: changes in types of, 64; family influence, 61; subject to multiple interpretation, 59; teacher fear of reporting, 53-54
Subcommittee to Investigate Juvenile Delinquency, 55, 61-62, 74n, 114, 119, 126, 129, 141. *See also* Bayh, Bingham, Dodd, *in author index*
Sullivan v. Houston Independent School District, 88
Suspensions, 71n; as affronts to minority cultures 77n; court cases, 87; for dress code violations, 89; research on, 19, 30; statistics on, 68: for truancy, 76n

Target-hardening: dangers of, 9; definition of, 15n
Teacher Opinion Polls, 18, 60-61, 95, 102n, 122, 131, 133, 149, 154n

Teachers: assaulted, 14n, 98; authority, 54, 68, 114-115; chronic versus acute, 51 *passim*, 75n; control in classes, 51, 54, 63, 67, 72n; as failing in eyes of pupils, 71n; fear of reporting incidents, 53-54; fear of students, 54, 72n; fired for not maintaining discipline, 67; pass problems to administrators, 67; socializing role, 67; views of crime, 114-116; views of disorders, 53, 54

Time periods: disorders, 58 *passim*; disruptions, 95

Tinker v. Des Moines School District, 69, 88

Trends: in crimes, 119-163; in disorders, 58-71; in disruptions, 92-101; overviews of, 161-163

Trespass, 33

Truancy, suspensions for, 68, 76n

Uniform Crime Reports, 37, 126-132, 135-136 (chart), 146-148 (charts); problems with using, 10, 131

Unrest in schools. *See* disruptions

U.S. News and World Report, 101n, 102n, 115, 150; crimes, articles about, 99, 120-122, 153n; crimes, cost of, 143; disruptions, 93-95; reasons for using, 103n

Values of school property, 139

Vandalism: cost, 142-145; data, 135, 138-142; definitions, multiple, 139; national concern, 122-123; research, 26, 38, 142; in specific cities, 141

Violence: administrators not reporting, 116; situational versus guided, 24-25, 101n. *See also* Vestermark *in author index*

Voight v. Van Buren Public Schools, 87

Walkouts. *See* disruptions

Weapons: carried by security officers, 13n; carried by students, 61-62; carried by teachers, 115

Williams v. Dade County School Board, 87

Withdrawal, 64

Wood v. Strickland, 69

About the Author

Robert J. Rubel received the B.A. in English and secondary school teaching from Colorado State University, the Ed.M. in urban education from Boston University, and the Ph.D. in urban educational policy studies from the University of Wisconsin. He has taught in one of Los Angeles' "special opportunity" schools for severely disruptive youths and worked as deputy staff director to the Federal Juvenile Delinquency Coordinating Council within the Department of Justice's Law Enforcement Assistance Administration. Dr. Rubel has been a Visiting Fellow in LEAA's Office of Juvenile Justice and Delinquency Prevention and he is currently director of research, Institute for Reduction of Crime, Inc. in College Park, Maryland.

/373.15R894U>C1/